CW01314118

Adobe Photoshop 2025 Handbook

A Comprehensive Guide to Mastering the Art of Image Editing with AI-Powered Tools and Generative Features for Professionals

Wyatt Porter

Copyright © 2025 by **Wyatt Porter**

All rights reserved

No part of this publication may be reproduced, distributed, or transmitted in any form or by any means, electronic, mechanical, photocopying, recording, or otherwise, without the prior written permission of the copyright owner. Specific exceptions are listed below. Excerpts or summaries for educational, commercial, or research purposes cannot be used without prior written permission of the copyright owner. Brief quotations for criticism, comment, or scholarly work are permissible, provided that proper acknowledgment of the author and source is maintained.

This book is copyrighted by the author under the copyright laws of the United States of America and international treaties. It may not be reproduced, distributed, or modified in whole or in part, without the express written permission of the copyright holder/author. The author has full rights to authorize use, reproduce, license, or publish any part of this work in all forms and media. Any infringement of these rights will be prosecuted.

Printed in the United States of America

TABLE OF CONTENTS

TABLE OF CONTENTS iii

INTRODUCTION 1

CHAPTER 1 2

GETTING STARTED WITH ADOBE PHOTOSHOP 2
- *OVERVIEW OF ADOBE PHOTOSHOP* *2*
- *HOW DOES PHOTOSHOP WORK?* *2*
- *WHAT'S NEW IN ADOBE PHOTOSHOP 2025?* *4*
  - Distraction Removal in the Remove Tool 4
  - Improved Generative Fill 5
  - Improved Generative Expand with Firefly Image Model 6
  - Generate Similar 7
  - Generate Image 8
  - Generate Background Tool 9
- *REQUIREMENTS FOR THE PERFECT RUNNING OF PHOTOSHOP* *9*
  - Other Factors 11
- *INSTALLING ADOBE PHOTOSHOP 2025* *11*
- *WORKSPACE OVERVIEW* *14*
- *UNDERSTANDING THE LEFT PANEL TABS AND BUTTONS ON THE HOME SCREEN* *17*
  - Menu Bar (Top of the Screen) 17
  - Left Sidebar 18
  - Welcome Section 18
  - Cloud Services and Account Options 19
- *FAMILIARIZING YOURSELF WITH THE PHOTOSHOP INTERFACE* *19*
- *UNDERSTANDING THE TOOLBAR* *21*
  - Selection Tools 22
  - Painting and Drawing Tools 23
  - Retouching and Healing Tools 23
  - Text and Typography Tools 24
  - Shape Tools 24
  - Navigation Tools 24

- Color Picker and Swatches ... 25
- Extra Hidden Tools ... 25

CUSTOMIZING THE TOOLBAR ... *25*

HOW PANELS WORK ... *26*
- Understanding Different Panels ... 26
- Docking, Grouping, and Moving Panels ... 27
- Collapsing and Expanding Panels ... 27
- Customizing Your Workspace with Panels ... 27
- Commonly Used Panels in Different Workflows ... 28
- Resetting Panels ... 28
- Hiding and Revealing Panels ... 29

PERSONALIZING YOUR TOOLBAR ... *29*

EXPANDING THE TOOL PALETTE ... *31*

HOW TO CHOOSE A TOOL FROM THE TOOLBAR ... *33*

WORKING WITH TOOL PROPERTIES IN THE OPTION BAR ... *34*

HOW TO CHOOSE A COLOR ... *34*

UNDERSTANDING THE STATUS BAR ... *35*

UNDERSTANDING THE CONTEXT MENUS ... *36*

WORKING WITH PANELS ... *37*

HOW TO RESIZE, EXPAND, AND COLLAPSE PANELS ... *38*
- Resizing Panels ... 38
- Expanding Panels ... 38
- Collapsing Panels ... 39

SHOW OR HIDE PANELS ... *39*

UNDERSTANDING PANEL CONTEXT MENUS ... *40*

USING THE UNDO AND REDO COMMANDS ... *41*

MAKING USE OF THE HISTORY PANEL ... *41*

GETTING A PORTION OF AN IMAGE BACK TO ITS OLD SAVED VERSION ... *42*

HOW TO ACCESS PHOTOSHOP PREFERENCES ... *42*

EXPORTING CLIPBOARD PREFERENCE ... *43*

INTERFACE PREFERENCES SETTINGS ... *43*

COLOR THEME *44*

SETTING THE HIGHLIGHT COLOR UNDER THE APPEARANCE *44*

UI FONT SIZE *45*

UNDERSTANDING THE SHOW TOOLTIPS FEATURE *45*

HOW TO USE SHIFT KEY FOR SWITCHING TOOL *45*

USING THE PERFORMANCE PREFERENCES *46*
    Understandung Memory Usage 46

CHAPTER 2 47

FUNDAMENTAL PREREQUISITE FOR IMAGE EDITING 47

THE IDEA OF PIXELS *47*
    How Pixels Work in Photoshop 47

EXPLORING IMAGE RESOLUTION AND DIMENSION *49*
    Width, Height, and Resolution Relationship 49
    The Idea of Pixel Dimensions 49
    Calculating the Total Number of Pixels in an Image 50

WHEN IS FILE SIZE AFFECTED BY RESOLUTION? *51*
    Resolution vs File Size: What is the difference? 51
    Higher Resolution vs File Size: A Better Look 52

SCREEN MONITOR AND PRINTING RESOLUTION DECISION *52*

HOW TO RESAMPLE AN IMAGE *54*

RESIZING VERSUS RESAMPLING *55*
    Resizing 55
    Resampling 55

IMPROVING A LOW IMAGE RESOLUTION AND RESAMPLING AN IMAGE
.... *56*

FILE SIZE VS PIXEL DIMENSIONS *57*

EXPLORING PRINTER RESOLUTION *58*

HOW PRINTER RESOLUTION WORKS *58*
    DPI vs. PPI 58
    Printer Technology 59
    Balancing Resolution with File Size 59
    Color Accuracy and DPI Impact 59

PRINT IMAGE RESOLUTION SPECIFICATIONS 59
Default Printing Resolution 59
Large-format prints (Banners, Billboards) 60
Printing of Magazines and Books 60
Flyers, Business Cards, and Brochures 60
Text-Dense Prints (Documents, Manuals) 60
Printing on Textiles or Fabrics 60
Preparing Files with Photoshop 60
Print Resolution Summary Table 61

PREVIEW ON-SCREEN PRINT SIZE 61

FILE COMPRESSION 61

FILE FORMAT SELECTION 62
PSD (Photoshop Document) Format 62
JPEG (Joint Photographic Experts Group) Format 62
PNG (Portable Network Graphics) Format 63
TIFF (Tagged Image File Format) 63
PDF (Portable Document Format) 63
GIF (Graphics Interchange Format) 63
EPS (Encapsulated PostScript) Format 63
BMP (Bitmap Image File) Format 64
SVG (Scalable Vector Graphics) 64

WORKING WITH RULERS 64

HOW DOES THE RULER TOOL FUNCTION? 65

WHEN TO USE THE RULER TOOL 65

WORKING WITH GUIDES IN PHOTOSHOP 66

CHAPTER 3 68

WORKING WITH LAYERS 68

HOW TO MAKE USE OF LAYERS 68
Understanding Layers 68
Creating and Managing Layers 68
Basic Layer Functions 69
Types of Layers 71
Non-Destructive Editing with Layers 71
Organizing Layers 72
Merging and Flattening Layers 73

Saving Layered Files 74
CREATING A BLANK AND ADJUSTMENT LAYER 75
EXPORT LAYERS 76
ASSIGN COLORS TO LAYERS 76
FLATTEN LAYERS 76
LEVELS ADJUSTMENT LAYER 77
UNDERSTANDING CURVE ADJUSTMENT LAYER 78
CREATING BLACK AND WHITE ADJUSTMENT LAYER 79
CREATING HUE/SATURATION ADJUSTMENT LAYER 80
HOW TO APPLY PRESET STYLES 81
UNDERSTANDING BLENDING MODES 82
MASTERING BLENDING MODES 83
USING MULTIPLY BLEND MODE 84
SCREEN BLEND MODE 84
OVERLAY BLENDING MODE 85
UNDERSTANDING COLOR BLENDING MODE 85
CREATING TEXT AND APPLYING SPECIAL EFFECTS 86
UNDERSTANDING GRADIENTS 87
   Types of Gradients 87
   How to Apply Gradients 87
   Edit Gradient Colors 88
   Using Gradients with Layers and Masks 88
   Practical Uses for Gradients 89
   How to Create a Gradient 89
HOW TO ADD BORDER TO AN IMAGE 91

CHAPTER 4 95

WORKING WITH SELECTIONS 95
OVERVIEW OF SELECTION? 95
SELECTING EVERY PIXEL ON A LAYER 95

- DESELECTING A SELECTION 96
- UNDERSTANDING OBJECT SELECTION TOOL 96
- OBJECT SELECTION TOOL FOR ADVANCED HAIR SELECTIONS............ 99
- EXPLORING SUBJECT SELECTION... 99
  - Using Select Subject... 100
- DISTINGUISHING BETWEEN THE SELECT SUBJECT COMMAND AND THE OBJECT SELECTION TOOL.. 100
- USING THE QUICK SELECTION TOOL.. 101
- ADD QUICK SELECT OPTIONS... 101
- MARQUEE TOOLS SELECTION... 102
- HOW TO MAKE A SELECTION.. 103
- MOVING A SELECTION USING SHORTCUT KEYS 103
- USING LASSO TOOLS FOR SELECTION... 104
  - When to Use the Lasso 105
- MAKING LASSO TOOL SELECTIONS... 106
- INTELLIGENTLY SWITCHING BETWEEN LASSO AND POLYGONAL LASSO TOOLS... 106
- SELECTING WITH THE MAGNETIC LASSO TOOLS 107
- HOW TO ROTATE AND SCALE A SELECTION 108
  - Rotating Selection... 108
  - Scaling Selection 111
- MAKING SELECTIONS WITH MAGIC WAND TOOL 111
  - Magic Wand Tool - How to Use It... 114

CHAPTER 5.. 115

EDITING IMAGES 115

- EXPLORING VARIOUS IMAGE EDITING OPERATION................................ 115
- SHARPENING IMAGES IN PHOTOSHOP WITH A HIGH-PASS FILTER.... 118
  - Exploring Image Processing Filter With High Pass..................... 119
- HOW TO USE GENERATIVE FILL INSTANTLY REMOVE PEOPLE OR ITEMS FROM PHOTOS.. 121

EXPANDING THE SELECTION.. *125*
CROP TOOL FOR IMAGE OPERATION.. *127*
SMOOTHING WRINKLES FROM AN IMAGE WHILE MAINTAINING A NATURAL APPEARANCE *131*
SMOOTHING SKIN IN PHOTOSHOP... *135*
HOW TO CHANGE EYE COLOR WITH PHOTOSHOP............................... *142*
HOW TO CHANGE HAIR COLOR IN PHOTOSHOP *148*
HOW TO WHITEN TEETH IN PHOTOSHOP *152*
HOW TO USE THE COLOR REPLACEMENT TOOL IN PHOTOSHOP....... *155*
HOW TO REMOVE BACKGROUNDS FROM IMAGES WITH BACKGROUND ERASER TOOL.. *159*
HOW TO REMOVE GREY BACKGROUND WITHOUT AFFECTING HAIR. *160*
HOW TO REMOVE THE BACKGROUND OF A PHOTO USING THE QUICK SELECTION TOOL *163*
HOW TO REMOVE PHOTO BACKGROUNDS IN ADOBE PHOTOSHOP USING THE PEN TOOL *165*
USING THE RED-EYE CORRECTION TOOL... *167*
USING DODGE AND BURN TOOLS FOR IMAGE OPERATIONS............... *168*
UNDERSTANDING THE BURN TOOL... *170*
UNDERSTANDING THE SPONGE TOOL *170*
UNDERSTANDING THE SPOT-HEALING BRUSH TOOL........................... *170*
    How the Spot Healing Tool Works 171
UNDERSTANDING THE PATCH TOOL... *172*
HOW TO ADD OR DUPLICATE OBJECTS BY CLONING WITH THE PATCH TOOL... *173*
WHAT CAN YOU DO WITH THE CLONE STAMP TOOL?........................... *174*
HOW FILTERS WORKS IN PHOTOSHOP *176*
WORKING WITH THE OIL PAINT FILTER... *177*
UNLEASHING THE POTENTIAL OF THE LIQUIFY TOOL......................... *178*
    Mastering the Liquify Tool and Advanced Features 179

HOW BLURRING WORKS IN PHOTOSHOP *180*

CHAPTER 6 .... **181**

EXPLORING THE TYPE TOOL **181**

WHAT CAN YOU DO WITH THE TYPE TOOL *181*

TEXT MANIPULATION IN PHOTOSHOP *182*

UNDERSTANDING CHARACTER PANEL IN PHOTOSHOP *185*

    Key Features of Character Panel 185

    How to Access the Character Panel in Photoshop 186

ORGANIZATION OF PHOTOSHOP TEXT ELEMENTS *186*

SELECTING CHARACTERS *187*

APPLYING UNDERLINE OR STRIKETHROUGH TO TEXT *188*

APPLYING ALL CAPS OR SMALL CAPS TO TEXT *188*

CREATING A POINT TYPE *189*

ALIGNING TEXT WITHIN A PARAGRAPH *190*

APPLYING JUSTIFICATION FOR PARAGRAPH TYPE *191*

CREATING A CLIPPING MASK AND APPLYING A SHADOW *192*

    Include Drop Shadow 195

    Including Additional Text 196

    HOW TO PUT TEXT ALONG A PATH IN PHOTOSHOP 196

APPLYING WARPING AND DISTORTION TO TEXT *200*

CHAPTER 7 .... **203**

UNDERSTANDING PHOTOSHOP DRAWING **203**

EXPLORING BITMAP IMAGES *203*

EXPLORING VECTOR GRAPHICS *205*

WHAT IS YOUR UNDERSTANDING OF PATHS? *206*

CREATING PATHS IN PHOTOSHOP *207*

CREATING A SHAPE USING THE PEN TOOL *207*

HOW TO DRAW A CURVE *208*

- *FAMILIARIZING YOURSELF WITH COLOR MODE* *211*
- *WHICH COLOR MODE DO I NEED TO SELECT?* *212*
  - RGB Mode, or Red, Green, and Blue 212
  - CMYK Mode: Cyan, Magenta, Yellow, Black 213
  - Lab Color Mode 213
  - Grayscale Mode 214
  - Bitmap Mode 214
- *HOW TO CHANGE COLOR MODE IN PHOTOSHOP* *215*
- *CALIBRATION AND PROFILING GRASPING* *215*
  - Understanding Calibration 215
  - Understanding Profiling 216
- *CONVERTING RGB IMAGE TO CMYK MODE* *216*
- *SAVING YOUR IMAGE AS PHOTOSHOP PDF* *218*
- *HOW TO EXPORT YOUR WORK* *218*
- *PRINTING YOUR WORK IN PHOTOSHOP* *219*

CONCLUSION **222**

INDEX **223**

INTRODUCTION

Welcome to Adobe Photoshop 2025 (Version 26.0), a game-changer in the world of digital design and photo editing. This version pushes the boundaries of what's possible, blending state-of-the-art AI tools with the trusted, powerful features that professionals rely on. Whether you're a seasoned photographer, graphic designer, or hobbyist looking to elevate your creativity, this release promises tools that make complex editing tasks simple and accessible to everyone.

This latest version introduces several groundbreaking updates, including the upgraded Remove Tool with Distraction Removal, which makes eliminating unwanted elements like tourists or wires a one-click task. The integration of Adobe's Firefly generative AI enhances this tool, ensuring seamless, photorealistic results by intelligently filling in missing areas. Firefly's influence extends across other tools, such as Generative Fill and Expand, giving users new ways to transform, resize, or creatively manipulate images using simple text prompts.

With version 26.0, Adobe also introduces the Generate Similar feature, allowing users to experiment with variations of visual elements without trial and error, and the Generate Background Tool, perfect for fast scene changes with realistic lighting and shadows. These enhancements are designed to accelerate workflows and unlock new levels of creative freedom.

Whether you're editing portraits, creating marketing assets, or developing artistic projects, Photoshop 2025 provides the precision, speed, and flexibility to bring your vision to life. This book will guide you through these exciting new features and offer step-by-step instructions to help you master the tools that are redefining the future of digital art. Let's fly in and explore the limitless possibilities that Photoshop 2025 has to offer.

CHAPTER 1

GETTING STARTED WITH ADOBE PHOTOSHOP

OVERVIEW OF ADOBE PHOTOSHOP

Adobe Photoshop is one of the big names in image creation, graphic design, and photo editing. This powerful graphical editor is a property of Adobe and brings with it a gigantic box of tools for editing pixel-based images, raster graphics, and even vector graphics. The facility has reached such heights from a modest beginning when it was launched in 1988 by Thomas and John Knoll for Macintosh computers to grow into the industry standard for digital image manipulation. Since its very first release, over the years, it has evolved to include both Windows and macOS. It does have a wide span of creative works that can be processed.

As a central member of the Adobe Creative Cloud software suite, Photoshop can easily integrate with other major programs, such as Adobe Illustrator, Lightroom, and Dreamweaver, in one workflow. In turn, this allows different programs to share files and communicate well in team situations for innovative, complex creative projects not limited by location. Be it professional photography, graphic design, or digital art, Photoshop has outstanding capabilities for cross-platform work creating amazing visual work to enhance your creative workflow.

HOW DOES PHOTOSHOP WORK?

Adobe Photoshop serves as a professional image editing application, designed for manipulating and enhancing digital images with advanced tools. The general concept behind Adobe Photoshop is as follows:

- **Layer-Based Editing**

Photoshopping fundamentally involves layers. Everything, from text to shapes to other parts of your photo, will be edited on a separate layer. This lets the user change active elements without altering the original image in any way. The flexibility provided by the layers allows for non-destructive editing, easy reordering, blending, and masking in creating complex compositions.

- **Pixel and Vector Manipulation**

Photoshop was originally designed to edit raster or pixel-based images. Raster images are made up of small, square building blocks called pixels. Zoom in close to an image, and reduce the size of it without losing sharpness, and it is at the core a tool for working with pixels. However, it also allows for vector shapes, meaning one can create designs that are scalable without loss of quality.

- **Selection Tools**

Photoshops Lasso, Magic Wand, and Quick Selection tools allow selecting part of the image to apply edits to. Items selected can be cut or copied from the rest of an image or their properties can be adjusted independently from the rest. Selections must be made to have exact control over applying filters, adjustments, or transformations to parts of an image.

- **Adjustment Layers and Filters**

With adjustment layers, edits such as brightness, contrast, and color correction are done without actually touching the original image. Blur, sharpening, and other distortion filters can be used either to refine or to stylize an image. A filter gallery in Photoshop allows users to see in real-time before applying such effects.

- **Retouching and Healing Tools**

This would also include the clone stamp, the spot healing brush, and the patch tool to remove imperfections from a picture. These tools will enable the user to smooth out blemishes, repair damaged areas, and seamlessly blend pixels so edits become invisible.

- **Text and Shape Tools**

Besides photo editing, Photoshop also supports both typography and vector-based design elements. Within it, the text tool allows users to add style and edit text; it also provides shape tools that enable constructing geometric shapes and vectors the ideal program for creating logos, posters, and web graphics.

- **Automation and Workflow Efficiency**

The key features used in Photoshop to automate repetitive tasks include actions and batch processing. Actions in Photoshop allow a user to record several edits applied to an image and then apply those edits to many other files. This saves a lot of time in post-processing.

- **File Export and Compatibility**

The file formats supported on Photoshop range from PSD-native to Photoshop, to JPEG, PNG, GIF, and TIFF. Such exporting of files has also been made available in settings meant for print, web, and other digital uses for compatibility with a wide range of platforms and usages.

WHAT'S NEW IN ADOBE PHOTOSHOP 2025?

Adobe Photoshop 2025 brings new features, additions, and enhancements aimed at pushing the boundaries of creativity and making it more efficient with your workflow. Whether a professional or a fresher, the recent version of Photoshop brings the ball of innovative tools to make designing easier, automate it, and increase usability. Here are the latest additions to Adobe Photoshop 2025:

Distraction Removal in the Remove Tool

The new feature in the Remove Tool allows you to click out some of the more common distractions, like people or wires and cables. This helps edit crowded scenarios, cityscapes, or event photos. It also aids in providing a fine image much sooner than manual ones. This feature is available with the updated desktop app and Photoshop on the web for flexibility across platforms.

How to Use:

- Select the Remove Tool from the toolbar.
- Click on the distraction you want to remove; for example, a person or wire.
- With one click, this cool tool will fill an area with content that will automatically match the background seamlessly.
- If that is not perfect, try over-brushing an object manually for refinement.

Improved Generative Fill

Generative Fill allows users to add or remove content using text prompts while maintaining natural lighting, shadows, and reflections for photorealistic results. The updated Firefly Image 3 Model makes this feature even more realistic, with a better comprehension of complex prompts and more variation. It can easily be used by users in creative ideation. For example, an artist may create a series of self-portraits, each with different royal accessories, to turn the images into magnets; another artist might take a photo and change its background to some sort of fantastic scene complete with mushrooms and trolls. New dimensions of creativity and precision, organic and life-like, are opened by this tool.

How to use:

- Select an area in your image where you want to add, remove, or extend content using either the Lasso Tool or the Rectangular Marquee Tool.
- These selection tools will allow you to isolate regions with precision.
- When your selection is active, click Generative Fill in from the Contextual Task Bar which is a menu that appears near your selection.

- Alternatively, if the Contextual Task Bar is hidden or disabled you can find Edit > Generative Fill from the top menu bar.

Improved Generative Expand with Firefly Image Model

Generative Expand will enable users to extend the edges of images by expanding the canvas and filling in new content that matches seamlessly. Such functionality is perfect for resizing images or fixing uneven edges without loss of quality. For example, it can extend a portrait to fit the 4:5 social media ratio or fill gaps in panoramic shots to soften jagged edges. The AI-powered model automatically ensures a seamless fusion of the new content with the old, maintaining consistency in lighting and texture. This makes it perfect for image refinement, composition straightening, or repurposing content across various formats and platforms.

How to use:

- Choose the Crop Tool from the toolbar.
- Drag the corner or edge handles outward until the size of the canvas reaches the required dimensions. The step will determine the area in which new content is to be generated.
- With the canvas expanded, in the Contextual Task Bar, choose Generative Expand.
- It enables this Photoshop tool to fill in the new areas with content that matches the lighting, color, and texture of the original material. Perfect for adjusting aspect ratios or extending scenes, such as taking a portrait and making it landscape by filling in new areas with relevant background information.

Generate Similar

Generate Similar enables the user to get every possible modification of certain elements in an image without going through trial and error. This tool works across multiple functionalities, including Generative Fill, Expand, and Background, enabling users to fine-tune their output efficiently. For instance, a creator might want to enhance a beach photo with grass realistically and then adjust it to perfection to generate multiple variations and find the perfect fit. It reduces guesswork, as it opens new creative possibilities to the user's initial choice and lets him/her explore alternative styles or effects with more confidence and greater precision.

How to use:

- From the toolbar, select the Rectangular Marquee Tool, and draw a selection where you would like new content.
- The size and shape of this selection inform Photoshop on how it will fill in the new elements.
- Open the Contextual Task Bar and select Generative Fill.
- As indicated below you will write a text prompt that indicates the kind of content you would like to generate.
- You can try the following prompts: "heirloom tomato" or come up with your own that best fits your creative needs.
- The interesting thing about this feature is that you can generate hundreds of assets in no more than a few minutes, be able to brainstorm new concepts in design, or even come up with multiple ideas and test them out simultaneously. It comes in handy in many cases for product

designers, artists, and marketers who would like to create multiple visuals without having to start from scratch.

Generate Image

The "Generate Image" feature, uses AI to generate custom visuals in an instant. This analyzes either text prompts or what is on the canvas, generating unique visuals for your project's needs. This simplifies workflows and allows you to quickly prototype and experiment with ideas right within the workspace.

How to use:

- Create a new black workspace in your Photoshop.
- Then, click on the Generate button from the Context menu.
- Type in your prompt and choose your options according to your preferences.
- Finally. Click on the Generate button.

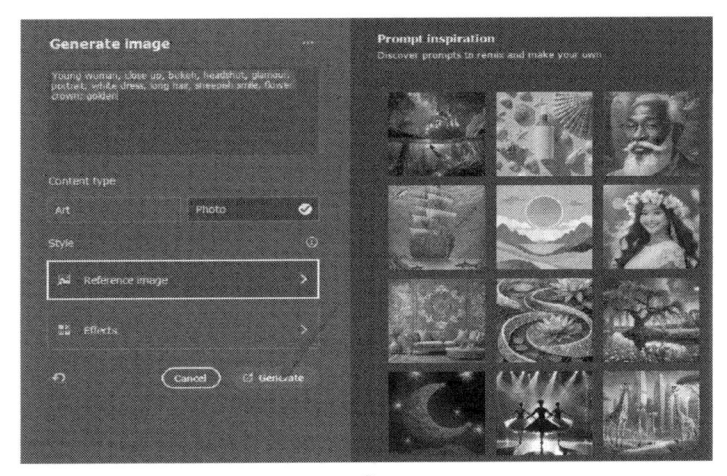

Generate Background Tool

The Generate Background tool uses AI to replace or change backgrounds without affecting natural lighting, shadows, and perspective. The feature is quite helpful for creatives who do fast scene changes with the need to keep the image quality intact. It may be used by a designer who wants to put themselves in a variety of different scenes for travel photos, or an interior designer might want to stage furniture against a variety of sceneries to create catchy advertisements. The tool provides endless creative freedom, allowing users to experiment with a wide range of settings and ideas while ensuring that the subject of the image stays well-integrated into the generated backdrop.

How to use:

- In the Contextual Task Bar, click Remove Background.
- Click Generate Background.
- Type a prompt for the background. You can make one up, or if you want, feel free to use something like: "Orchids and oranges."
- Let me know if you have any other questions about this feature!
- Click Generate to generate the background.
- In the Properties panel select your favorite variation.

REQUIREMENTS FOR THE PERFECT RUNNING OF PHOTOSHOP

To have smooth operation and good performance with Adobe Photoshop 2025, meeting or going above the recommended system specifications is key. The following are the best system requirements to run Photoshop 2025 effectively:

1. **Operating System**
   - **Windows**: Windows 11 or Windows 10 (64-bit) with version 20H2 or later.
   - **macOS**: macOS 12.4 (Monterey) or later.
2. **Processor (CPU)**
   - **Minimum**: Multi-core Intel processor with 64-bit support, 2 GHz or faster.
   - **Recommended**: Intel Core i7 or AMD Ryzen 7 or higher for optimal performance while dealing with heavy editing tasks and large files.
3. **Graphics Processor (GPU)**
   - **Minimum**: For Windows, a DirectX 12 compatible GPU is needed, while for macOS, use a Metal-compatible GPU.
   - **Recommended**: NVIDIA GeForce GTX 1060 or AMD equivalent; 4 GB of dedicated VRAM ensures smooth performance while dealing with 3D rendering, filter effects, and AI-powered tools.
   - **For the best results**: The NVIDIA GeForce RTX 20 series or AMD Radeon RX 5000 series with a minimum of 8 GB of VRAM.
4. **RAM**
   - **Minimum**: 8 GB of RAM.
   - **Recommended**: 16 GB or higher, usually for normal editing along with multitasking.
   - **Optimal**: 32 GB of RAM for heavy tasks such as working with large, high-resolution images, 3D rendering, and video editing.
5. **Hard Drive Space**
   - **Minimum**: 4 GB of available hard disk space for installation; additional free space required during installation (cannot install on a volume that uses a case-sensitive file system).
   - **Recommended**: SSD (Solid-State Drive) with at least 50 GB free for project files, scratch disks, and faster boot time
   - **Optimal**: NVMe SSD would be ideal for faster opening and handling of files. This will be much more evident in the case of large image files.
6. **Display Resolution**
   - **Minimum Display**: 1280 x 800 at 100% UI scaling
   - **Recommended**: Display - 1920 x 1080 or higher for a more comfortable editing workspace.
   - **Optimal**: 4K display - 3840 x 2160 for viewing and editing ultra-high-definition images, and for more detailed views of fine details.

7. **Internet Connection**

Required for software activation, access to the Adobe Creative Cloud libraries as well as other services such as Adobe Stock, cloud storing, and updates.

8. **Graphics Card Compatibility**

Only the performance of Photoshop can be enhanced with the latest GPU drivers. For improved results from AI-powered features, filters, and rendering of 3D models, Adobe recommends the use of Photoshop performance-certified GPU.

Other Factors

- **Input Devices**: Digital artists or those who want complete control over brush strokes and other tools will find a pressure-sensitive tablet very useful.
- **External Monitor**: A second monitor or widescreen monitor is useful for those who need extra screen space for multitasking among different tools, palettes, or reference images.

The above specification will enable optimum performance of Adobe Photoshop 2025 without lag in a smooth workflow and full utilization of powerful tools that also include AI enhancements, 3D features, and real-time collaboration.

INSTALLING ADOBE PHOTOSHOP 2025

Once you have satisfied the minimum installation requirements, proceed with the installation process. To install Adobe Photoshop 2025, you must initially acquire an Adobe membership, which is available through monthly or yearly subscriptions. This membership includes a license that provides access to the complete suite of Creative Cloud applications, encompassing Photoshop and various other creative tools.

It is important to note that an active internet connection, possession of an Adobe ID, and agreement to the license terms are obligatory prerequisites for product activation and usage. To install Adobe Photoshop 2025, adhere to the outlined procedures below.

- First, you'll need to create a free Adobe Creative Cloud account to install Photoshop 2025.
- Open the official website of Adobe and click on the Sign In button.

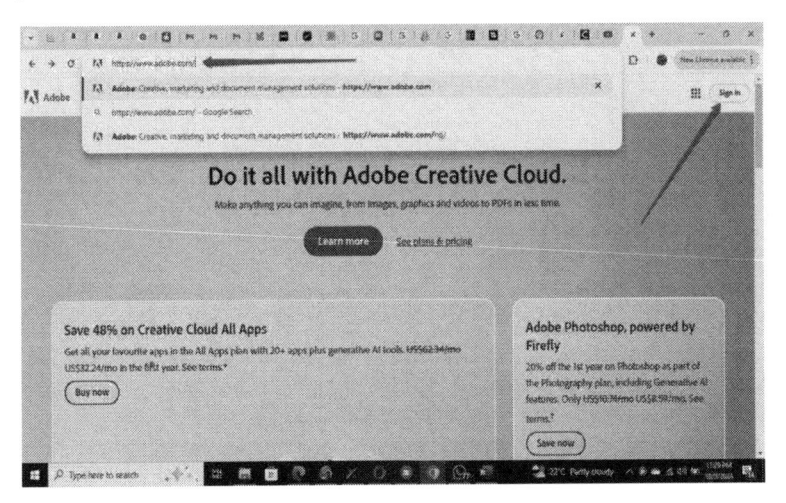

- If you do not have an account, just click on the link labeled Create an Account and follow the onscreen directions to create one.

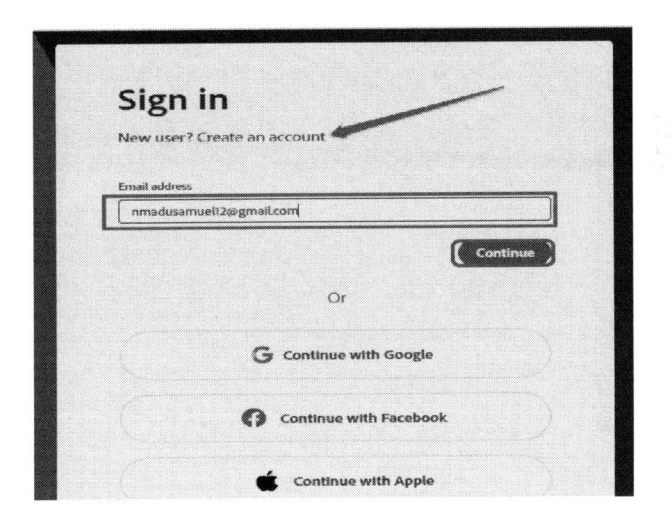

- Sign in using your credentials after creating your account.
- Locate Adobe **Creative Cloud**, and click the **Download** button; this will download the installer for Creative Cloud. In the window that opens, begin the installation process for the Creative Cloud Desktop app on your computer.

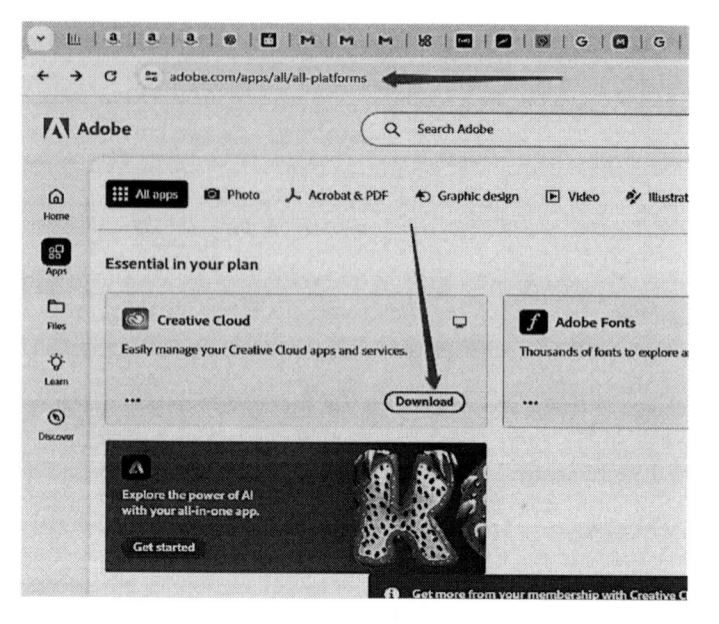

- Install Adobe Photoshop 2025 when the Creative Cloud app has been installed, launch the Creative Cloud Desktop app on your computer, and then sign in using your Adobe credentials. Locate Photoshop from within the Creative Cloud app.
- Click the free trial option or buy, then fill in your payment details and proceed.
- The application will now download Photoshop and install it. It can take anywhere from a few minutes up to an hour depending on one's connection speed.
- While this installs, make sure your internet connection is stable.

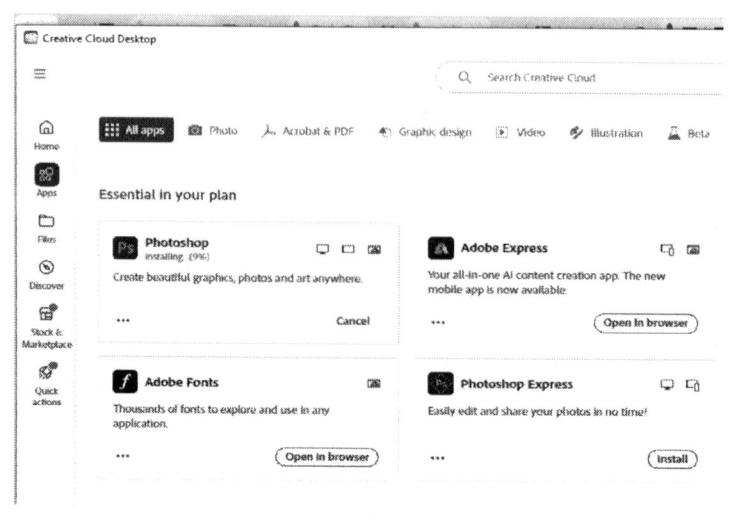

- When it finally downloads, double-click on it to launch the application.

If you like to use any third-party plugins or Adobe extensions after the launch, do the following to activate them:

- Go to Edit > Preferences > Plug-ins > (for Windows users) or Photoshop > Preferences > Plug-ins (in case you work on macOS).
- Turn the plug-ins option on, and install the extensions if needed from Adobe Exchange or other third-party providers.

WORKSPACE OVERVIEW

The workspace of Adobe Photoshop 2025 is the core of your creative environment, intuitively laid out with the placement of tools and panels in such a way that helps to streamline your workflow. The ability to position and access essential tooling with ease is accomplished with very customizable workspaces inside Photoshop. Whether one is editing a photo, designing graphics, or creating digital artwork, here is a general overview of the main workspace components to show you how to easily navigate this interface.

- **Application Frame**

Mac Users Only: The Application Frame keeps all Photoshop panels and windows within a single unified window, making it easier to manage your workspace. It can be resized, moved, or minimized like any other window.

- **Menu Bar**

Located on the top of the screen, the Menu Bar contains drop-down menus for File, Edit, Image, Layer, Select, Filter, View, Window, and Help. It gives access to basic Photoshop features that include new file creation, filtering, and working with layers.

- **Tools Panel (Toolbar)**

The Tools Panel is the column of tools that, by default, is located on the left side of the screen. These contain all basic tools that assist in editing or creating:

   a. **Selection Tools**: Move Tool, Lasso Tool, Quick Selection Tool.
   b. Drawing and Editing Tools: Brush Tool, Clone Stamp Tool, Eraser Tool.
   c. **Navigation Tools**: Zoom Tool, Hand Tool.
   d. **Color and Gradient Tools**: Fill, Gradient, Eyedropper. Most of the tools offer additional options if you either long-press or right-click on the tool icon, etc.

- **Options Bar**

Below the Menu Bar, the Options Bar displays the settings of the currently active tool. As you have clicked on one of the tools from the Tools Panel, the Options Bar will update to the selected tool and will display the tool-specific settings, such as brush size, opacity, blending mode, and so forth. It is the location from where you may do any modification related to the selected tool.

- **Document Window**

The Document Window is the actual window where your opened image or project is displayed. This is the main, central area where you will edit your photo or design in real-time. You may open several documents in one session in Photoshop, set up in tabs.

Across the bottom of the Document Window, there is a status line showing information about zoom percentage, file size, and document color profile.

- **Panels and Palettes**

The workspace of Photoshop is strewn with panels for managing everything related to layers, colors, adjustments, and so on. Some of the important ones include:

a. **Layers Panel**: This is a panel where you deal with the layers in your project. You can arrange, hide, lock, and group layers.
b. **Properties Panel**: Well, this panel shows you advanced options depending on what you've selected it a layer or an object.
c. **Adjustments Panel**: The panel offers quick access to color correction and image adjustment tools, such as Brightness/Contrast, Levels, and Curves, among others.
d. **History Panel**: This will allow you to step back or revisit previous steps that you have taken so far in your workflow.
e. **Brush Settings Panel**: Advanced brush dynamics and characteristics control.
f. **Character and Paragraph Panels**: These panels are very important while manipulating text as these allow changing the font, size, kerning, and paragraph alignment.

Panels can be docked, rearranged, stacked, and minimized to customize your workspace. Other panels can be opened from the Window menu at the Menu Bar.

- **Workspaces**

There are several sets of predefined Workspaces in Photoshop to perform specific tasks, such as Photography, Graphics and Web, Motion, and 3D. These show and hide some tools and panels depending on what you are doing.

You can choose any one of these workspaces from the Window > Workspace menu or create your own by organizing your panels and then saving the arrangement for later use.

- **Layers Panel**

The Layers Panel arguably is the most important section of the workspace, which allows stacking of images, text, and effects; to apply non-destructive edits to them. You can also rename every layer and group, and hide, or lock layers for better organization.

You can also apply blending mode, masks, and effects directly from the Layers Panel to achieve complex image manipulations.

- **The Properties Panel**

Context-sensitive settings are displayed in the Properties Panel according to the layer or tool at hand. If one is working on a Shape Layer, for example, in the Property Panel, one will see options to change fill and stroke and the dimension of the shape.

- **Navigator Panel**

The Navigator Panel allows you to scroll around and zoom in or out of parts of your image without affecting the document zoom level. This is particularly helpful when working with high-resolution images where you will, for the most part, work on details.

- **Workspace Customization**

Photoshop gives you options to customize your workspace. Therefore, you can move, dock, and float panels, and save your customized workspace for later use too. Just open the menu Window > Workspace > New Workspace and save your layout.

- **Context Menus**

The context menus that appear by right-clicking on any elements in your workspace give quick access to tools and commands relevant to what you have selected. Saving you a lot of time, potentially.

UNDERSTANDING THE LEFT PANEL TABS AND BUTTONS ON THE HOME SCREEN

Here, we will explore the Home Screen of Adobe Photoshop, and the things visible on this screen:

Menu Bar (Top of the Screen)

The menu bar is at the top of the screen, and through it, one may access a variety of tools and settings within Photoshop, including:

      a. **File**: Open and save, export files.
      b. **Edit**: Allows access to undo, redo, and other editing actions.
      c. **Image**: Allows changing image settings, such as size, mode, and rotating images.
      d. **Layer**: Offers layer controls-which means you can add, change, or delete layers.

e. **Type**: Used in adding text layers and modifying them.
f. Select: Allows selecting the selection tools for the refinement of your images.
g. **Filter**: Allows access to Photoshop filters for blurring or artistic effects.
h. **3D**: Related to 3D objects and layers in Photoshop.
i. **View**: Changes the view and layout of the workspace.
j. **Plugins**: Access third-party plugins.
k. **Window**: Controls the different panels in Photoshop.
l. **Help**: Opens tutorials and troubleshooting inside the application.

Left Sidebar

- **New File / Open**: These are your very first options in the sidebar. By clicking "New File", you will be able to create a new project whereas "Open" will let you browse for any existing files.
- **Home**: This brings you back to this home screen, which will be a launch point for projects, tutorials, and files.
- **Learn**: Opens learning resources inside Photoshop-in-app tutorials and guides for new users.
- **Your Files**: It gives you a list of recently opened and shared files using Adobe's cloud services:
- **Shared with You**: These are files other Adobe users have shared with you; it makes collaboration easy.
- **Deleted**: This will show recently deleted files from which you can recover if needed.

Welcome Section

Here at the top middle of the screen, you will find a banner stating "Welcome to Photoshop" along with the "Name." Below that, there are options like

- **Edit your photos**: This is where some ideas for photo editing are given out, and also tutorials to be found right in the app.
- **Recent Files Section**

Below the Welcome Section, your recent files worked on are displayed. The files are shown as thumbnails, which you may click to reopen your recent projects.

a. **Sort/Filter Options**: Sorting will be enabled on the "Sort" section by date modified, file type, etc.
   b. **Filter**: Filtering shall be available for showing all kinds of projects, like "All Files" or "Recent Files."
- **Search Bar (Top Right Corner)**

The magnifying glass icon opens a search in Photoshop for a file, tool, or help topic. It is a quick way of finding how to do something or where a feature is located within Photoshop.

Cloud Services and Account Options

The cloud icon beside your profile opens up your Adobe Creative Cloud storage and syncs files and assets across devices.

The icon of your profile allows you to manage account settings or switch between accounts.

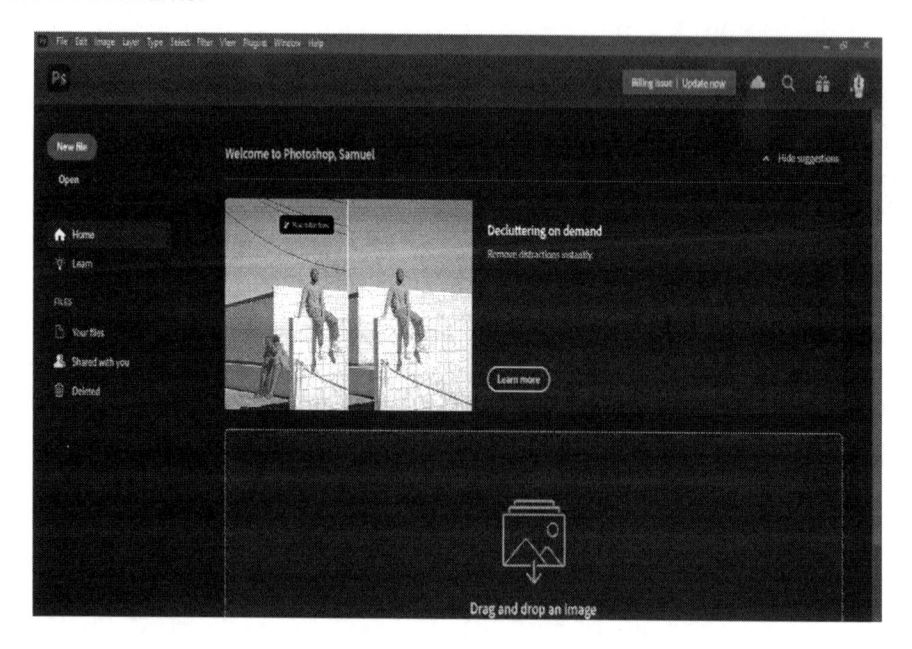

FAMILIARIZING YOURSELF WITH THE PHOTOSHOP INTERFACE

In Adobe Photoshop, a workspace is a named configuration of many of the components in the Photoshop interface. It includes which panels are open and where they are positioned on your screen. Workspaces can also modify the contents and arrangement of the Toolbar, including custom menu items that have been added in the Menu Bar, and even custom keyboard shortcuts. All or any of these options can be saved into a workspace.

Adobe interface involved various options and features, including:

- **Options Bar**: Positioned just below the main menu bar in Adobe Photoshop, the Options Bar functions as a dynamic toolbar that showcases context-sensitive settings for the currently selected tool. Users can swiftly access and modify various controls related to the active tool, such as brush size, opacity, blending modes, and more.
- **Home Screen Button**: The Home Screen Button within Photoshop serves as a gateway to the Home Screen, offering convenient access to recent files, and creative options. It acts as a central hub for initiating new projects, opening recent documents, exploring Adobe Stock assets, and accessing learning resources.
- **Toolbar**: Comprising a collection of tools, the Toolbar in Photoshop empowers users to execute diverse actions like selection, painting, cropping, and retouching. Each tool within the Toolbar serves a distinct purpose, allowing users to switch between them by clicking on the corresponding tool icon. Common tools include the Move Tool, Brush Tool, Pen Tool, and others.
- **Status Bar**: Situated at the bottom of the Photoshop interface, the Status Bar furnishes information about the current document, such as dimensions, color mode, and zoom level. It incorporates helpful icons for tasks like toggling layers, adjusting screen mode, and more.
- **Working Area**: Also known as the canvas or workspace, the Working Area is the central zone in Photoshop where users create and manipulate images. It constitutes the region enclosed by the application's interface, serving as the space for activities like drawing, editing, and applying various effects to projects.
- **Share Button**: The Share Button simplifies the process of sharing work directly from Photoshop. It offers options to share files via email, social media, Adobe Creative Cloud, and other platforms, streamlining the showcasing and collaboration of creative projects.
- **Search and Help Button**: This feature aids users in swiftly locating tools, menu items, and information within Photoshop. The Search and Help

Button also grants access to contextual help and tutorials, enhancing the user's ability to learn and navigate the software effectively.

- **Workspace Menu**: Providing predefined layouts and arrangements of panels, tools, and other elements, the Workspace Menu allows users to switch between different workspaces tailored for specific tasks like photography, design, or 3D modeling. Users can also customize and save their preferred workspaces.
- **Panels**: Resizable, collapsible, and dockable containers located on the right side of the interface, Panels in Photoshop house various functions and features, including layers, adjustments, brushes, and more. Users can organize panels to align with their workflow, offering essential controls and options for different aspects of image editing and design.

UNDERSTANDING THE TOOLBAR

The toolbar in Photoshop is the virtual workplace where you will be holding all of your artistic tools. This tall, thin palette on the left side of the workspace holds some of the most basic tools for drawing, painting, erasing, and other manipulative work with images.

It also has a set of associated tools that allow the user to manipulate and enhance the quality of images. When a tool is selected from the palette, the mouse pointer and mouse functions take on the characteristics of the tool selected. In summary, Photoshop's tool palette contains a vast variety of tools that are organized by their primary functions.

Let's take a closer look at some of the main groups and their tools in the Photoshop toolbar:

Selection Tools

Selection tools are some of the most important tools for users who want to extract portions of an image that are to be worked upon individually. These tools will provide the user with the ability to choose pixels, shapes, or objects, which can then be manipulated, moved, or adjusted in further detail.

- **Move Tool**: This tool is used to move the objects or selections around the canvas. This is commonly used when you have been working with layers, to simply rearrange content.
- **Marquee Tools**: These are rectangular, elliptical, and so on, which create selections of the aforementioned shapes. You can thereby select only a part of your image to edit.
- **Lasso Tools**: The lasso tools are a set of freehand selections that, by drawing around an area, will isolate it. The polygonal lasso creates a straight-edge selection, while the magnetic lasso will cling to the edge of an object.
- **Quick Selection and Magic Wand Tools**: These tools help in making selections of color and texture. While the Magic Wand Tool selects all pixels of a similar color, the Quick Selection Tool detects and selects objects based on texture edges.

Painting and Drawing Tools

This segment of the toolbar provides various tools that can help users apply creative touches to an image, such as color, brush strokes, and gradients. These are simple tools but see broad applications in artistic design, digital painting, and retouching.

- **Brush Tool**: Most likely, this is one of the most used tools in Photoshop. The Brush Tool lets you paint on your image. You can use other effects by adjusting brush size, hardness, and opacity. It's good for retouching or adding creative elements. Pencil Tool: A similar tool to the brush tool but with hard, pixelated strokes. It's way much better if you want to do some rough sketches or create some pixel art.
- **Gradient Tool**: The Gradient tool is used for a gradient mix of many colors. The Gradient tool is utilized to create backgrounds for filling selections and for creating smooth color transitions.
- **Paint Bucket Tool**: It fills an area of similar colors with the selected foreground color or with a specified pattern. It sees its wide usage in giving color to big areas of an image with less effort.

Retouching and Healing Tools

These tools serve to straighten out and further improve images by removing defects or unwanted objects. They find rampant usage in photo retouching, especially in portrait photography and restoration works.

- **Spot Healing Brush and Healing Brush**: Both of these brushes automatically sample nearby pixels to mask blemishes, scratches, or other unwanted elements in your image. The Healing Brush allows more control because you can manually select the source pixels.
- **Clone Stamp Tool**: Applied for duplicating parts of an image by sampling an area. One can "paint" over another part of the image with the selected pixels. Works well in removing big objects or duplicating areas of an image.
- **The Patch Tool**: Works just like the healing tools but provides far more control over the area you want to patch. Drag a selected area over another part of the image to replace it seamlessly.

Text and Typography Tools

Text can be considered one of the most critical aspects of graphic design, where Photoshop possesses some of the best options for inserting text into an image or a design.

- **Type Tool**: The Type Tool is going to enable you to add text to your images. You can create both point text and paragraph text. Once added, text can be fully customized with options like font style, size, alignment, color, and many more.
- **Text Mask Tool**: This allows the creation of a text selection that can be filled with images, patterns, or gradients to bring special creativity to your designs.

Shape Tools

Shape tools provide some basic vector shapes that can be useful in creating graphics, logos, or design elements that scale with no loss of quality.

- **Rectangle, Ellipse, and Polygon Tools**: These three basic shape tools create solid vector shapes on your canvas. Great for designing simple graphics, frames, or buttons.
- **Custom Shape Tool**: This is a tool that consists of several different pre-defined vector shapes, such as arrows and stars, among others. You can drag these onto your canvas. You are also able to load other custom shapes you have created or downloaded from somewhere else.

Navigation Tools

Navigation tools make the process of moving around on your canvas easier than if you were working without them on large images or fine details.

- **Zoom Tool**: With it, you will be able to zoom your image in and out. This is effective whenever you want to have a better look at small details or look at the bigger picture of your whole project.
- **Hand Tool**: This tool is used to move the canvas around when you are zoomed in. You can then drag the image around in different directions to navigate across your workspace.

Color Picker and Swatches

The Color Picker at the bottom of the toolbar allows the user to pick foreground and background colors to use for painting, filling, or other effects.

- **Foreground/Background Color**: The foreground color is used with which you paint or draw, while the background color is used in fills and for other purposes. You can click to toggle between them.
- **Swatches**: Photoshop has a default panel of color swatches to select from, but you can also save custom colors that you create for later use.

Extra Hidden Tools

Some hidden tools are grouped with other tool icons in the Photoshop Toolbar. To access them, click, and right-click to view the hidden tools. For example, holding the Eraser Tool active will provide you with a host of tools like the Magic Eraser and Background Eraser, each set to a special function.

CUSTOMIZING THE TOOLBAR

You can customize the toolbar in Photoshop according to your needs and workflow. Access its menu via Edit > Toolbar and remove, add, or reorder the tools. Such customization will keep all your commonly used tools at your fingertips for easy editing. Below is a detailed screenshot of all the tools you can use for your Photoshop editing works.

```
A Selection tools              Eraser (E)                  Path Selection (A)
  Move (V)*                    Background Eraser (E)       Direct Selection (A)
  Rectangular Marquee (M)      Magic Eraser (E)
  Elliptical Marquee (M)                                   Rectangle (U)
  Single Column Marquee        Blur                        Rounded Rectangle (U)
  Single Row Marquee           Sharpen                     Ellipse (U)
  Lasso (L)                    Smudge                      Polygon (U)
  Polygonal Lasso (L)                                      Line (U)
  Magnetic Lasso (L)           Dodge (O)                   Custom Shape (U)
  Quick Selection (W)          Burn (O)
  Magic Wand (W)               Sponge (O)                  Navigation & 3D tools
                                                           3D Object Rotate (K)†
  Crop and slice tools         Painting tools              3D Object Roll (K)†
  Crop (C)                     Brush (B)                   3D Object Pan (K)†
  Slice (C)                    Pencil (B)                  3D Object Slide (K)†
  Slice Select (C)             Color Replacement (B)       3D Object Scale (K)†
                               Mixer Brush (B)             3D Rotate Camera (N)†
  Measuring tools              History Brush (Y)           3D Roll Camera (N)†
  Eyedropper (I)               Art History Brush (Y)       3D Pan Camera (N)†
  Color Sampler (I)            Gradient (G)                3D Walk Camera (N)†
  Ruler (I)                    Paint Bucket (G)            3D Zoom Camera (N)†
  Note (I)
  Count (I)                    Drawing and                 Hand (H)
                               type tools                  Rotate View (R)
  Retouching tools             Pen (P)                     Zoom (Z)
  Spot Healing Brush (J)       Freeform Pen (P)
  Healing Brush (J)            Add Anchor Point
  Patch (J)                    Delete Anchor Point
  Red Eye (J)                  Convert Point
  Clone Stamp (S)              Horizontal Type (T)
  Pattern Stamp (S)            Vertical Type (T)
                               Horizontal Type Mask (T)
                               Vertical Type Mask (T)
```

HOW PANELS WORK

Panels are a key factor in managing your workspace. They provide easy access to the tools and options to manipulate layers, colors, history, etc. Position by default along the right side of your screen, panels are dockable, collapsible, and resizable and their configuration can be adjusted to fit the needs of your workflow.

To understand how panels work and how they help in enhancing the user experience in Photoshop, here's a closer look:

Understanding Different Panels

There are a host of different panels that exist in Photoshop, each designed to give you control over another aspect of your project. Some of the most commonly used panels include:

- **Layers Panel**: Arguably the most crucial panel in all of Photoshop, the Layers panel is where you will control and work with each of the layers in your document. Here you can turn on and off the visibility for layers, toggle different blending modes, work with masks, and organize layers through grouping.
- **Properties Panel**: This panel provides different contextual options depending on which tool or object is being chosen. For example, on a text layer, via this properties panel, one can edit font size, color, and alignment. When working with an adjustment layer, it is here where settings are modified such as brightness, contrast, or exposure.
- **Color and Swatches Panels**: These panels will help you organize your colors. The Color Panel allows you to pick foreground and background colors, while the Swatches Panel offers a library of pre-defined colors that you can use with just one click.
- **Adjustments Panel**: This panel comprises options to add adjustment layers to your image, such as brightness/contrast, hue/saturation, and curves. These adjustment layers give you the power to make edits to your image in a non-destructive way.
- **History Panel**: This is your history panel-so you use this to go back in time, to any previous states of your project. So, every time you change something, it's gonna log in here in the History panel, and you can go back to an earlier step in your workflow.

- **Brushes and Presets Panels**: These panels offer a massive range of different brush tips, sizes, and presets for creating your custom brushes for painting and design.

Docking, Grouping, and Moving Panels

Panels can be personalized to fit your working preference. Here's how you can manage them:

- **Docking Panels**: You can dock panels by dragging them to the right side of the screen where other panels reside. Docking panels help organize your workspace to better access the tools you will need.
- **Panel Grouping**: Several panels can be grouped within a tabbed window. For example, the Layers Panel, Channels Panel, and Paths Panel can all be grouped so that you quickly switch between those three panels without cluttering your workspace.
- **Moving Panels**: To do that, simply click and drag the panel to a new position. Place it in another location on your screen or undock it and let the panel float free. That's extra good if you work with several monitors.

Collapsing and Expanding Panels

You can also minimize a lot of space taken up by panels by collapsing them into icons or small bars that are accessible, yet only take a minimal amount of screen space. If you click on one of your panels that have been collapsed, it temporarily opens up so you can use it, and then minimizes again when you're done. This feature helps maximize your canvas area without losing easy access to essentials.

Customizing Your Workspace with Panels

In Photoshop, you can save your personalized workspace depending on what panels you use most. For example, a Photography Workspace would include panels such as Layers, Adjustments, and Histograms, but for a Design Workspace, you may only need Brushes, Swatches, and Paths.

To create and save a workspace:

- Open the required panels by navigating to the Window menu and then selecting the panel you need.
- Organize the panels by either docking or grouping them accordingly.

- Save your workspace by going to Window > Workspace > New Workspace. Name it something relevant to your work, and you can already enable this whenever you want.

Commonly Used Panels in Different Workflows

- **Photographers**: The most used panels are those of Layers, Adjustments, History, Histogram, and Navigator. These will help photographers make fast, non-destructive edits and see the list of changes while keeping the image properly exposed.
- **Digital Artists**: Brushes, Layers, Paths, and Swatches panels are used to work on brush settings, digital painting, and illustration.
- **For Graphic Designers**: In a typical process, Characters, Paragraphs, Layers, and Color panels help designers in handling typography, shapes, and colors in designs.

Resetting Panels

If your panels become disorganized or lost, you can easily revert them to their default location. To do so, at any time you can select Window > Workspace > Reset Essentials, which will allow you to return to the original setting of your working environment and save you from the hassle of manually readjusting the panels.

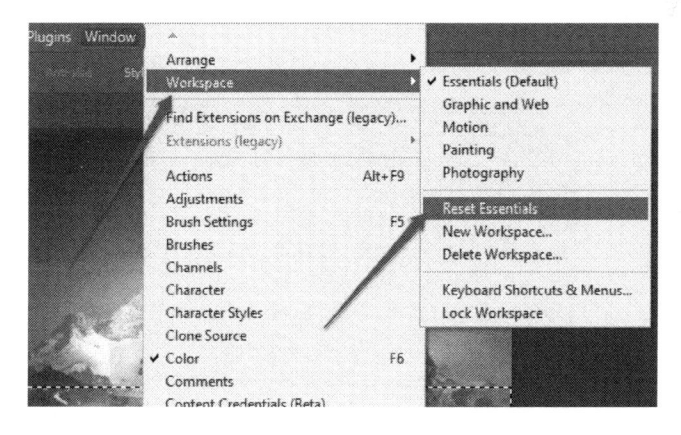

That is the default selection, and it is called the Essentials workspace. The Color Panel, the Properties Panel, and the Layers Panel are included in the workspace.

The other way is through the Window tab, where you can access any of the panels by selecting which one you want to open.

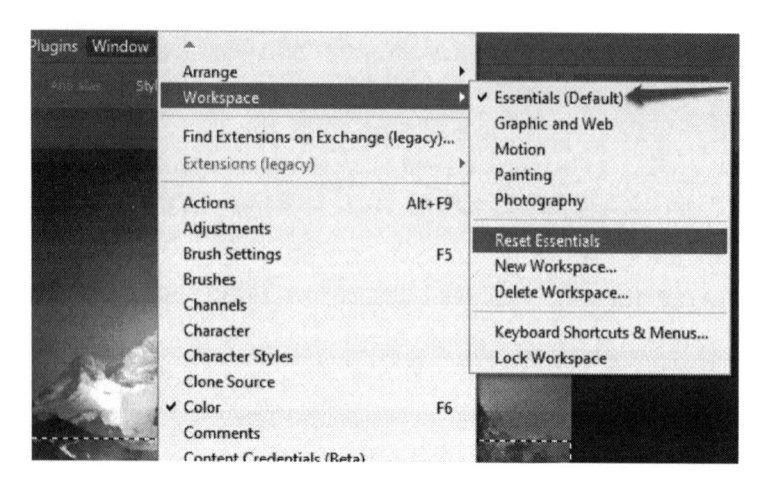

Hiding and Revealing Panels

Pressing the **Tab** key on your keyboard will instantly hide or show all of your panels. This is useful when you need a clear view of the canvas on which you may be working. You can bring the panels back with another press of the Tab key.

PERSONALIZING YOUR TOOLBAR

To personalize the tool palette that aligns with your preference, follow these steps:

- Right-click on the three dots in the toolbar, and click on the Toolbar.

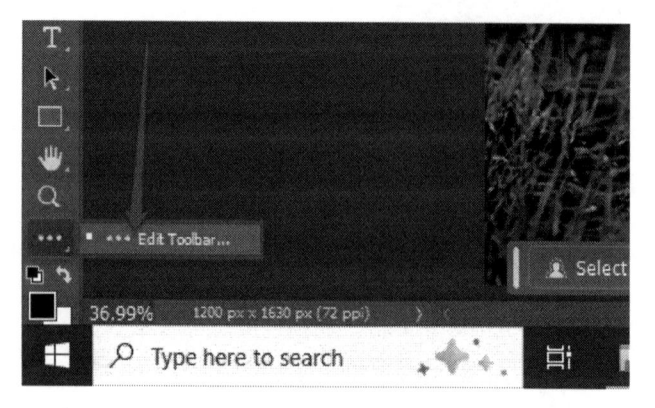

- After clicking the "Edit Toolbar...", a dialog box will appear, as depicted below.

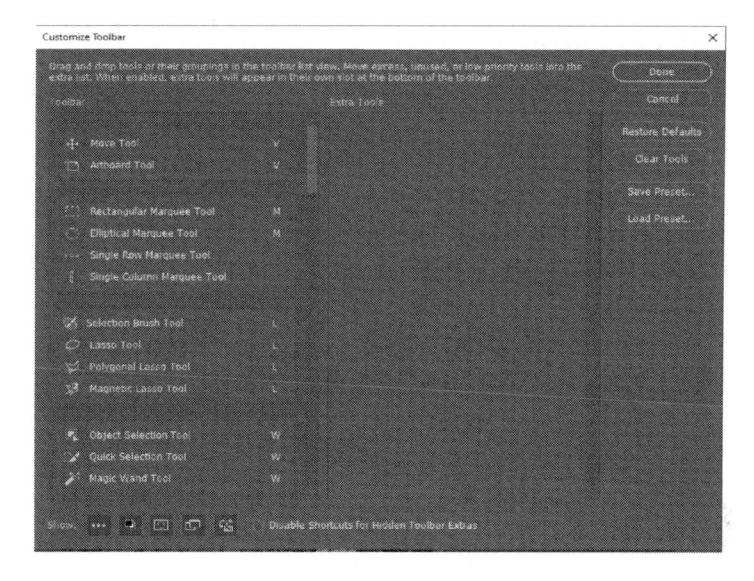

- In the dialog box, drag the tools wanted in the "Extra Tools" panel from the toolbar and select "Save." The chosen tools will be moved from their existing locations and will be available in the "Extra Tools" sub-menu in the toolbar.
- Below the "Edit Toolbar" dialog box, you shall find the "Show" option as shown below.

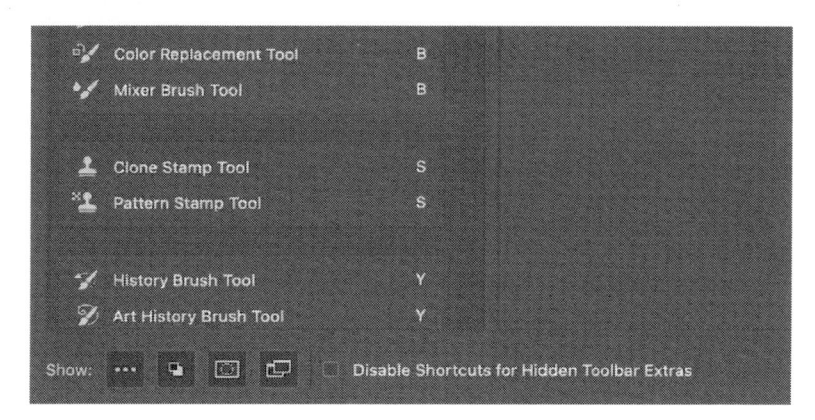

To work on customizing the Adobe Photoshop toolbar, to hide or organize tools according to preference, follow the instructions below.

To access the Toolbar customization:

- Go to the menu option Edit > Toolbar.
- Long-press the bottom of the toolbar and select "Edit Toolbar."
- Customize the Toolbar

The Customize Toolbar dialog box opens. You can make changes to the layout of the toolbar:

- Reorganize tools by drag and drop in different positions or create tool groups.
- Move seldom-used tools to the "Extra Tools" section accessed via the bottom of the toolbar long-press.

Save and Load Presets:

- Save the preset once the toolbar has been customized, using "Save Preset."
- To go back to a previously saved custom toolbar, use "Load Preset."

Restore Default Toolbar:

- If you want to restore the original default arrangement of tools in Photoshop, click "Restore Defaults."

Clear Tools:

By clicking "Clear Tools," all the tools will be moved to the "Extra Tools" area and it will completely clean up the toolbar.

EXPANDING THE TOOL PALETTE

You can always adjust the orientation of the tool palette in Photoshop to your liking. One column is the Photoshop default for the tool palette, but it can be so, so overwhelming with all those tools on it when you go to find the one you want. Well, you can change the orientation to two rows, which many people like. Here's how you would do it:

- Opening of a document in Photoshop.

- Go to the little icon, shaped like ">>", located on the top left in the tool palette.

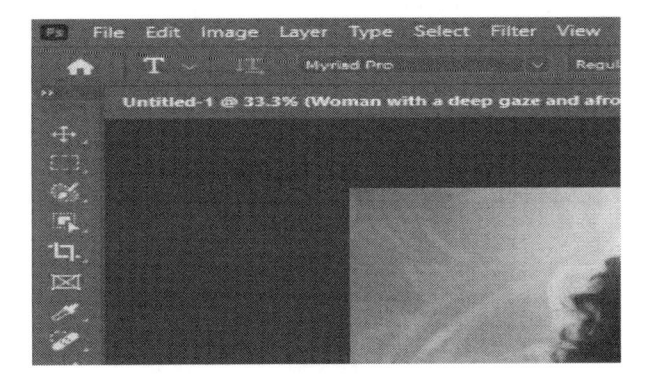

- This button splits your tool palette into two rows for an easier, more intuitive arrangement.

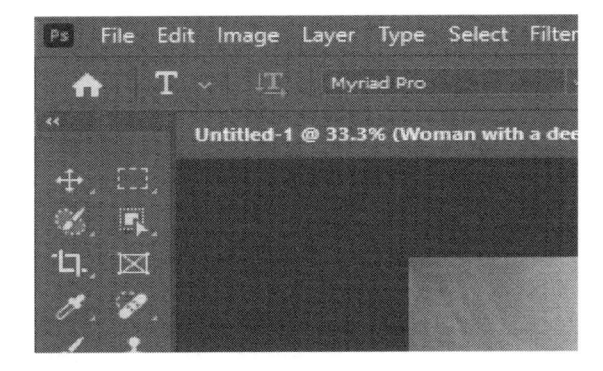

HOW TO CHOOSE A TOOL FROM THE TOOLBAR

The default is the Move tool, which will allow you to move either a selected area or the entire layer if no area is selected. To activate it, either choose the Move tool from the tool palette by holding down the Ctrl key in Windows, or the Command key on a Mac. Or, simply click on your desired tool to make the selection.

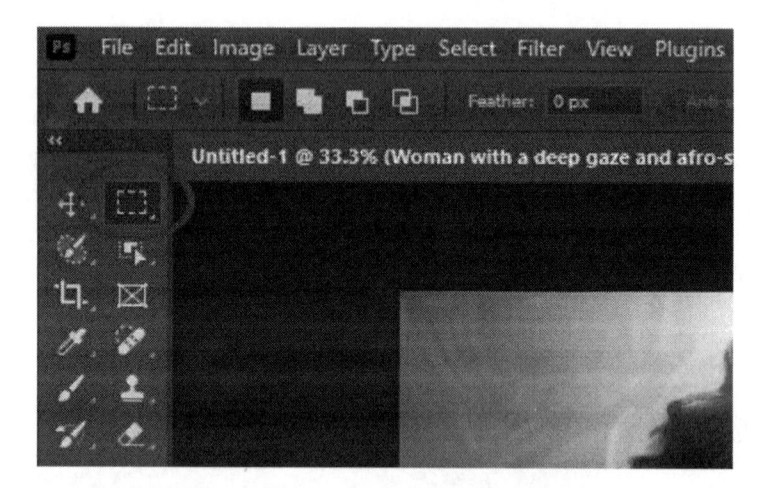

To view a hidden tool, you only have to right-click on the tool to show the hidden tool. Thus, it opens a fly-out menu that displays all the tools that are included within this group. Then, you can choose the needed tool either by clicking on the selected tool or by using a shortcut key, for example (P), to select the Pen tool.

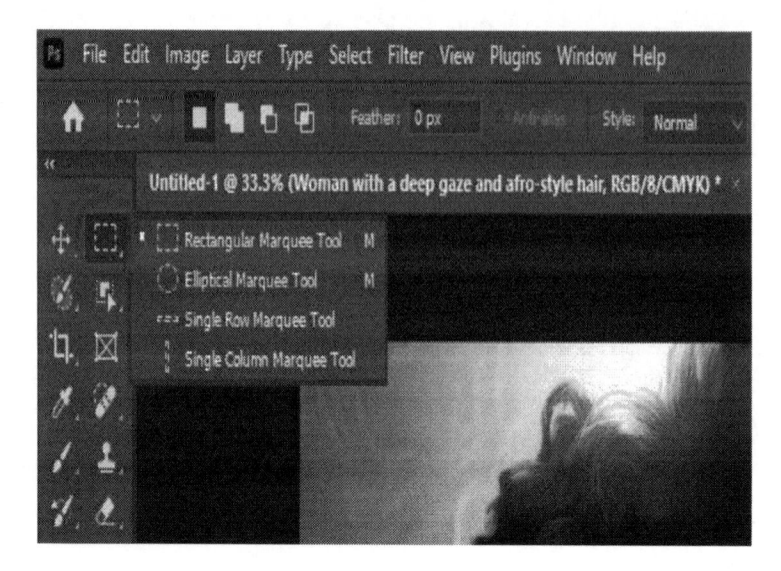

WORKING WITH TOOL PROPERTIES IN THE OPTION BAR

Various parameters about the currently selected tool are displayed in the Options bar. Some of these parameters are exclusive to a particular tool, while many are shared between more than one tool. For example, the Zoom tool is the only tool that has options like zooming in and out; you will not see these options in any other tool's Options bar. On the other hand, since they are common features shared among the majority of selection tools, actions, like select plus or deselect, will fall under the Options bar.

The context-sensitive tool options bar changes depending on which tool is currently chosen and is located below the menu bar at the top of your workspace. Some of the elements on the options bar, such as opacity and painting modes are specific to only one tool, though other parameters are utilized across more than one tool. You can dock the options bar to the top or bottom of your screen in your workspace using the grayed-out gripper bar. Tooltips show up when the pointer is rolled over a tool. To display or hide the options bar, choose **Window** > **Options**.

To reset your tools to their default setting, right-click say in Windows-control-click in macOS and select the tool icon in the options bar. Click the context menu, then select either "Reset Tool" or "Reset All Tools."

HOW TO CHOOSE A COLOR

Along the bottom of the Toolbar are the Foreground and Background Color Swatches. These are frequently referred to as color chips. The default for the foreground color is black, and for the background color, white. If you paint in Photoshop or fill an area with color, it will use the foreground color. The background color becomes a backup or secondary choice to rely on when creating a gradient or erasing part of a locked Background layer.

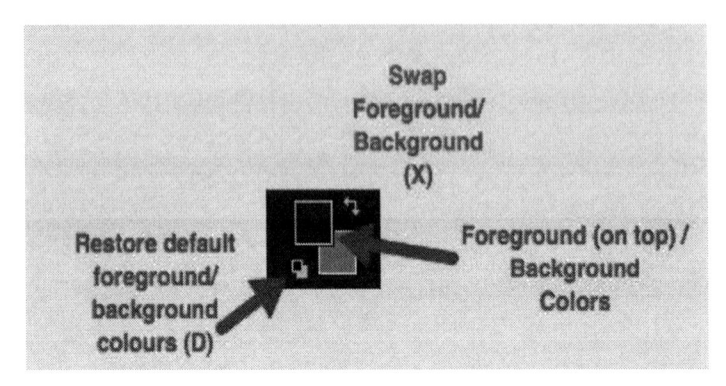

- Just click on the color's swatch once to open the Color Picker where you can play with millions of shades.
- You can exchange the colors of the foreground and background by clicking the "X" key on your keyboard or by the circular double-headed arrow a little above the foreground and background swatches.
- Clicking any of the small swatches, or using the "D" key to return both color swatches to their default settings of black and white.

- The Screen Mode and the Quick Mask Mode The final two items on the Photoshop Toolbar are buttons, which are found at the very end.

UNDERSTANDING THE STATUS BAR

The status bar is the area at the very bottom of the document window that contains much valuable information. For one, it provides the percentage or level of zoom or magnification of the image in the workspace. It also allows you to see the file properties of the active document. You can set the zoom by typing a new value in the zoom box.

Also, you can choose what to show on the status bar. You do this by clicking on the Status Bar arrow and choosing whatever you want to show.

UNDERSTANDING THE CONTEXT MENUS

A contextual menu, like other menu types, is context-sensitive, appearing when you right-click (on Windows) or Control-click (on Mac) an element within the application. The term "contextual" indicates that the menu's content depends on the specific object or item you right-click (Windows) or Control-click (Mac).

For example, when you invoke a contextual menu while the cursor hovers over an image, it will display commands related to that image. Conversely, if you right-click (Windows) or Control-click (Mac) on the background of a document, you'll typically encounter options that pertain to the entire document rather than a specific element within it.

This functionality enables you to choose relevant commands tailored to the item you've selected. In the accompanying figure, you can observe a contextual menu that appears when you right-click (Windows) or Control-click (Mac) an object in Photoshop.

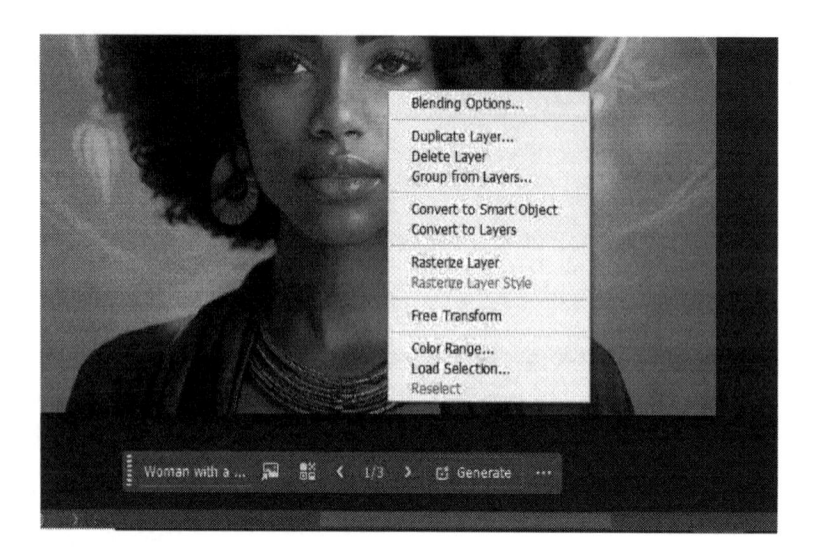

WORKING WITH PANELS

On the right-hand side of the application frame sit a set of short windows called panels. These panels house some of the most commonly used features in the application, including color controls, adjustments, layers, and so much more. You can drag and move these panels around, which allows you to position them wherever you would like them to sit. Panels can either be free-standing and moveable windows, or docked to the left, right, top, or bottom edges of your screen. You can also combine panels, enabling you to move them as one object. Each panel has its menu called a "panel menu," which is located in the upper right corner. This is a well-labeled menu, and it's rather easy to recognize since it has an icon that looks like four small lines with a downward-pointing triangle.

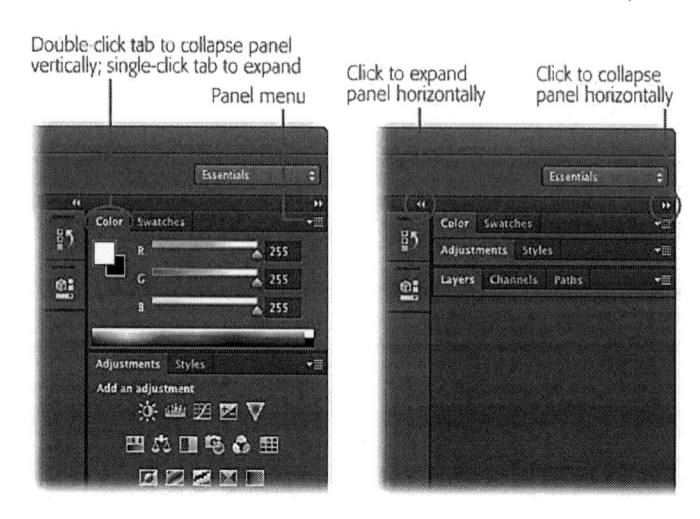

HOW TO RESIZE, EXPAND, AND COLLAPSE PANELS

Resizing Panels

You can click and drag any of the corners or the right or bottom edges of a Photoshop Panel or Panel Group size using your mouse. Double-clicking on an edge when the cursor changes to a double arrow will also allow you to adjust the size.

Expanding Panels

Clicking once on any tab in the panel group opens a previously collapsed panel group and restores the panels to view. Here, one click on the Swatches panel tab has restored visibility to the entire group. The Color panel below the group has returned to its original smaller size. Overview In other words, double-clicking the tab will collapse the panel group; a single click will expand it.

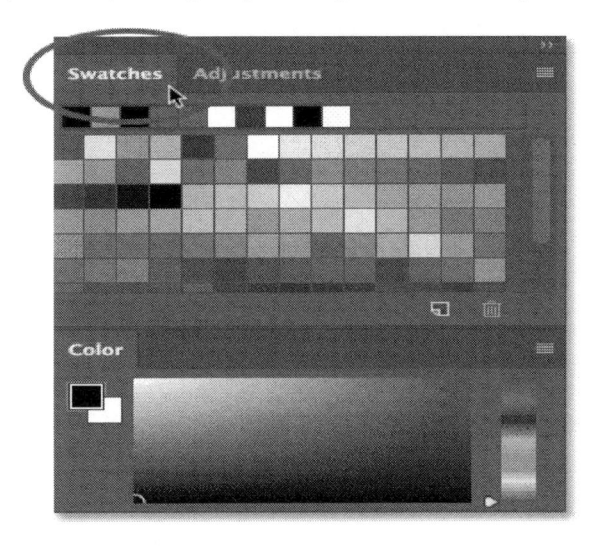

Collapsing Panels

Manage your panel area effectively by collapsing and expanding panel groups. Collapse a panel group temporarily into a tabbed area at the top so that there is more room for panels in other groups. To collapse a panel group, double-click anywhere on any tab in that group. This will collapse all the panels in that group, regardless of which tab you clicked. For example, here we have double-clicked on the Swatches tab. Now, the Swatches panel and the Adjustments panel next to it are collapsed so that just their tabs show. Also, notice how the Color panel underneath them has expanded to take advantage of the freed-up space.

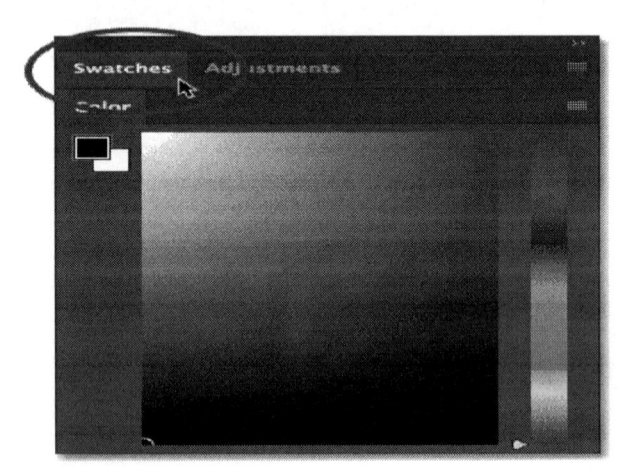

Additionally, as shown below, you can choose the collapse to Icon button.

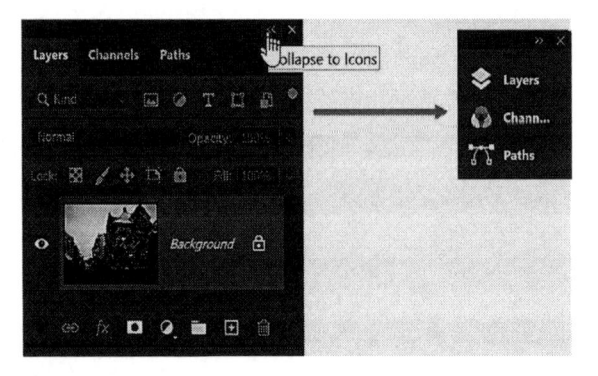

SHOW OR HIDE PANELS

Some panels in the workspace allow you to access information and make changes to the current file. For instance, the Layers panel allows you to view the document's layers. Navigate to the Window menu, select the panel you wish to reveal or conceal (visible panels have a checkbox next to them) and click OK. In the image below, the Window menu is used to open the History panel.

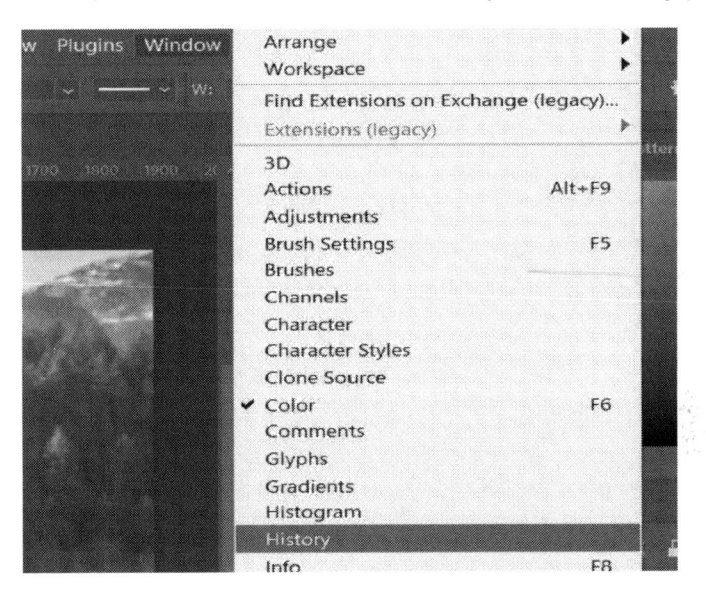

UNDERSTANDING PANEL CONTEXT MENUS

Context-sensitive menus appear in most panels in Photoshop. Click the triple lines in the top right to access them.

The following sample shows you the complete array of menu options when you use the Character panel. If you were to click the tab for the Paragraph making it active then pull up the menu-you would find a whole other set of options.

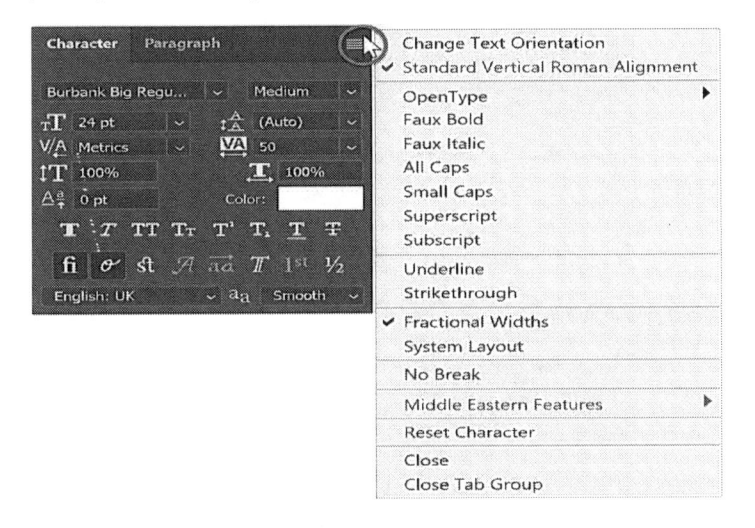

USING THE UNDO AND REDO COMMANDS

To undo and redo things, do the following:

- **Undo**: Edit > Undo or Control + Z - Windows, Command + Z - Mac Moves one step back in the undo chain.
- **Redo**: To undo one step further, go to Edit > Redo, or use the Shift + Control + Z (Windows) or Shift + Command + Z (Mac) keyboard shortcut. In addition, the Undo and Redo choices on the Edit menu are also an indication of what action will be undone. For example, Edit > Undo Edit Type.

MAKING USE OF THE HISTORY PANEL

One convenient tool for stepping through recent changes you have made to an image as you continue to work on it is the History panel. This panel saves the most recent version of an image after each edit.

For instance, every time something is done to part of a picture, it writes a separate entry in the panel. You can then go back to these states and when you select one of them, the image goes back to how it looked at the time the change was originally made so that you can resume where you were before.

The History panel also offers controls to delete image states and, for Photoshop users, to open a document from any selected state or snapshot. Click the History panel tab or choose Window > History to open the History panel.

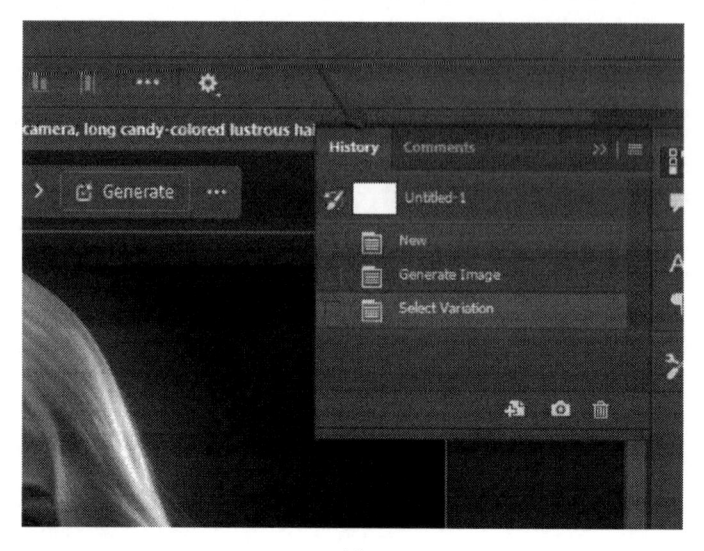

GETTING A PORTION OF AN IMAGE BACK TO ITS OLD SAVED VERSION

To restore part of an image to a previously saved version perform one of the following actions:

- Use the History Brush tool to apply the selected state or image of your History panel.
- Make sure to select the "Erase To History" option when the Eraser tool is in use.
- Identify which area of the image needs to be restored, then select "Fill" under the "Edit" menu. From there, under "Use" select "History" and click "OK."

HOW TO ACCESS PHOTOSHOP PREFERENCES

Photoshop Preferences contain endless options to customize the appearance, behavior, and performance of the application. Even though there is a big list of settings in Photoshop Preferences, we will highlight some of the most important ones that will be crucial for your work with Photoshop. These options will allow you to personalize the interface, help you optimize your workflow, and fine-tune for maximum performance of Photoshop and your computer.

Opening up the Photoshop Preferences is pretty straightforward. On a Windows PC, navigate to the top Menu Bar, click on Edit, scroll down to the bottom of the list then click on Preferences > General. On a Mac, in the Menu Bar click on the Photoshop menu, choose Preferences then select General.

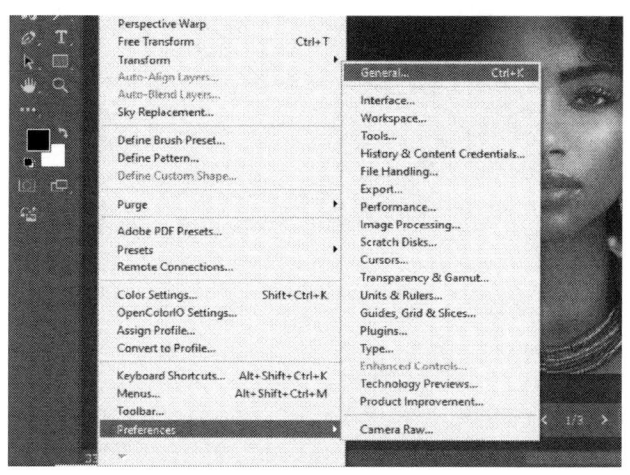

The General Preferences section offers you the following choices.

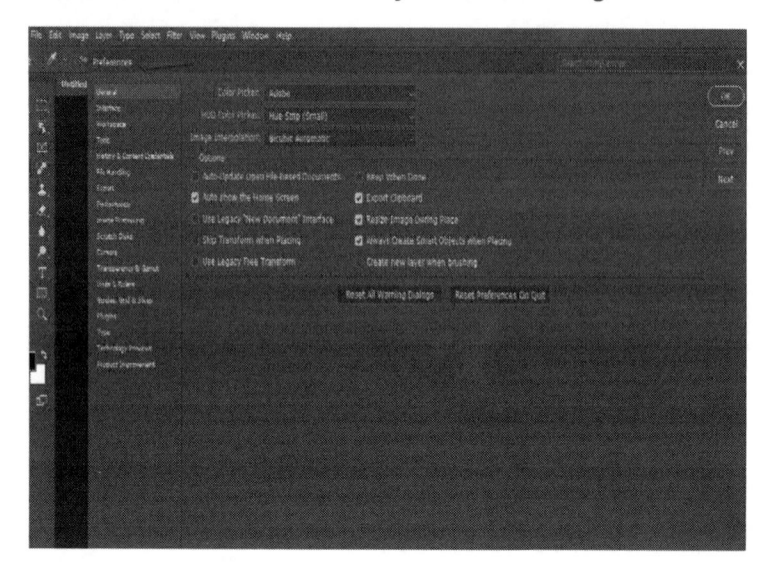

EXPORTING CLIPBOARD PREFERENCE

Your computer's performance is greatly affected by the Export Clipboard choice, particularly when it comes to copying and pasting items from Photoshop's clipboard to your computer's clipboard. Enabling this option could cause performance problems because Photoshop files can be quite huge. In general, to guarantee seamless operation, it is best to disable this setting. It is advised to save a file in Photoshop and then open it in the intended application if you need to transfer files from Photoshop to another program.

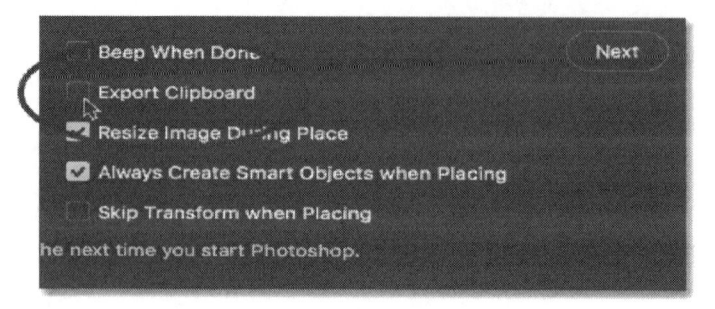

INTERFACE PREFERENCES SETTINGS

Let's explore the several settings that allow us to personalize the interface of Photoshop. Navigate to the Interface category located on the left:

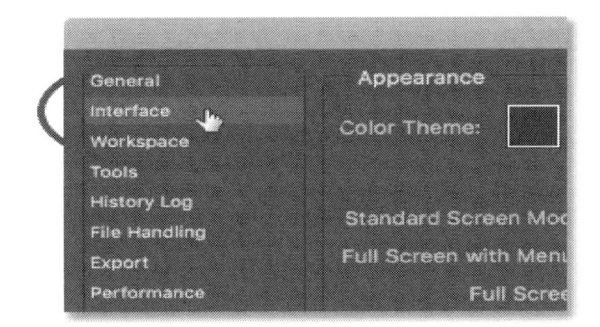

COLOR THEME

This preference determines the color of the Photoshop interface. You can select one of four different colored themes, one of which is the dark theme that was new for CS6 and continues in CC. Here you will choose which one you prefer to work with. The Darker theme was designed by Adobe to minimize distractions and increase your focus on your image.

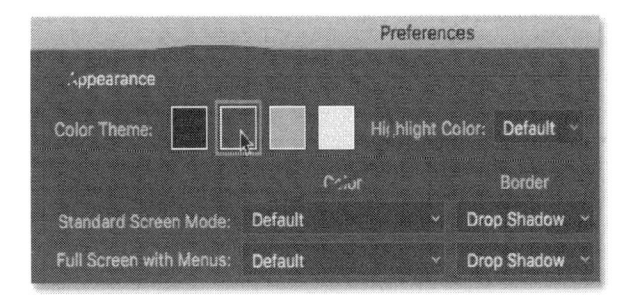

SETTING THE HIGHLIGHT COLOR UNDER THE APPEARANCE

Exclusively available in Photoshop CC, this feature enables you to select the color used to highlight the currently selected layer in the Layers panel. You can stick with the default gray or opt for blue, tailoring it to your preference.

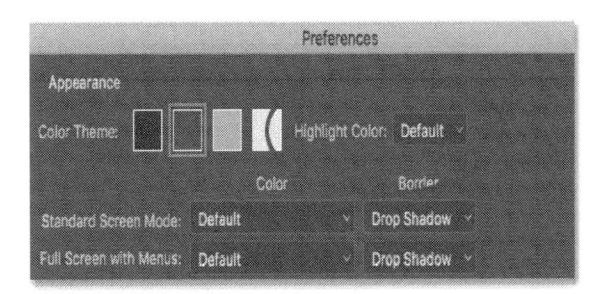

UI FONT SIZE

You can adjust the font size in Photoshop's user interface by changing this parameter. Small, Medium, Large, and even Tiny are available as options to suit your needs and reduce eye strain while working.

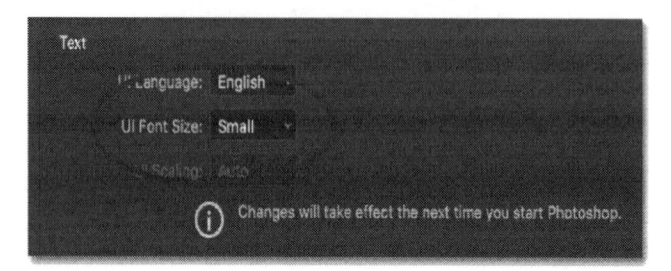

UNDERSTANDING THE SHOW TOOLTIPS FEATURE

Tooltips are information boxes that show up when you hold your cursor over the tool and options in Photoshop. These are very useful to learn with but can be disabled once you have learned the names and uses of the different tools.

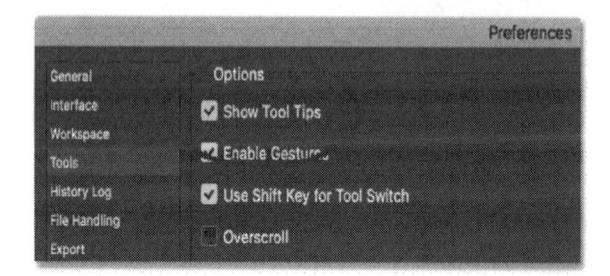

HOW TO USE SHIFT KEY FOR SWITCHING TOOL

This preference controls how you tab through tools via hotkeys. If this is enabled then to access tools that share the same hot key you need to hold down the Shift key along with the tool's hot key.

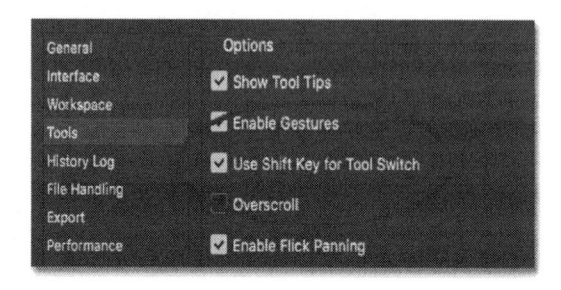

USING THE PERFORMANCE PREFERENCES

By choosing the "Performance" category on the left and customizing the settings to suit your tastes, you may access the Performance preferences.

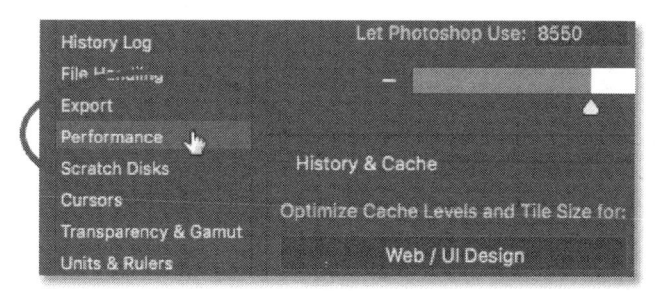

Understandung Memory Usage

Set the Memory Usage setting to specify how much RAM Photoshop is allocated. The default is 70%, but this can be changed if your computer's capabilities and needs warrant it.

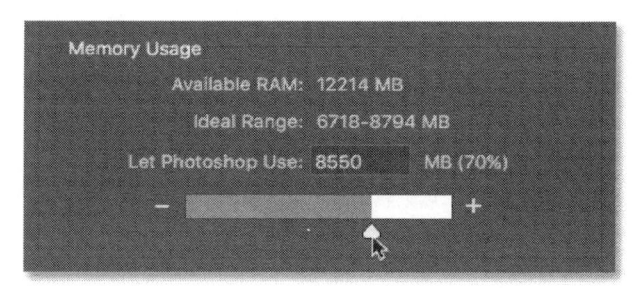

CHAPTER 2

FUNDAMENTAL PREREQUISITE FOR IMAGE EDITING

THE IDEA OF PIXELS

In digital imaging, the pixel is the basic building block of any digital picture or graphic. A pixel, a portmanteau of a picture element, is a single point in an image that helps create its resolution and clarity. Each pixel has color and brightness information; together, these create the visual content you see on screens or printed images.

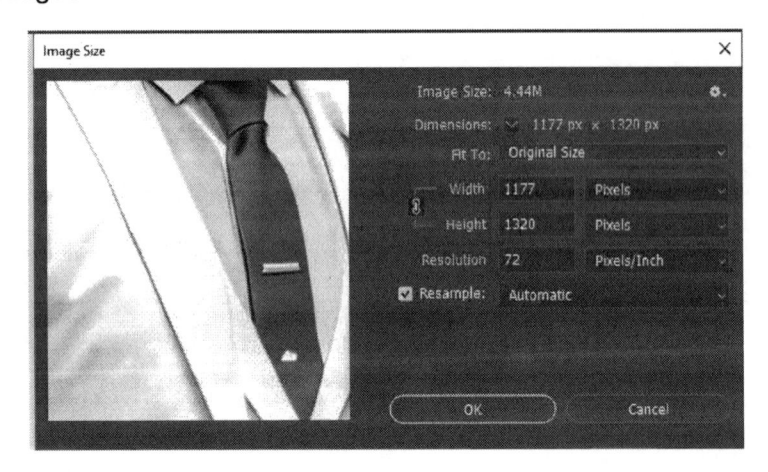

How Pixels Work in Photoshop

- **Pixel-Based Editing**: All images in Photoshop are made up of minute units of pixels, showing the image resolution and detail. Zooming into any given image allows you to view how each pixel is a minute square, hence offering pixel-perfect editing. While zooming in closely, a once seamless image gradually turned into a collection of minute squares, each representing a pixel. Every closer glance, every pixel would show its unique color. Wholly, the entire image effectively constitutes a grid of these single-colored squares. Though our eyes blend these colors seamlessly while viewed from some considerable distance, a close look just ensures that the pixels serve as the building blocks of our digital World.

- **Color and Tone**: Each pixel in Photoshop has a combination of RGB- red, green, and blue values that can create millions of colors.

The brilliance, contrast, or saturation adjustment affects the underlying data at the pixel level.

- **Resolution and DPI (Dots Per Inch):** Higher resolution entails quality images, with a greater number of pixels per inch. Low-resolution images always come out blurry and pixelated. Photoshop enables you to change the resolution through the Image Size dialog box to fit your printing or web needs.

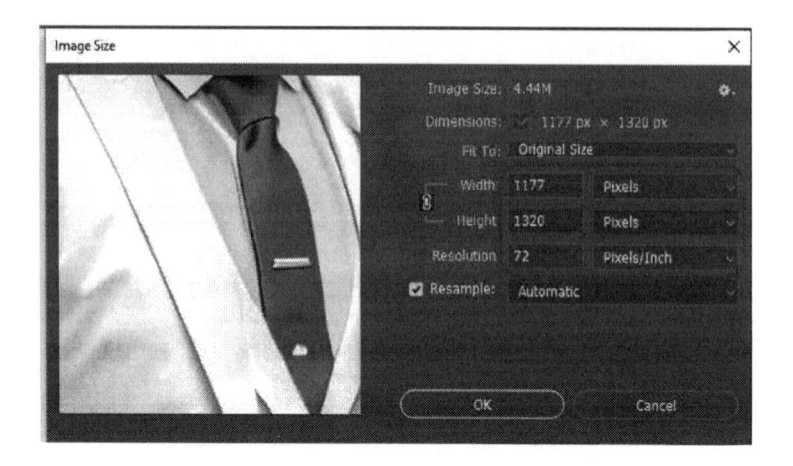

EXPLORING IMAGE RESOLUTION AND DIMENSION

Understanding the resolution of an image requires one to know that the small colored squares in digital images are called pixels. The size of the image is determined based on the number of pixels in width and height. The image resolution, though, pertains to how the photo is going to appear if it were printed based on its current image size. More importantly, image resolution only affects the size of the printed image, leaving the screen view unaffected.

Width, Height, and Resolution Relationship

In the Image Size dialog box, under the "Dimensions" heading, you have the Width, Height, and Resolution fields. These fields don't just show you what your current settings are but you can make the necessary adjustments.

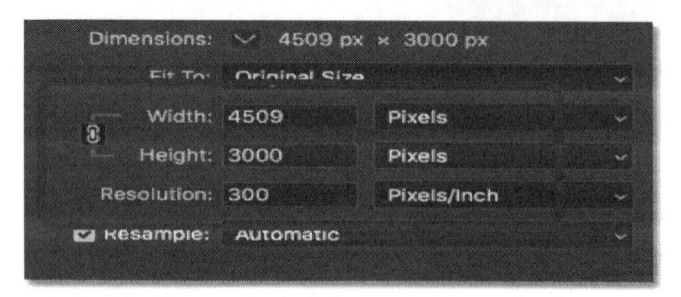

The Idea of Pixel Dimensions

In Photoshop, the pixel dimensions of a picture refer to its width and height in pixels, and are called "pixel dimensions." You can locate these dimensions near the top of the dialog box under the label "Dimensions." You can see that the image width is 4509 pixels (px) and the height is 3000 pixels.

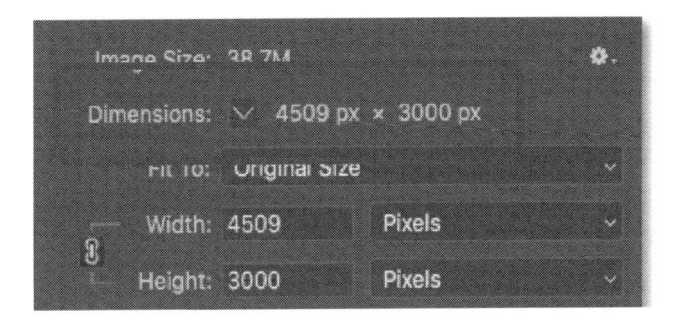

If the measurements are in some other unit of measurement, such as inches or percents, this is easily changed by clicking the small arrow to the right of the word "Dimensions" and then selecting "Pixels" from the pop-up list.

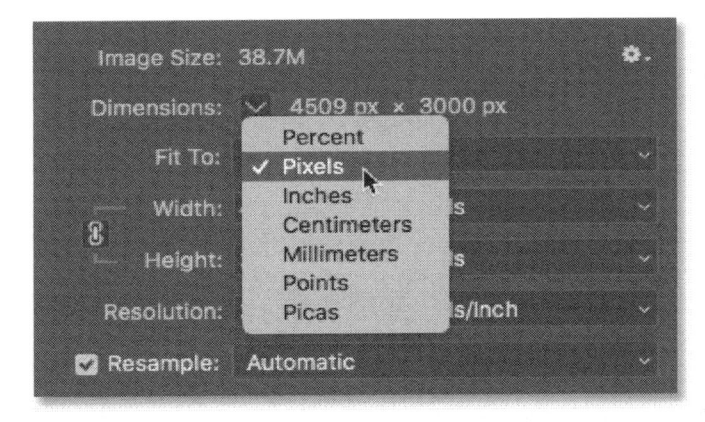

This shows that my picture is 3000 pixels high and 4509 pixels wide.

Calculating the Total Number of Pixels in an Image

Multiplying the number of pixels in width × the height in pixels yields the total number of pixels in the image. In this case, 4509 × 3000 = 13,527,000 pixels, approximately 13.5 million total pixels. Having a specific number of pixels is helpful to determine the possible print size of an image as will be discussed in the next section on image resolution, although it is not always necessary.

WHEN IS FILE SIZE AFFECTED BY RESOLUTION?

Some of the common fallacies regarding image resolution: many people believe that resolution affects the file size of an image. They believe, for this reason, that their photo resolution should be lowered before emailing or uploading it to the web to reduce the file size. The belief is wrong because changing the resolution does not affect the number of pixels in an image and hence it has no relation with the file size.

The number under the heading "Image Size" at the top of the dialog box is the amount in megabytes (M). Mine says 38.7M. This number is an indication of the size of the image as a computer file in your computer's memory. When you open an image in Photoshop, it is essentially copied from your hard drive and decompressed from its original file format into the memory (RAM) for faster editing. The figure that is presented in the Image Size dialog box shows the actual, uncompressed size of the image.

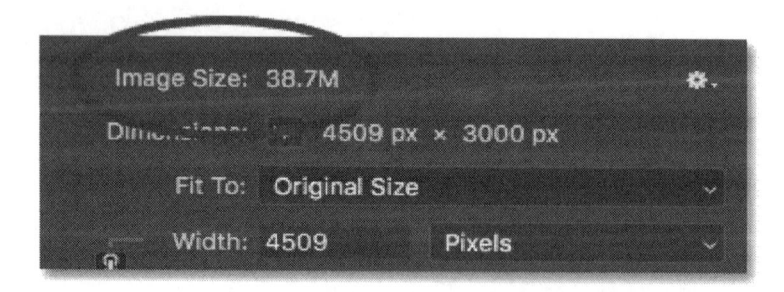

Resolution vs File Size: What is the difference?

It's easy to show that changing image resolution does not change file size. Just watch the file size as you change the resolution, but be sure the Resample box is not checked - you want the number of pixels to stay constant. Here I have lowered the resolution from 300 pixels/inch to 30 pixels/inch. Even with a reduced pixel concentration per inch on paper, the memory size of the image would still be 38.7 M.

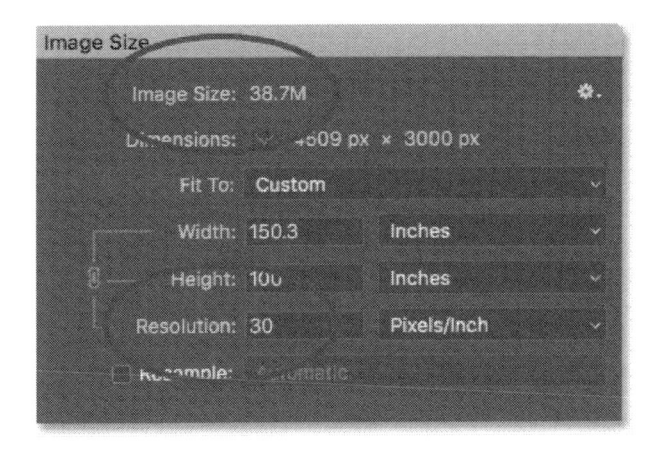

Higher Resolution vs File Size: A Better Look

In contrast, I have amplified the resolution to 3000 pixels/inch. That knocks the print size down to a scant 1.503 inches × 1 inch, but of course, the file size has not changed and is 38.7M. It is important to understand that a change in the print resolution alone will not affect whatsoever on file size. You need to either reduce the number of pixels in an image, by using Resample, save the image in a format that supports compression such as JPEG, or use both options to decrease the file size.

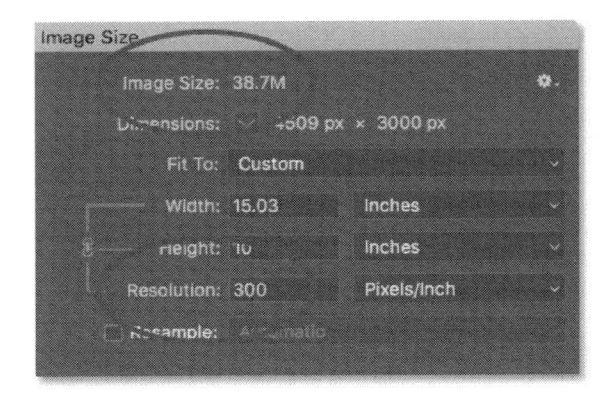

SCREEN MONITOR AND PRINTING RESOLUTION DECISION

To find the print dimensions of the picture, we simply have to divide its width and height currently recorded in pixels by the value of resolution. Coming back to the top part, Dimensions, it would be noticed that the image width is still 4509 pixels.

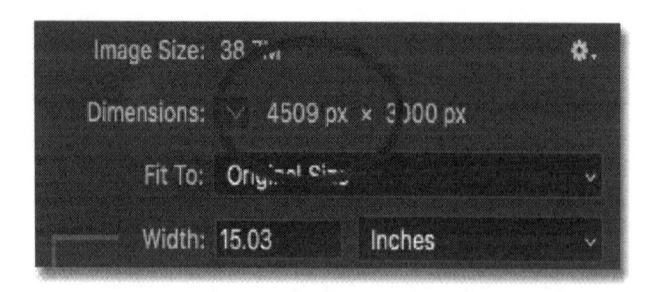

The existing width in pixels is targeted in the Image Size dialog box now opened in Photoshop. Dividing 4509 by the existing resolution of 300 yields 15.03. In other words, the image will be printed 15.03 inches wide, which perfectly matches the value in the Width field.

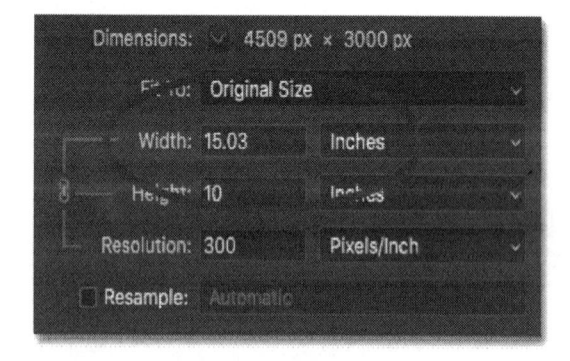

In the Image Size dialog box, the print width of the image is calculated as 4509 pixels divided by 300 pixels/inch, so its width is 15.03 inches, while under Dimensions, the height is 3000 pixels.

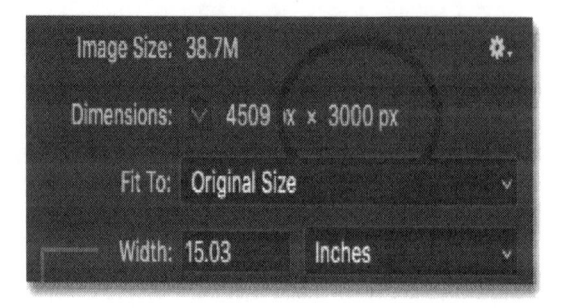

Now, in the Photoshop Image Size dialog box, the document's print height is calculated by dividing 3000 pixels into 300 pixels/inch to yield 10 inches. This is what appears in the Height field. Additionally, the picture width in pixels, as appearing in the Width field, remains set to 4509 pixels.

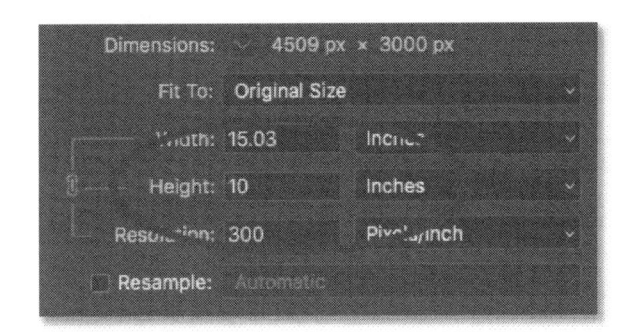

HOW TO RESAMPLE AN IMAGE

Before we proceed, notice the Resample option that is located just beneath the Resolution value. The resample is on by default. We will have more to say about the Resample option when we learn about image resizing. For now, suffice it to say that Resample allows us to adjust the total number of pixels in the image.

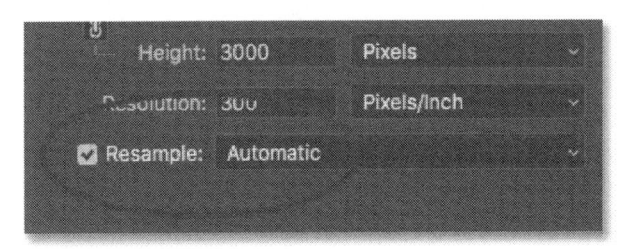

But why would you want to change the pixel count? If the image dimensions in their current form aren't sufficient to print your photo at your intended size, Resample lets you increase the pixel count by upsampling. Conversely, if you want to e-mail your photo to friends or post it on the web and the current size is more than you need, Resample lets you decrease the pixel count by downsampling.

Once again we will cover upsampling, and downsampling when we cover resizing images. But for now, to view a comparison of how resolution affects the print size of the image, simply uncheck Resample to turn it off.

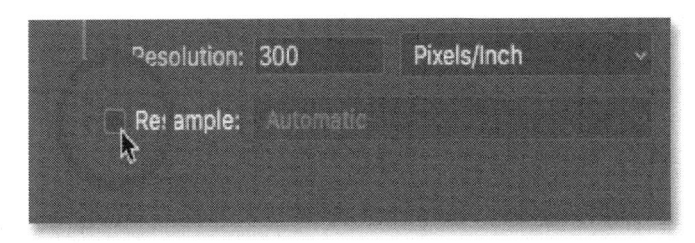

RESIZING VERSUS RESAMPLING

The terms "resizing" and "resampling" are both used in digital images. Each of them denotes two different kinds of processes that alter the size and dimensions of an image. Here's the difference between resizing and resampling:

Resizing

- Resizing mainly refers to changing the physical dimensions of an image, such as the width and height of the image, while the number of pixels remains the same.
- When resizing, you are making the image larger or smaller in terms of its printed or displayed size-not adding or removing pixels from the image.
- Resizing can also be performed without discarding any pixel information whenever you want to change its size for printing, web display, or other purposes without affecting image quality.
- This mostly would prompt for the new dimensions in inches or centimeters and can be done without resampling, provided the resolution remains constant.

Resampling

- Resampling refers to the alteration of the actual number of pixels in an image; therefore, this always leads to an increase-upsampling or a decrease-downsampling-in pixel count.
- Resampling means altering the pixel information of an image. Upsampling will introduce new pixels, and downsampling will reduce the number of pixels in the image.
- Resampling is normally used to modify the resolution of an image or to fit into a certain output size. For example, upsampling is done to bring out the best in an image for high-quality printing, and downsampling is carried out to decrease file size for web usage.
- You will have to define new dimensions here, and also the resolution wanted in pixels per inch or centimeter.

In other words, resizing is about making the image size bigger or smaller either when printing or displaying without changing the pixel information. On the other hand, resampling has to do with the change of pixel count by either adding more or reducing some pixels, which may affect the quality of an image. Which is which between resizing and resampling depends on your different needs for different uses of the image.

IMPROVING A LOW IMAGE RESOLUTION AND RESAMPLING AN IMAGE

Improving a Low Image Resolution in Adobe Photoshop Each time the resolution setting is changed, an important preliminary step to printing, as print quality will not be good without it. To change the resolution setting of any image,

- Open any image.
- Along the top menu bar, click on "Image" and select "Image Size."
- A new window called "Image Size" will open.
- Check off "Resample Image" to change only the resolution.

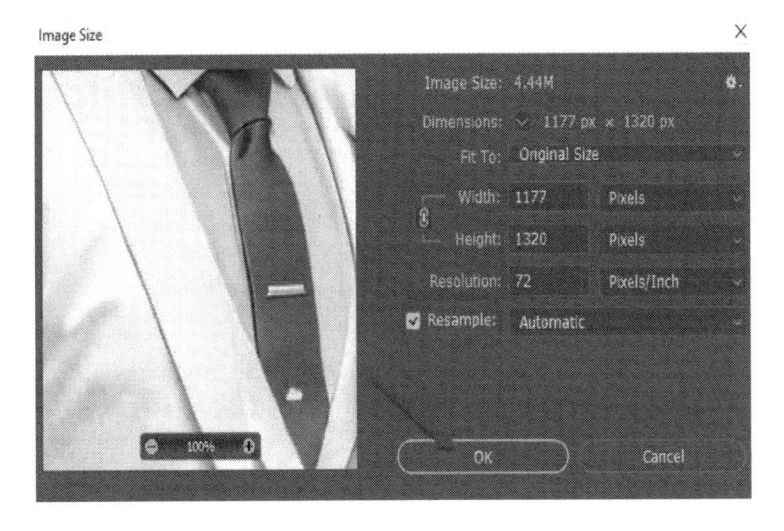

- This tells Photoshop not to add or remove any pixels from the image. Adding or removing pixels usually takes place when one resizes an image to make it larger or smaller. In changing the resolution, you are not affecting the total number of pixels but rather specifying how many pixels will be shown per inch. Now, type the intended resolution number in the "Resolution" field.

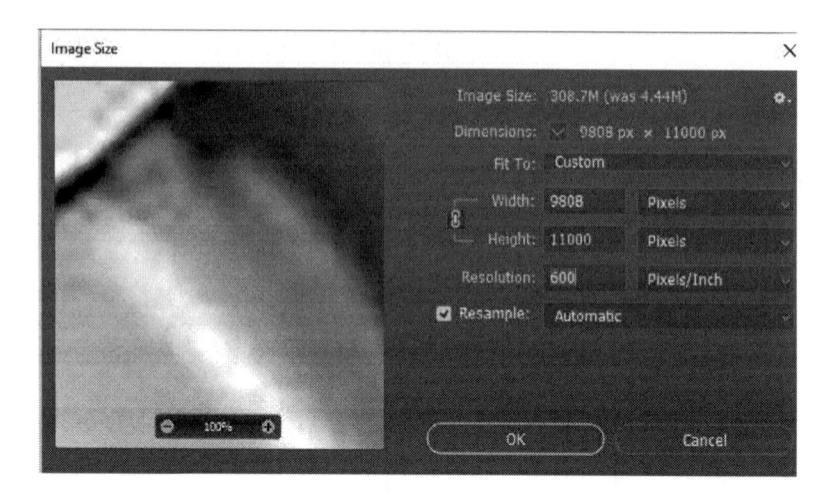

- Type a value in the "Resolution" field. Note that the width and height of the document automatically change. Click "OK" to confirm

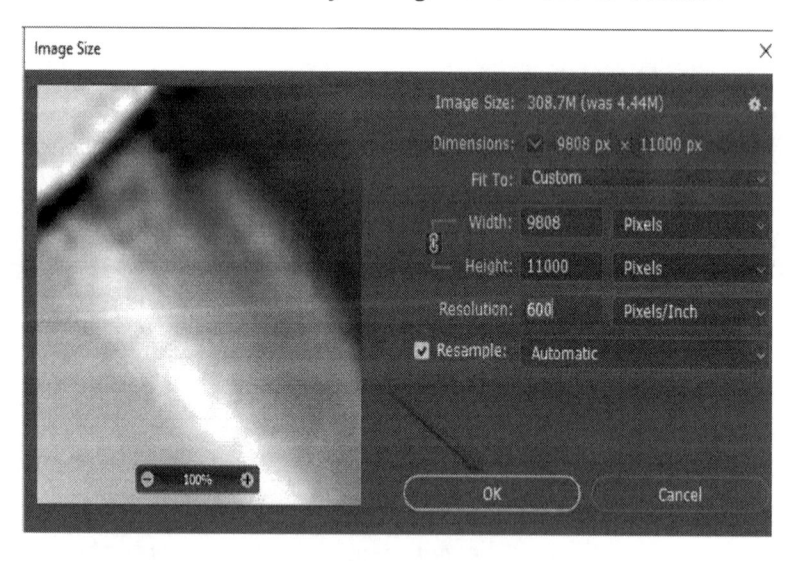

FILE SIZE VS PIXEL DIMENSIONS

The size of a picture, sometimes referred to as kilobytes (K), megabytes (MB), or gigabytes (GB), is the digital file size. The file size is invariably connected with the pixel dimension of an image. The more pixels, though welcome for greater detail when printing, comes at the cost of space and, in extreme cases, can slow down the editing and printing processes. That image resolution is a delicate balance between getting all the necessary information and the highest quality of an image and file size.

Also, file sizes can vary significantly because of the selected file format. In these regards, various file formats, including GIF, JPEG, PNG, and TIFF, all use different forms of compression that can be extremely effective in changing the file sizes of two images with the same number of pixel dimensions. Other variables that will continue to affect an image's file size include color bit-depth and whether the image has layers and channels.

Image files are restricted to a maximum pixel dimension of 300,000 by 300,000 pixels. This limits the maximum size an image can be printed and at what resolution.

EXPLORING PRINTER RESOLUTION

The resolution of a printer is basically how fine or detailed a printer can reproduce on paper. This is measured in DPI or dots per inch. It determines how many small ink dots can be printed within one inch of space. The resolution directly affects the quality and clarity of the final print. Hence, understanding and managing printer resolution with Photoshop will ensure your digital work looks just as sharp and vibrant as it does in print.

HOW PRINTER RESOLUTION WORKS

DPI vs. PPI

- The resolution is what measures the density of the ink dots used by the printer, measured in DPI.
- PPI stands for Pixels Per Inch, and that is the resolution of the digital image. The greater the PPI, the more detail the printer has to work with.

- While 300 PPI is the standard for professional printing, with higher DPI settings, printers can yield even finer details.

Printer Technology

Most inkjet printers come with 300-1200 DPI, depending on how one wants to print out pictures. Laser printers are lower-DPI printers that work fine for texts and documents, anything between 300 to 600 DPI.

Balancing Resolution with File Size

- The higher the resolution, the better the print quality. Resolution images above 300 PPI produce large-sized files, which may slow down the printing process.
- Lower-resolution images (72-150 PPI) save on the file size but will become pixelated if printed too large.
- Choose the right balance by considering what the print is for some prints, such as flyers, might use 150 DPI, while professional photo prints may require 300 DPI or even more.

Color Accuracy and DPI Impact

Different printers rely on the inks of CMYK-Cyan, Magenta, Yellow, and Black to reproduce colors. In Photoshop, one can convert RGB files to CMYK for printing purposes. A high value for DPI ensures smooth gradients, sharp text, and no evident dots or banding issues.

PRINT IMAGE RESOLUTION SPECIFICATIONS

Knowing and using the correct resolution in preparing digital artwork for print means sharp, high-quality outputs. Image resolution simply describes the pixels per inch, or PPI, of your digital file, which needs to correspond with the printer's dots per inch or DPI, capability to avoid blurry or pixelated prints. Below are key resolution specifications for different printing scenarios.

Default Printing Resolution

It follows the industrial standard, with 300 PPI, for high-quality prints such as brochures, posters, and photo books. This resolution allows the print to be sharp enough without showing pixels when this is viewed up close. Most printers use a resolution of 300 DPI to 1200 DPI to create the ink or toner dots from the digital image.

Large-format prints (Banners, Billboards)

For large prints that are viewed from a distance, such as billboards or banners, 150 ppi is usually sufficient. Here, a lower PPI is acceptable, since it is difficult to detect the minute details from a distance. Example: the same 24x36 inch poster can be 150 PPI and retain a much smaller file size with no apparent loss of quality.

Printing of Magazines and Books

Especially, magazines and books require 300–600 PPI for images with complicated details. For high-end prints (e.g., art books), use 350 PPI or higher to maintain perfect detail and color fidelity.

Flyers, Business Cards, and Brochures

With 300 PPI, business card-sized prints or brochures will be clear as far as text and image details are concerned. The fine print on business cards benefits from 400 PPI, especially with the use of small fonts.

Text-Dense Prints (Documents, Manuals)

For essentially text documents, 150 PPI to 200 PPI would be enough, especially if printed on laser printers. Laser printers usually work within the 300–600 DPI range, which gives enough sharp text output.

Printing on Textiles or Fabrics

Print resolution for fabric prints is often lower, around 72–150 PPI, since textiles naturally diffuse ink. Even a design file for a T-shirt or any apparel should also be at 300 PPI, considering the quite small print size.

Preparing Files with Photoshop

Image Size Settings: Within it, go to Image > Image Size and set the PPI without compromising the print dimensions. Color Mode CMYK: Convert files to this color mode for correctness in the colors of prints. Use RGB mode only when using digital displays. Bleed Settings: Add 1/8 inch (0.125") bleed to prevent image cutoff during trimming.

Print Resolution Summary Table

Print Type	Recommended PPI	Printer DPI
Photo Prints	300 PPI	300–1200 DPI
Posters and Banners	150 PPI	300–600 DPI
Magazines and Art Books	350 PPI or higher	600–1200 DPI
Business Cards	300–400 PPI	600–1200 DPI
Text Documents	150–200 PPI	300–600 DPI
Fabric/Textile Prints	72–150 PPI	300–600 DPI

PREVIEW ON-SCREEN PRINT SIZE

To see approximately how the image will appear on screen at its print size, do one of two things: Go to View > Print Size, OR Select either the Hand tool or Zoom tool and click "Print Size" in the options bar.

This will reopen the image in a view close to the image's actual printed size, according to the Document Size area of the Image Size dialog box. Remember that the size and resolution of your monitor determine how the onscreen print size is displayed.

FILE COMPRESSION

Image compression uses special algorithms that intentionally reduce file size. Many types of image file formats exist, including JPG, TIF, and PNG, each using a unique algorithm that changes how the image data are stored to reduce its byte size. When appropriately compressed for the intended purpose, such modified files may retain good enough image quality while their overall size is significantly reduced.

Both applications can perform an equal amount of photo compression. Photoshop can export your file as an image file in GIF format. However, for the most part, JPG is the best image file format when it comes to photo sharing or storage.

Compress an image in Photoshop by doing the following:

- Open a picture in Photoshop.
- Go to File > Export As.
- Under "Export As.", choose the file type of JPG.
- Left-click the Quality slider toward the left to reduce file size at the expense of image quality. Note that you can preview the resulting file size in the left-hand section of the "Export As." window.
- Click the blue "Export Photo" button at the end and specify a location to save your compressed file.

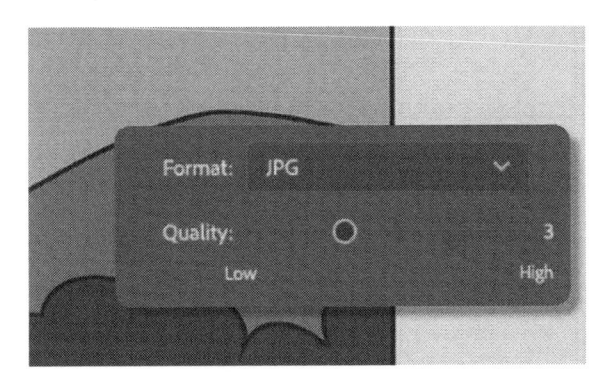

FILE FORMAT SELECTION

You should also choose an appropriate file format whenever saving your work through Photoshop. This helps in maintaining compatibility and quality, besides meeting the various requirements of different outputs. Each has its purpose-be it for displaying on the Web, printing, or editing. Here is a rundown of common file formats and their use cases.

PSD (Photoshop Document) Format

- **Purpose**: Photoshop file format default to save projects containing layers.
- **When to Use**: Perfect for projects with continuous work in which you want to retain layers, masks, and adjustments.
- **Pros**: Virtual editing allows non-destructive editing, supporting Smart Objects for high-quality content.
- **Cons**: Large file size, limited compatibility with non-Adobe software.

JPEG (Joint Photographic Experts Group) Format

- **Purpose**: Best for web display and digital sharing of photos.

- **Compressed images are best for;** Web graphics or digital portfolio items.
- **Pros**: Small file size and widely supported across devices and platforms.
- **Cons**: Lossy compression reduces quality with each save.

PNG (Portable Network Graphics) Format

- **Purpose**: Ideal for web graphics that require transparency.
- **When to Use**: Applies to logos, icons, and images that leverage transparent backgrounds.
- **Pros**: Supports transparency and lossless compression.
- **Drawbacks**: larger file size as compared to JPEG.

TIFF (Tagged Image File Format)

- **Purpose**: Ideal for printing and archiving purposes.
- **When to Use**: When sending very high-quality photo prints, or when sharing with printers.
- **Pros**: supports layers and transparency; best quality is preserved.
- **Cons**: Large file size.

PDF (Portable Document Format)

- **Purpose**: Best suited for documents that have to retain the layout integrity across platforms.
- **When to Use**: Design brochures, presentations, or digital booklets.
- **Pros**: Keeps layout consistent across various devices and platforms.
- **Cons**: Limited editing capabilities once saved.

GIF (Graphics Interchange Format)

- **Purpose**: Best used for simple animation and low-resolution web graphics.
- **When to use**: Apply to short animations or web-based icons.
- **Pros**: supports basic animation, supports transparency.
- **Disadvantages**: Poor color gamut; not intended for high-quality images.

EPS (Encapsulated PostScript) Format

- **Use**: Best for vector graphics for large-scale printing.
- **When to Use**: Apply on logos and print materials that need scalable vector content.

- **Pros**: It retains vector data to scale without losing quality.
- **Disadvantages**: larger file size and not widely supported by web browsers.

BMP (Bitmap Image File) Format

- **Purpose**: To hold simple, uncompressed raster images.
- **When to Use**: Rarely used today, except when compatibility with really older systems is desired or needed.
- **Pros**: Excellent image retention.
- **Cons**: File size too large.

SVG (Scalable Vector Graphics)

- **Overview**: Online Scalable Vector Images.
- **When to Use**: Apply to web elements that need to scale, such as logos or icons.
- **Pros**: Resolution independent, perfect for the web.
- **Cons**: Limited support for complex raster images.

A swift approach to diminish image size revolves around the transformation of the file format, particularly advantageous when working with raw photos (i.e., the uncompressed originals captured by a digital camera).

Converting your image to a different file format efficiently compresses the image data across all your pictures, facilitating effortless posting, publishing, sharing, or storage. However, it's crucial to acknowledge that not all file formats exhibit equal efficiency in terms of compression.

WORKING WITH RULERS

The rulers within Photoshop are a very useful utility to use in aligning pictures or objects with supreme precision. Once turned on, rulers appear; they stretch horizontally on top and vertically along the left side of the active window. Along these rulers, markers continuously give the pointer position as it moves down the workspace. The origin of the ruler-that is the (0,0) reference point on both the top and left rulers-adjusts to allow you to measure distances from a specific location within the image. The origin of the ruler also provides the starting point for the grid.

- To show or hide the rulers, select the menu "View" and click "Rulers."

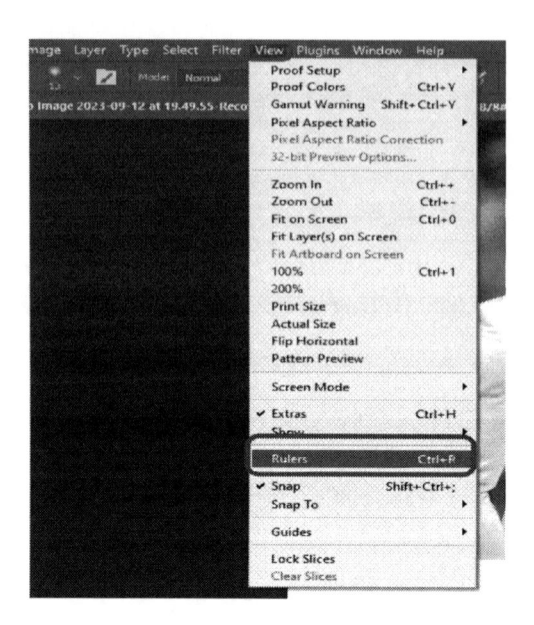

HOW DOES THE RULER TOOL FUNCTION?

The Ruler Tool in Photoshop consists of two rulers: one vertical on the left side and one horizontal on top of the document window. These rulers provide a visual guide to measure elements within your project, such as width, height, angles, and distances. Photoshop does most of the geometric calculations for you, so advanced math skills are not required.

Cleverly enough, it also boasts a range of refinements that allow one to set dimensions, have multiple start and end points, and lock measurements to ensure your objects remain aligned. Vertical and horizontal guides track along the X and Y axes as you move your cursor, giving precise coordinates.

WHEN TO USE THE RULER TOOL

The Ruler Tool is useful in a range of functions and applications including:

- **Measure Angles**: Just change to Protractor Mode and measure angles by adding a second distance line.
- **Image rotation**: This is used to define the exact rotation of an image.
- **Straightening Images**: Allow for straightening alignment of elements before cropping for accuracy.
- **Exact Crop**: No more guessing; determine exact cut points when cropping.

This scale can be customized with specific values for fine-tuning when default measurements may be off. Example: using D1 and D2 in protractor mode.

WORKING WITH GUIDES IN PHOTOSHOP

Guides will enable you to align elements precisely. Ensure rulers are on by selecting View > Rulers or using Ctrl+R (Windows) / Command+R (Mac).

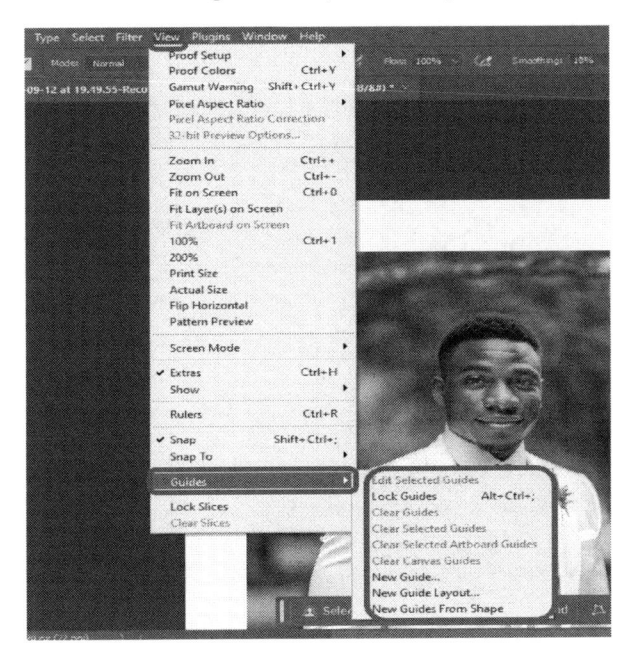

Guide Creation and Management:

- **Dragging**: To do this simply drag from the vertical or horizontal ruler onto the canvas. A thin guideline will appear where you release it.
- **Move Guide**: hover the cursor over a guide and click and drag to move it.
- **Show/Hide Guides**: To activate/deactivate guides go to View > Show > Guides.
- **Guides Delete**: Either drag guides back into the ruler, or press Delete with the Move Tool selected.

Customize Guide Appearance:

- Go to Edit > Preferences > Guides, Grids, and Slices.
- Change the color of the guide or line style to your liking.

Setup and Erase Instructions:

- **Reposition a Guide**: Using the Move Tool drag it to the desired position.
- **Remove a Guide**: Drag it back into the ruler, or use View > Clear Guides to delete all.
- **Locking guides provide stability**: Avoid accidental changes by selecting View > Lock Guides. The Ruler Tool, along with guides, provides the precision one needs in alignment, measurement, and arrangement within a Photoshop project.

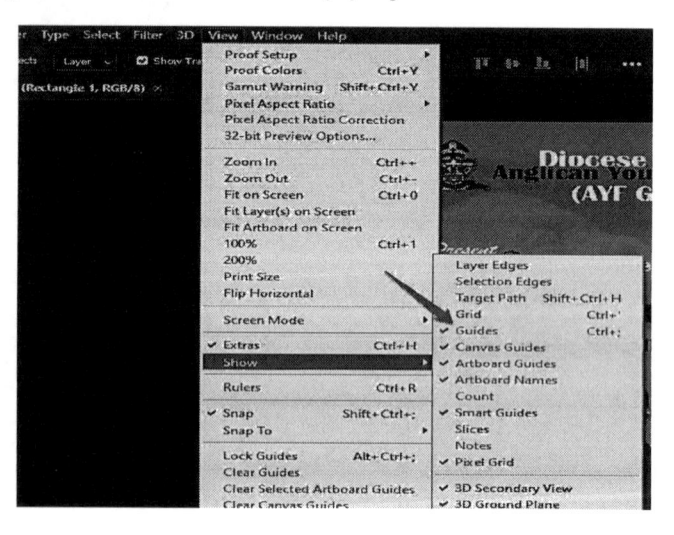

CHAPTER 3

WORKING WITH LAYERS

HOW TO MAKE USE OF LAYERS

Layers in Adobe Photoshop are probably one of the most great and important features. You may work on an image in parts, paying more attention to whatever you need, be it modifying some objects, taking photos, or just making a picture look more beautiful without destroying other elements of the picture. In real life, mastery of using layers is critical for everyone who deals with Photoshop, either for the first time or regularly.

The following provides a detailed explanation of how to use layers effectively:

Understanding Layers

Think of layers as transparent sheets laid on top of each other. Any of these sheets may carry a different part of your image, text, or adjustments. Layers enable you to work on individual elements without affecting the whole image.

You might edit a photograph in separate layers if you want to add text or effects. In that way, it leaves the base image intact, making the process of editing or removing part of your project easier without having to redo everything.

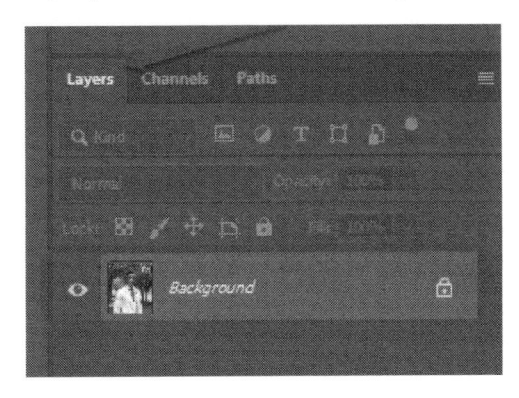

Creating and Managing Layers

To create a new layer, go to the Layers panel, usually on the right-hand side, and click the bottom icon that says New Layer. You could even use the Ctrl + Shift + N for Windows or Cmd + Shift + N on Mac to create a new layer in one second.

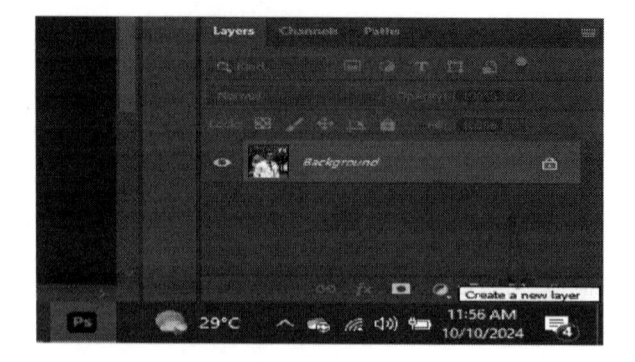

- **Layer Order**: The higher the layer order in the stack, the higher it appears over the lower layers. To change a layer order up or down, simply click and drag the layer in the Layers panel.
- **Naming Layers**: You need to be in the habit of naming your layers so that you can keep track of them easily when you are working on complicated projects with multiple layers. To rename a layer, simply double-click the name of the layer in the Layers panel and type the name you want to give it.

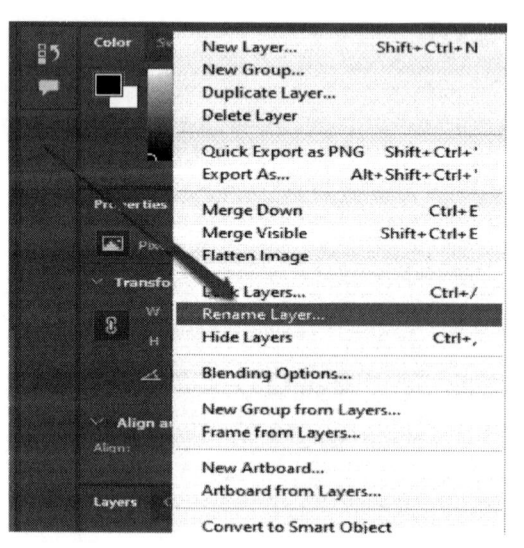

Basic Layer Functions

- **Opacity and Fill**: Every layer has an Opacity setting that determines how much it is seen through. If the opacity is decreased, the layer(s) underneath begins to show through. Similarly, Fill controls the transparency of only the content in the layer, without affecting any layer styles applied to it, like shadows or glows.

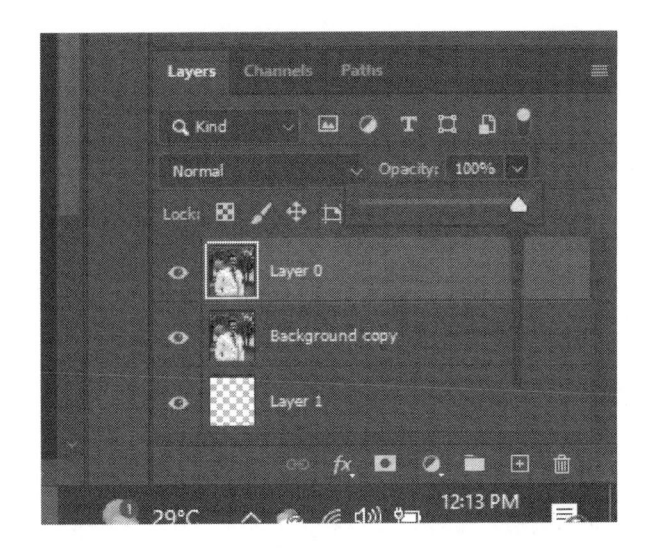

- **Blending Options**: Layers also support Blending Modes, which determine how colors on one layer will interact with colors on the underlying layer. You can set other blending modes like Multiply, Screen, Overlay, etc. For a variety of effects. To do this, right-click on the layer and choose Blending Options from this window that appears, and choose according to your preferences by clicking on the box to select. Click on the ok button when you are done.

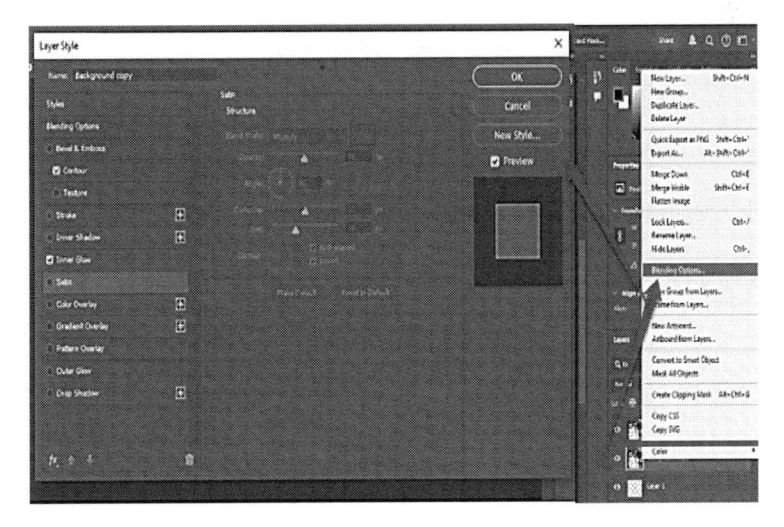

- **Layer Visibility**: Next to each layer in the Layers panel, there is an eye icon. Clicking the eye icon toggles the visibility of the layer without having to delete the contents that are on that layer.

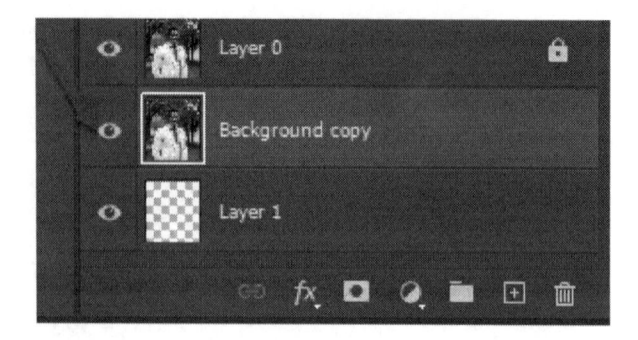

Types of Layers

- **Image Layers**: These are the default layers that would contain picture content, such as photos, graphics, or drawings.
- **Adjustment Layers**: An adjustment layer is used to make color and tone adjustments without permanently editing your picture. You can go ahead with making adjustments on an adjustment layer by using brightness/contrast, hue/saturation, or color balance, and at any time, you may go back and edit or discard the adjustments.
- **Text Layers**: Anything you type in Photoshop automatically opens a text layer for itself. The text layers are completely editable and allow you to apply font, size, and style.
- **Shape Layers**: These layers consist of vector shapes created with the use of shape tools, such as rectangles, ellipses, and custom shapes among many others. They are always sharp and never pixelated or soft because they are vectors.

Non-Destructive Editing with Layers

Perhaps the best thing about working with layers is non-destructive editing. This means that all the editing effects applied on any layer will not affect the original underlying image. For example,

- **Layer Masks**: A Layer Mask is a way to reveal/hide parts of a layer without deleting the pixels. It provides exact control over what is visible; hence, it's ideal when you want to blend objects or apply an effect to only a part of an image. To do this, choose the Object Selection tool select your image to mark out image edges, and then click on Layer Mask. You should have your result as shown below.

- **Smart Objects**: A Smart Object can be made by converting a layer in such a way that the original data is preserved. Converting is helpful when you want to resize, rotate, or filter an image multiple times without degradation.

Organizing Layers

- **Layer Groups**: It's good housekeeping to have your layers organized into groups. You can create a layer group either by making a selection of numerous layers that you want to keep together and using Ctrl+G for Windows or Cmd+G for Mac, or by simply clicking the folder icon in the Layers panel. A Layer Group will easily help you manipulate and organize even the most elaborate projects.
- **Locking Layers**: To prevent changes to a layer inadvertently, you can lock an image layer against changes by selecting it and then clicking the Lock icon at the top of the Layers panel. You may only want to lock the position, or lock the whole layer, or just other specific attributes of the layer.

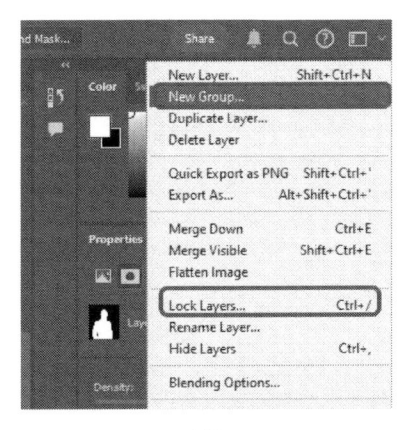

Merging and Flattening Layers

Once you're done working on your layers, you may want to merge them to simplify your file. You can:

- **Merging Layers**: To merge layers, select the clicking and holding down the Ctrl key. Right-click on any of the layers and choose the Merge layers option, or use Ctrl + E keys on the keyboard.

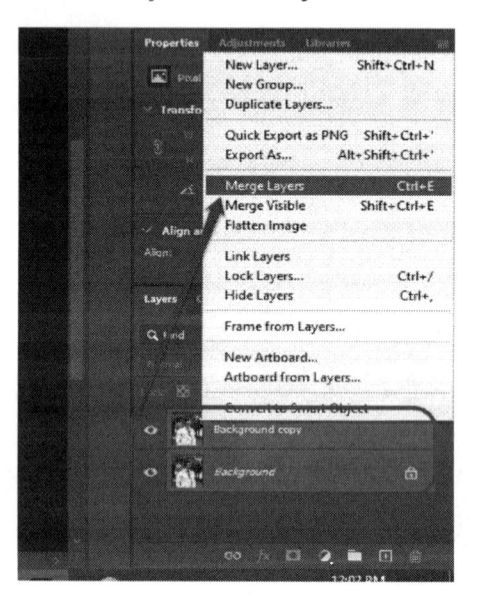

Merge Visible:

Merges layers that are on by hiding the ones not to be merged and selecting a pixel layer as the bottom layer.

- To perform this operation, select Layer > Merge Visible, or from the menu of the Layers panel, choose Merge Visible. Alternatively, press Shift+Cmd+E (macOS)/Shift+Ctrl+E (Windows).

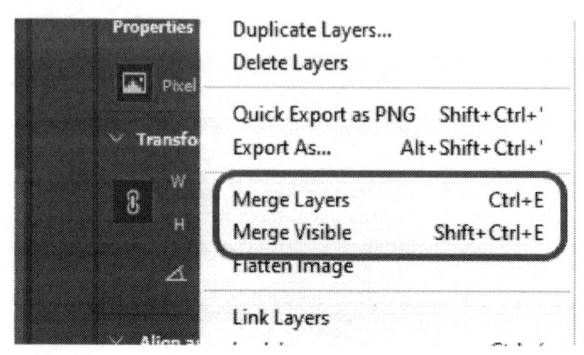

73

Note: An adjustment or fill layer cannot be a target layer for merge.

- **Flatten Image**: When you are done with all the edits and you want to finalize the image, you can flatten it by going to Layer > Flatten Image. It will combine all the layers into a single background layer.

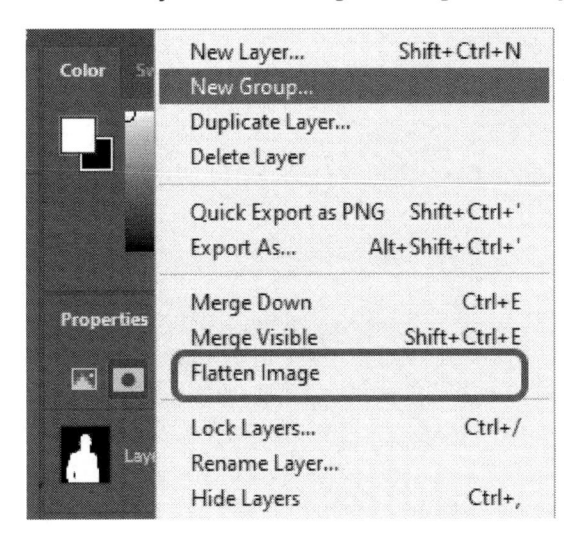

Saving Layered Files

If you are working with layers, you'll want to save your file in a format compatible with layers such as PSD or TIFF. Both of these formats allow you to reopen and edit the layers later. Saving it as a JPEG or PNG will flatten your file. You will no longer be able to edit any of the layers.

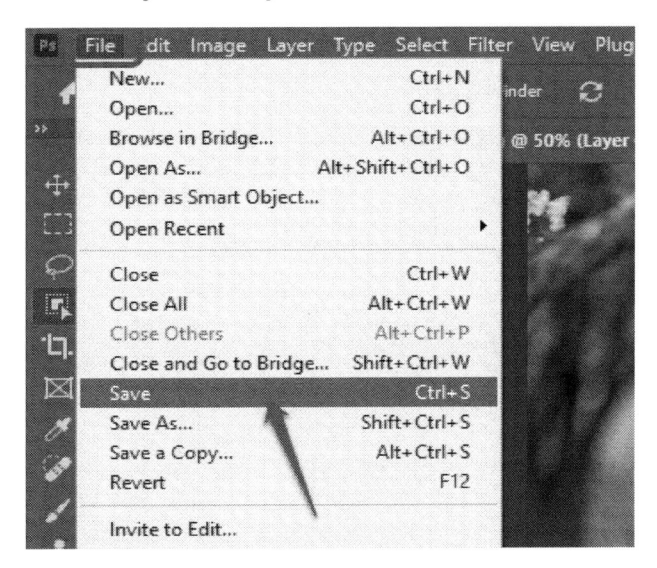

CREATING A BLANK AND ADJUSTMENT LAYER

Sometimes you need to make a new layer from scratch. This option is useful when you want to use the Brush for editing an image. In such cases, you can create a new layer and proceed with your work in your artistic project. To add a new layer, click the icon "New Layer" at the bottom right of the Layers panel. Immediately, a new layer will appear in the Layers panel.

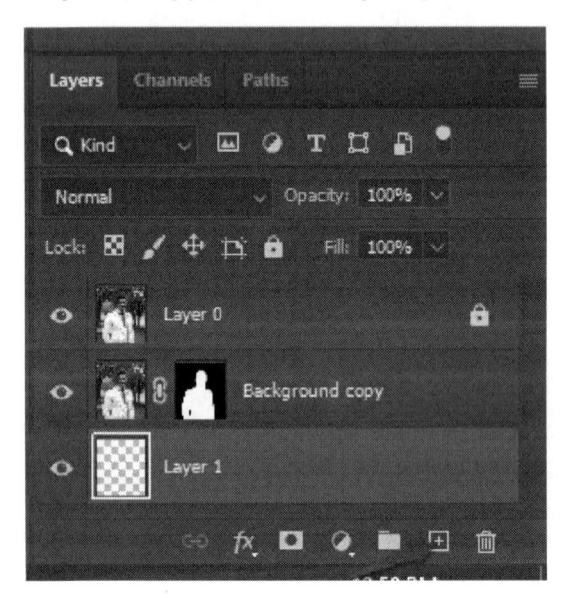

An Adjustment Layer is a great way to work on the color and tone of your image without touching it. The beauty of adjustment layers is that they do not permanently alter the pixels of your original image, allowing you to tweak or remove changes at any time.

EXPORT LAYERS

You can use File > Export to export all layers or just visible layers to other files. Or, Right-click on any of the layers and choose Export from the options.

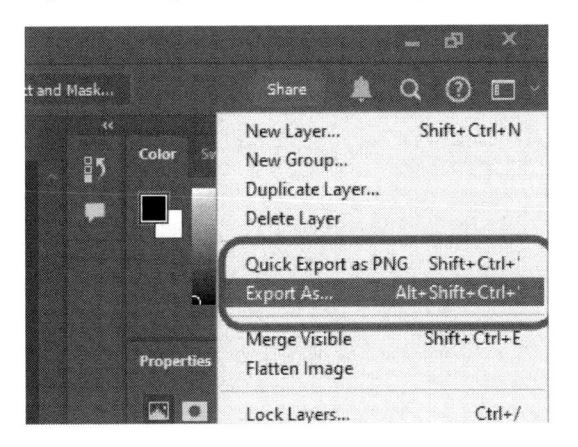

ASSIGN COLORS TO LAYERS

Color-coding-related layers can help you find them quickly in the Layers panel; just right-click on a layer or group and select a color.

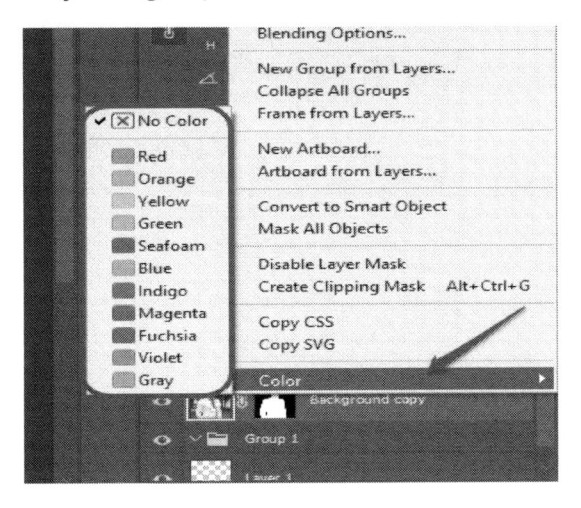

FLATTEN LAYERS

By flattening, hidden layers are removed, transparent portions are filled with white, and visible layers are blended into the background. Once saved, the unflattened state cannot be recovered. Choices consist of:

- **Flatten Image**: Use Layer > Flatten Image or choose Flatten Image from the Layers panel menu to flatten the entire image.
- **Flatten All Layer Effects**: Choose File > Scripts > Flatten All Layer Effects to just flatten layer styles.
- **Flatten All Masks**: Choose File > Scripts > Flatten All Masks to permanently apply masks to related layers.

LEVELS ADJUSTMENT LAYER

Refining the intensity of shadows, mid-tones, and highlights in an image can be effortlessly accomplished with the Levels adjustment layer. This tool allows for precise adjustments to color balance and tonal range, offering a level of control that goes beyond what the Contrast slider can provide.

To incorporate and apply the Levels adjustment layer:

- Go to the Layer tab.
- Click on Create Fill or New Adjustment layer.
- Choose Levels from the options available.

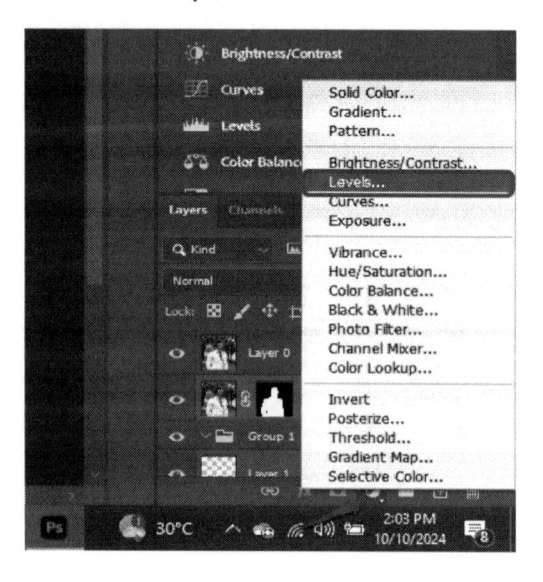

- The color balance of the image is shown on the middle graph, also referred to as the Levels histogram. The White Level is shown on the right, and the Black Level is on the left.
- Avoid using the second slider, the Output Level Slider, and instead use the input level sliders to adjust the color tone.

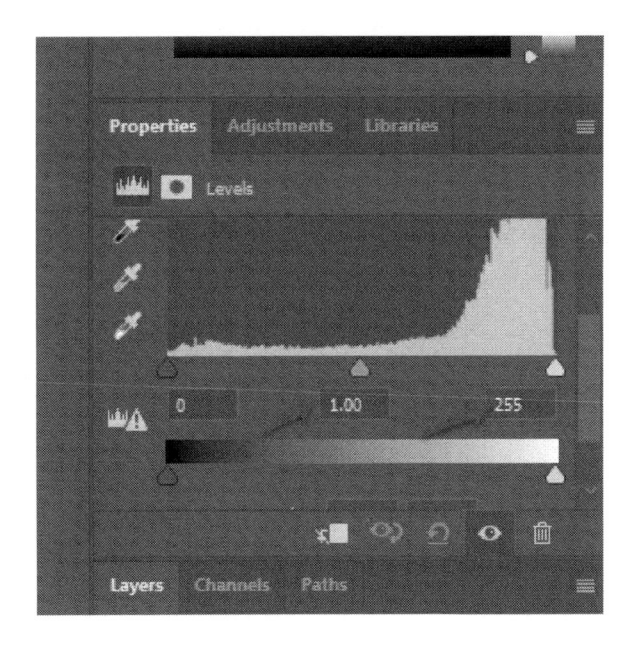

UNDERSTANDING CURVE ADJUSTMENT LAYER

Although the Curves tool and the Levels tool are similar, the Curves tool allows for more precise control over highlights, shadows, and mid-tones. You can work with the straight-line default appearance to produce different color temperatures at different places in your image.

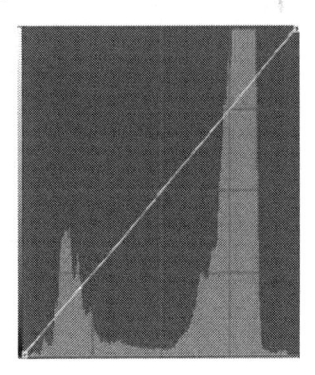

The following is how curves can be added and modified:

- Choose Curves from the menu when you click the Create New Fill Or Adjustment Layer symbol.

- To draw the desired curves, draw points at any position on the line and then drag them.

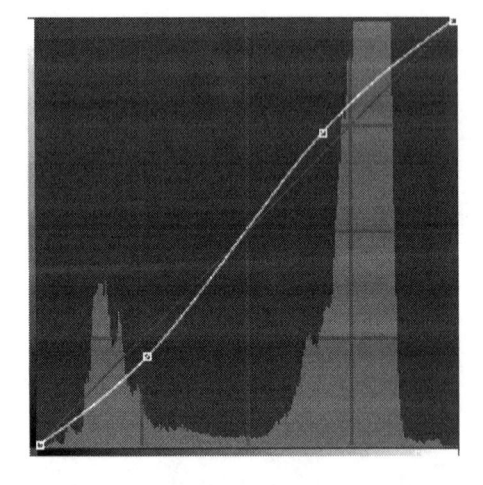

- You can use the Delete key or select an option from the Preset drop-down menu to delete points.

CREATING BLACK AND WHITE ADJUSTMENT LAYER

The Black and White Adjustment Layer simplifies the process of creating black-and-white photographs or adjusting brightness. It is also flexible, allowing you to change the gray components in your picture. The Black and White Adjustment Layer can be applied by:

- Click the Create New Fill Or Adjustment Layer icon and select Black/White;

- Adjust the black-and-white portions of the image by sliding sliders for various color ranges.

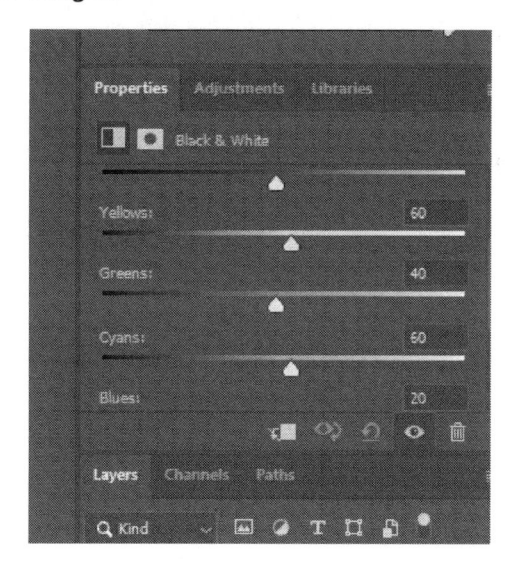

CREATING HUE/SATURATION ADJUSTMENT LAYER

The Adjustment Layer Hue/Saturation is used when some color correction is required with high accuracy. This allows for precise adjustments of Luminance, Saturation, and Hue for various color channels. This is especially useful for the focus on separate colors that do not touch the general color tone in the image.

- Click on the Create New Fill Or Adjustment Layer icon and choose Hue/Saturation Adjustment Layer.

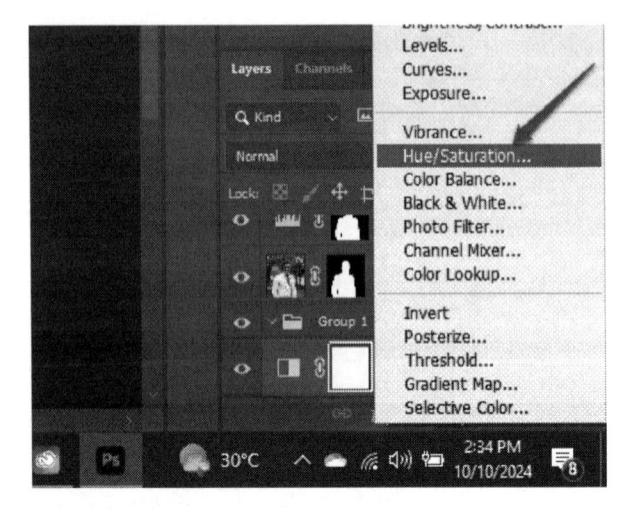

- Choose Hue/Saturation from the menu that appears from this point on.
- Adjust the hue more with sliders if needed.

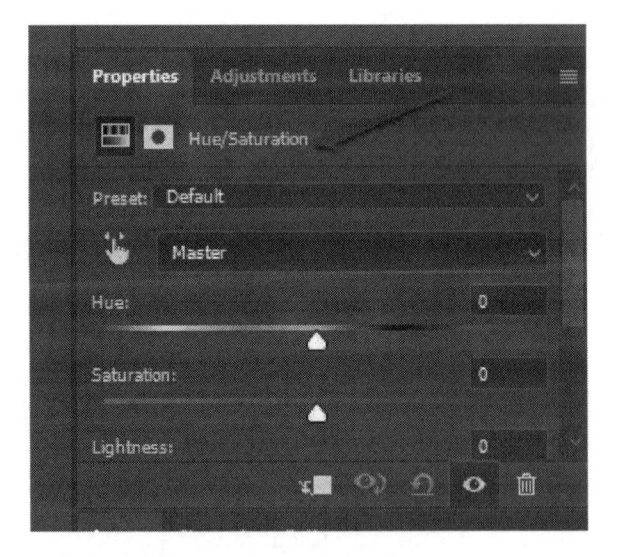

HOW TO APPLY PRESET STYLES

In Photoshop, layer styles are organized into libraries based on their uses. For example, styles in one library might be strictly for the creation of web buttons, while those in a different library might be strictly for enhancing text effects.

- To apply Preset Styles, go to Window > Styles and open the Styles Panel.
- The following window will load the library that will be used with these styles.

Remember that layer styles can't be put on either a backdrop, locked layers, or groups.

UNDERSTANDING BLENDING MODES

Blending modes will combine the pixels in one layer with the pixels in the underlying layer to achieve special effects. The base layer will interact with the blend layer; adjustments are non-destructive.

To apply blending modes:

- In this exercise, you'll practice with modes starting with "Normal" at the top left of the Layers panel.
- Click a layer, then use Shift + and Shift - to cycle through various layer blending modes for a range of effects. Apply the intensity via the layer opacity.

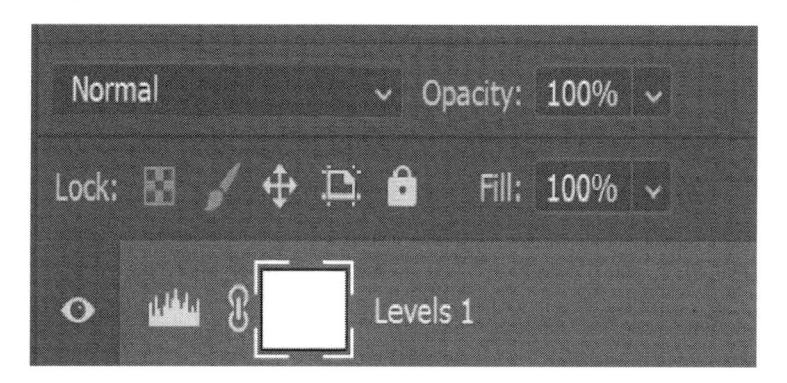

MASTERING BLENDING MODES

It's important to understand the structure of blending modes and identify basic differences. Although it's fun to experiment with blending modes, which can often yield cool results, a little understanding goes a long way.

The blending modes are divided into six groups, as separated by the thin rules: Normal, Darken, Lighten, Contrast, Inversion, and Component.

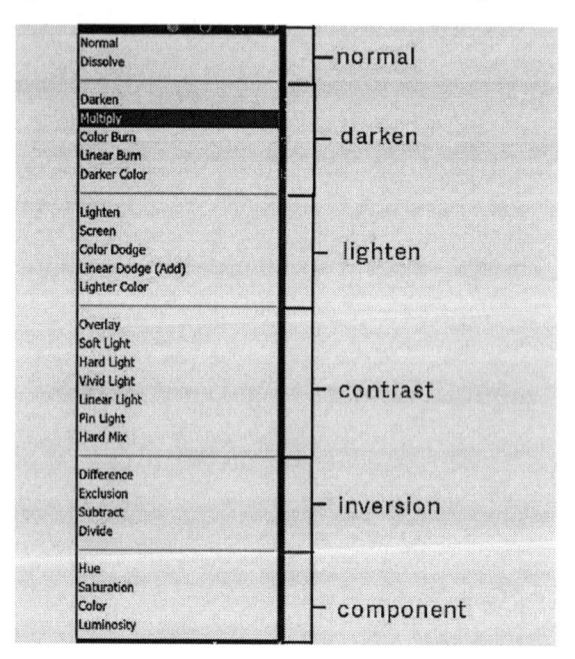

Making these categories simpler:

- **Normal Blending Mode**: Preserves the current appearance of the layer.
- **Darken Blending Modes**: These blend modes turn transparent white pixels into darker ones.
- **Brighten Blending Modes**: Brighten light pixels and give black pixels transparency.
- **Contrast Blending Modes**: Highlight lighter and darker pixels by making 50% of the gray pixels transparent.
- **Inversion Blending Modes**: Produce a contrast between the layer above and below the blend layer.
- **Component Blending Modes**: To achieve blending effects, use hue (color), saturation (color intensity), and luminosity (brightness).

Examining the following four popular blending modes:

- **Multiply**: Makes the mixture darker.
- **Screen**: Makes the mixture lighter.
- **Overlay**: Strengthens the blend's contrast.
- **Color**: Concentrates on combining different hues.

USING MULTIPLY BLEND MODE

One of the commonly used blending modes, Multiply uses dark pixels to darken the underlying layer while rendering white pixels transparent. In this regard, adding a compass to a photo and, with its blending mode set to Multiply, removes the white background of the compass, leaving just the compass.

SCREEN BLEND MODE

Unlike Multiply, Screen uses light-colored pixels to lighten up the layer below it while making the black pixels transparent. This is shown in the screen blend option, where black pixels are removed from an image of falling snow in a scene to allow for its inclusion in the overall composition.

OVERLAY BLENDING MODE

The overlay blend mode is peculiar because it lightens lighter pixels while darkening the darker ones, and it creates a 50% gray transparent area. When applied to an added texture image of a photo, this mode gives the resulting image that gritty look.

UNDERSTANDING COLOR BLENDING MODE

The Color blending mode instantly replaces the color of a layer, without affecting its luminosity and saturation relative to the underlying layer. For example, if you want to change the color of a car, you could select the car, fill the selection on a new layer with a solid color, and then apply the Color blending mode. What this ensures is that the newly applied color will smoothly integrate with the luminosity and intensity of the original photo.

CREATING TEXT AND APPLYING SPECIAL EFFECTS

There are two main methods of applying the text effects in Photoshop; first, using Layer styles, and second, using Character panel.

To use layer styles:

- Select a layer and then click the "Add a Layer Style" icon at the bottom of the Layers panel.
- A menu will pop up with a list of many different effects. Scrolling through the menu, select the effect that you would like to use and click on it to choose, then modify the various settings as desired. To add additional effects, click on the "Add Layer Style" button again.

To open the Character panel:

- Within Menu Bar go to Window > Character.
- In this panel, you will be modifying the font, size, color, and spacing of your text layer.
- Several text effects can be applied through the "Character Styles" menu. For applying one, a style needs to be selected from the list, and then "Apply" should be clicked.

Both of these have advantages and disadvantages. Using layer styles allows you to apply much faster, but it is less flexible than making use of the Character panel, which allows more detailed adjustments for each character. It depends on what exactly is needed for your design.

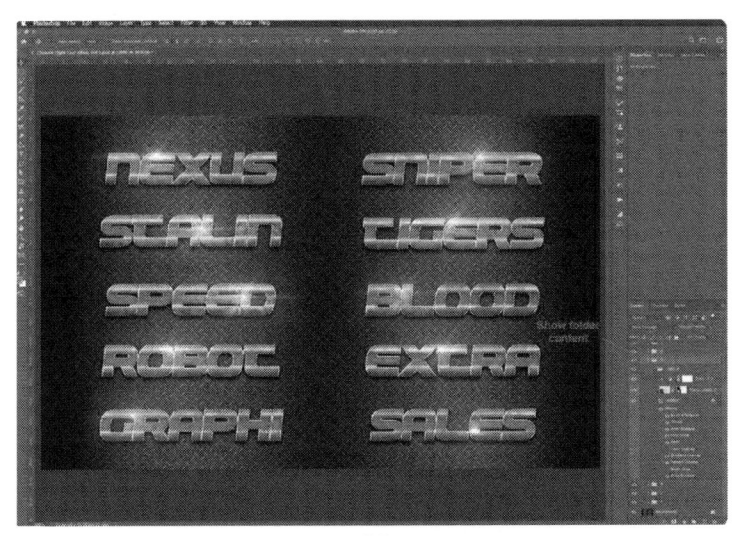

UNDERSTANDING GRADIENTS

One of the important features of Adobe Photoshop is the gradient, which allows smooth transitions of colors. These transitions can be from a simple blend between shades to complex color shifts that may involve several colors. Gradients are used in many design projects, adding depth, enhancing backgrounds, or even applying soft effects to images and text. Here's an explanation of how gradients work and how you can use them effectively.

Types of Gradients

Photoshop has a couple of gradient types, each operating in its unique way of blending colors, as shall be seen below.

- **Linear Gradient**: It contains colors that transition in a straight line from one point to another. This is usually used for backgrounds and shading effects.
- **Radial Gradient**: Colors radiate from a focal point, creating a circle-like blend. It's usually used to create spotlight or lens flare effects.
- **Angular Gradient**: Colors are spread in a counterclockwise manner around a starting point, resulting in a rotating color effect.
- **Reflected Gradient**: This type of gradient creates a mirrored linear gradient so that colors reflect equally on either side of a starting point.
- **Diamond Gradient**: Colors merge from the middle of a point outwards in a diamond shape and offer a special geometric effect.

How to Apply Gradients

- In the Toolbar, click the Gradient Tool icon or use the keyboard shortcut G. If the gradient tool icon is not visible as it may be hidden behind other tools such as the Paint Bucket, click and hold on the Paint Bucket icon and it will appear.

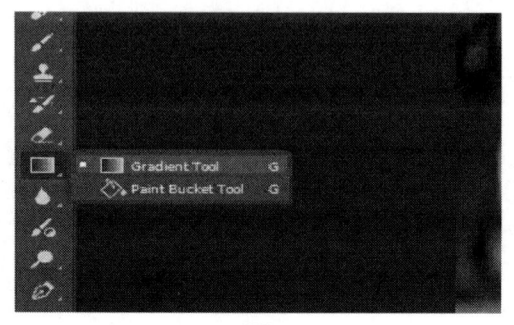

- You can choose one of several preset gradients via the Gradient Picker in the Options Bar along the top, or you may create your custom gradient. Some of the presets within Photoshop include simple colors Oranges, Clouds, Greens, and much more.

Edit Gradient Colors

If you are using a custom gradient, clicking the gradient bar in the Options Bar opens the Gradient Editor. You can use it to change any color stops, change the opacity of your gradient at any point, and add colors to your gradient.

Using Gradients with Layers and Masks

Gradients can be applied to layers or used with layer masks for more creative applications. For example:

- **Gradient Fill Layers**: It allows you to fill the layers with gradients independently. This will make it easy to edit them without necessarily having other elements of your design involved in the editing process. You can fill an entire layer with a gradient by following the command, Layer > New Fill Layer > Gradient.
- **Gradient and Layer Masks**: The application of gradients to the layer masks enables a soft transition in a layer from the visible to the invisible area. It also finds its use in image blending, creating fade effects, or feathering of edge areas.

Practical Uses for Gradients

- **Backgrounds**: Gradients make excellent background elements in web designs, posters, and digital arts. These will serve to add depth and visual interest compared to using flat colors.
- **Text Effects**: Applying gradients to texts would make your typography pop. For merging colors into text, one could utilize clipping masks or effects of gradient overlay.
- **Layer Blending**: One could employ gradients together with the blend modes of Photoshop for cool effects: laying a gradient over an image for light or color effects.
- **Image Blending**: Doing a gradient on layer masks to meld two images seamlessly into one by gradually transitioning from one image to another.

Gradients can be colors or tints that graduate smoothly into others, thereby adding subtle nuances of shading or shadow to an image. The real creativity behind gradients comes in layering and blending them. The Gradient Tool fills a selected area or active layer with linear, radial, angular, reflected, or diamond gradients. Here's a simple tutorial on how to create and use a gradient in Photoshop:

How to Create a Gradient

- Select the gradient tool from the toolbar.

- To access the Gradient Editor, click the wide gradient icon located on the top bar.

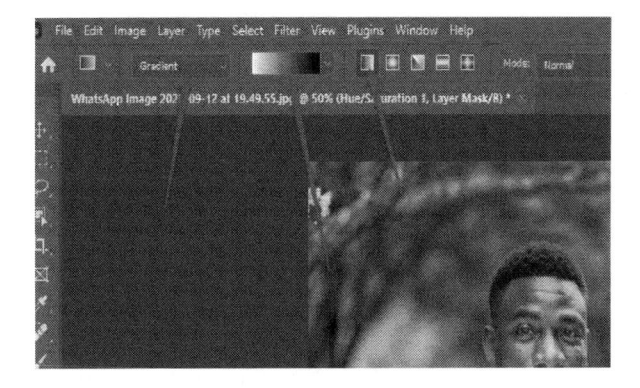

- Choose a preset from the organized options or customize from the "Basics" folder.

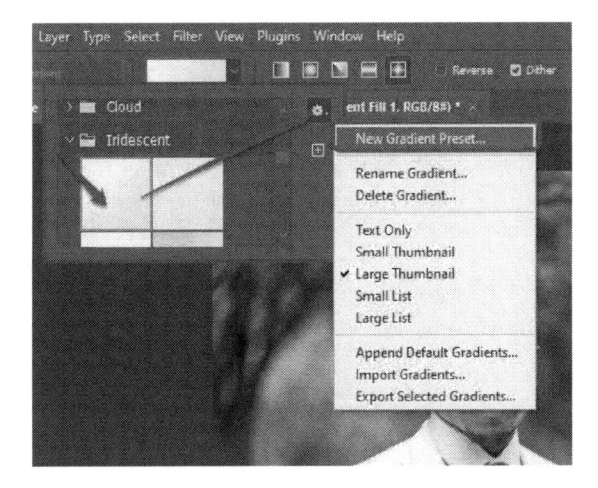

- Use the preview bar or Properties panel to change the colors, blending, and position until you're satisfied.

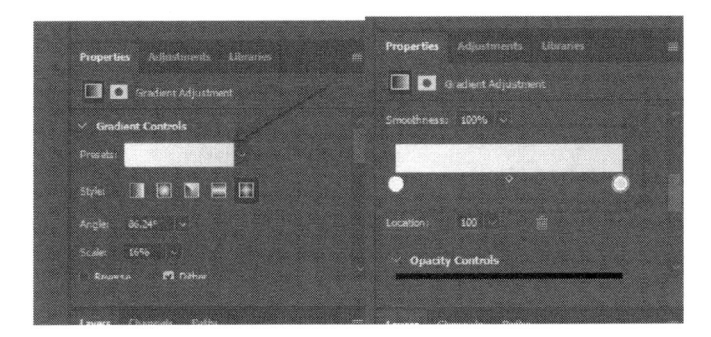

- Use the Opacity and the "Smoothness" option to alter the Opacity Control for smoother transitions.

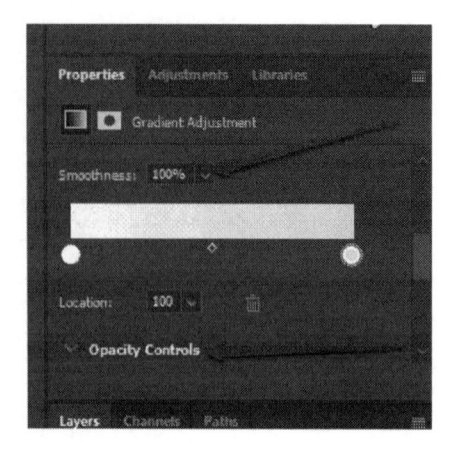

Go through the Preset preview options and choose your setup according to your preferences, and in the end, Save your Preset or click Ok.

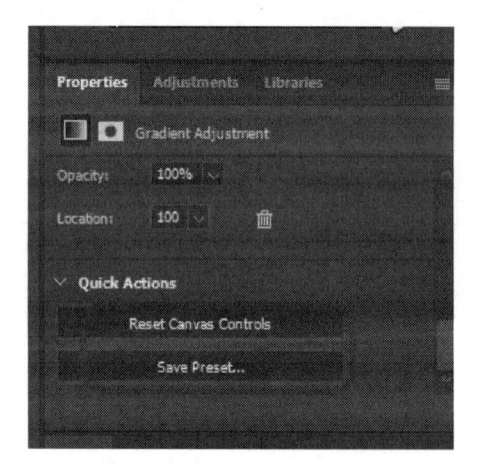

HOW TO ADD BORDER TO AN IMAGE

Adding a border to an image using Adobe Photoshop to enhance the look of the photograph. This adds an internal matte appearance and is super effective when an image is ready for an actual frame.

- **Start with just one background layer.**

Open Photoshop and then take a look at the Layers tab of the image. If there's more than one layer from other adjustments you may have done, you can go to Layer > Flatten Image to merge all of the layers down into a Background layer which is shown with a lock icon. If it already is a background layer, then proceed accordingly.

- **Advance in bringing the background to the front**

Go to Layer > New > Layer from Background. Click OK on the dialog box that opens. This will enable easy color modification of the border.

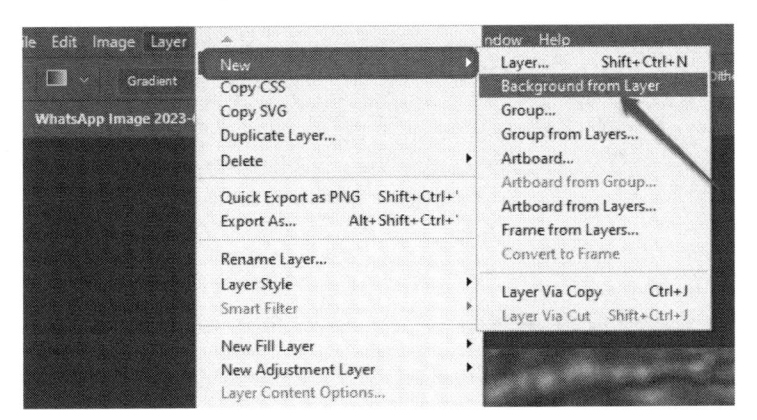

- **Enlarge the Image Canvas**

To enlarge the image around it, navigate to Image > Canvas Size, ensure that the Relative option is selected, and then enter the desired amount of pixels. Every edge has an equal distribution of the given value. For instance, if 200 pixels are entered into each field, a border width of 100 pixels will result. Click OK after making sure the Anchor is set to the center square.

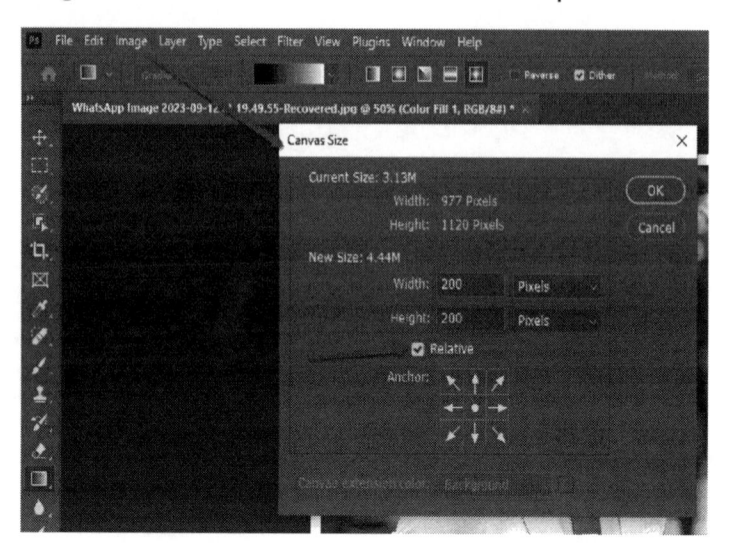

- **Create a Border Color**

To create the border, click the "Create a new fill or adjustment layer" icon in the Layers panel, and select "Solid Color". If the color is already on, which will be white, click OK.

- **Reposition the border color to the background**

In the Layers panel, drag the color fill layer beneath the picture layer.

- **Explore various aesthetics**

Double-click the color swatch in the adjustment layer and choose a new color to see what your border looks like in various colors. You can also create some interesting framed effects by playing with the settings in the Width and Height fields in the Canvas Size dialog box. Negative numbers yield a smaller border while positive numbers yield a larger border. The colored border seamlessly follows the shape adjustment because it was created with a fill layer.

- **Keep the flexibility**

Just as you wouldn't permanently glue a picture into an actual frame, you should be able to make changes to the border of your digital image at any time. Go back and open the border document again, then choose File > Save As and save the file in a new version that will allow you to easily go back to the original unbordered version of the document whenever you want to

CHAPTER 4

WORKING WITH SELECTIONS

OVERVIEW OF SELECTION?

A selection is the designation of an area in an image to better suit a range of manipulations. This enables the user to independently manipulate sections of the image without affecting those areas that are not selected. Selections are created through various tools and commands, in addition to the Select and Mask workspace. Once a selection is made, a border around it provides the ability to move, copy, or delete pixels within the border. Outside this selected region, no changes can be made until the selection is de-selected.

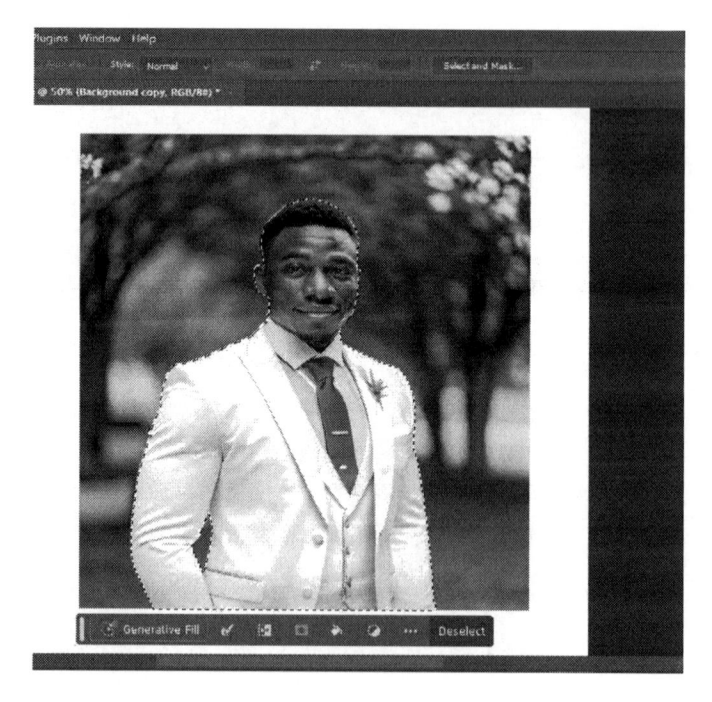

SELECTING EVERY PIXEL ON A LAYER

To select all pixels on a selected layer that fall within the bounds of the canvas, follow these steps:

- Select the layer you want via the Layers panel.
- Go to Select >> All.

DESELECTING A SELECTION

To deselect an active selection:

- Click Choose > Deselect.
- Control+D for Windows, and Command + D for Mac for Setting it.
- If the Rectangle Marquee tool, the Elliptical Marquee tool, or the Lasso tool was used to select, click anywhere in the image outside the selected area.

UNDERSTANDING OBJECT SELECTION TOOL

The Object Selection tool will help you through the easy selection of an object or area of your image that includes people, cars, pets, sky, water, buildings, mountains, and many more. You can choose to draw a rectangle or freehand select over an object or area manually, or you can let the tool automatically detect and select an object or area in your image. Selections made with the Object Selection tool provide enhanced precision and preserve fine details along the edges of the selection, which reduces the time and effort taken to achieve perfect selections.

The Object Selection tool can be accessed via:

- Availability within the application toolbar in Photoshop.
- Located on the toolbar in the Select And Mask workspace.

Steps for object selection with the use of the Object Selection tool are presented as follows:

- To start working, pick the Object Selection tool.
- Click on the Object Selection tool inside the toolbar.

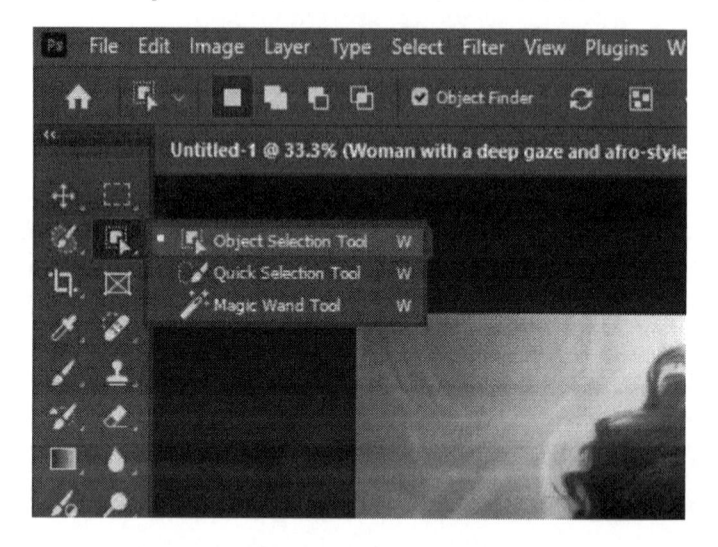

Select using the Object Selection tool as follows:

- On the Object Selection Options bar make sure the Object Finder is checked. When the Object Finder is turned on, there is a little spinning refresh icon beside the Object Finder option. Move your mouse over and click on your intended object or image area that The Object Finder is typically on by default.
- To do a manual selection without the auto aid, in the Options bar uncheck the Object Finder check box then choose either Rectangle or Lasso object Mode. Now drag over your desired selection with the currently chosen mode.

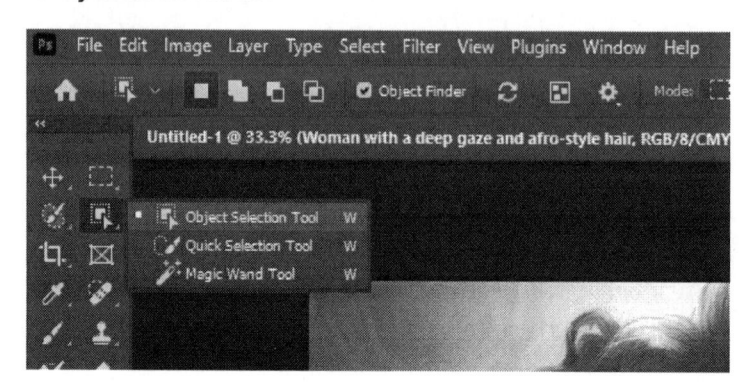

Object Select tool options bar choices include the following:

- **Rectangle**: After selecting the tool drag the cursor to draw a rectangular region around an object or area.
- **Lasso**: After selecting the tool draw by freehand a lasso around the outside edge of the object or area.

To subtract, or to add to the selection.

- In the options bar, select one of the following options; New, Add To, Subtract From, or Intersect With the selection. The default is New with no previous selection; once the first selection has been made, this automatically changes to Add To.
- **Add to selection**: With the Shift key active, or click Add To Selection in the option bar Drag over or draw a new rectangle or lasso over the area you want to add. Repeat for each of the other regions to add in.
- **Subtract From Selection option in the Options bar**: Click the Option [Mac] / Alt [Win] key or, if already selected click Subtract From Selection in the options bar then hover over, or draw a rectangle or lasso around the boundary of any area you would like to subtract from the selection.
- Click on the gear icon in the options bar to turn it on to view more options, then click on Object Subtract; The Object Subtract option comes in pretty handy when cleaning background areas within a selected object boundary.

Object select settings:

- **Sample All Layers**: A selection will be made considering all layers, not just the active ones.
- **Hard Edge**: Turn hard edges on along the edge of the selection.

Refine the selection edge further in the Select and Mask workspace:

- Click the Select And Mask button in the options bar, to further refine the selection edge, to view the selection against various backgrounds, or to see the selection as a mask.
- Further refine using the Selection Feedback dialog to supply information about your selection, and hence improve your success with the Object Selection tool.

OBJECT SELECTION TOOL FOR ADVANCED HAIR SELECTIONS

Object Selection has been vastly improved to give better hair selections on human portrait images. It now does a much better job of identifying portraits and offers advanced hair refinement, giving a mask of similar quality to what is possible using the Select Subject feature. To use this enhanced capability, follow these easy steps:

- Open your portrait image.
- From the toolbar, select the Object Selection tool.

Selection is to be done either by directly clicking on the portrait or drawing a lasso/marquee on the person. It will mask out all the minute details of hair and thus a very refined and fine selection can be achieved.

EXPLORING SUBJECT SELECTION

The "Select Subject" feature has now become more content-aware; new custom algorithms are used, especially around the detection of people in images. Notice significantly improved treatments in the area of hair. To temporarily disable the content awareness, press and hold the Shift key while using "Select Subject."

The Select Subject feature automatically selects the main subject of a picture. Powered with the power of advanced machine learning, this feature can select everything from people, animals, vehicles, and toys to many others in your pictures.

Using Select Subject

With the Image Editing Lab, you can select a subject using one of the following methods:

- Click "Select" > "Subject."
- While using the Object Selection, Quick Selection, or Magic Wand tool, click the "Select Subject" in the options bar.
- In the Select & Mask workspace, while selecting any of the Object Selection or Quick Selection tools click "Select Subject" in the options bar.

Once "Select Subject" has been applied, the selection can be further refined by doing the following:

- Employ selection tools to add to or subtract from a selection. Refine selections more precisely by opening the selection in the "Select and Mask" workspace via "Select" → "Select and Mask." Additional tools and sliders in this workspace are tailored for more detailed refinement of selections.

DISTINGUISHING BETWEEN THE SELECT SUBJECT COMMAND AND THE OBJECT SELECTION TOOL

The Object Selection tool and the Select Subject command are a couple of useful image selections, as both serve different purposes during an image selection in Photoshop. These are as follows:

- **Object Selection Tool**: This option shall be used when you want to select a specific object or a part of an object that is present in the picture along with other objects
- **Select Subject Command**: This will select all the primary subjects that are present within the image.

USING THE QUICK SELECTION TOOL

The Quick Selection tool is super convenient for making selections quickly by "painting" with a dynamically adjusting round brush tip. As you drag the brush, the selection automatically extends, pulling itself along defined edges within the picture.

How to use the Quick Selection tool:

- The Quick Selection tool Choose the Quick Selection tool from the toolbar. If you don't see the tool, click and hold on the Magic Wand tool.
- In the options bar, choose one of the options: New, Add To, or Subtract From. "New" is the default selection option when there is no active selection. Once an initial selection has been made, it

ADD QUICK SELECT OPTIONS

- **Sample All Layers**: This option allows you to make a selection that is based on all of the layers not just the selected layer.
- Sharpen Edge: This refines the rough edges and adds to edge smoothness. This option automates some refinement to the edges, which is also manually editable within the Select and Mask workspace.

What to Do Next:

- To make a selection, click and drag the image over the area where you want the selection to be. This will auto-extend the selection just keep painting until it's large enough. If it is taking a long time to refresh, simply continue dragging until the selections take some time to catch up. You can paint near the edge of a form and the edges will be sampled through the selection area.

- To subtract from an already existing selection, choose "Subtract From" from the options bar and drag through the image where the selection already exists.
- Temporarily switch between add and subtract modes by holding the Alt key (Windows) or Option key (Mac).
- To modify the tool cursor, select Edit > Preferences > Cursors (Windows) or Photoshop > Preferences > Cursors (Mac), and then select "Painting Cursors." The "Normal Brush Tip" icon displays the default Quick Selection cursor, with its selection mode indicated by a plus or minus sign.

MARQUEE TOOLS SELECTION

The marquee tools in Photoshop allow selections of all shapes and sizes. You can choose to draw rectangle ellipses, as well as rows or single columns of pixels.

- Select a marquee tool:
    - **Rectangle Marquee**: Creates rectangular selections- it will also create squares if you hold the Shift key.
    - **Elliptical Marquee**: Creates elliptical selections- it will create circles if you hold the Shift key.
    - **Single Row or Single Column Marquee**: Sets the border as a 1-pixel width row or column.
- In the options bar, choose how you want to view your selection with one of the settings: A. New, B. Add To, C. Subtract From, D. Intersect With
- You can also adjust feathering, in the options bar, to produce softer selection edges as well as turning anti-aliasing on and off.
- For the Rectangular Marquee tool or the Elliptical Marquee tool, in the options bar choose a style:
    - **Normal**: The marquee's proportions are set as you drag.
    - **Fixed Ratio**: Requires an exact height-to-width ratio of the selection. Type in your values, including decimal values for the aspect ratio.
    - **Fixed Size**: Allows the entry of exact pixel values for the height and width of the marquee. Note: Other units can also be used, such as inches, centimeters, etc.

- To align your selection precisely to guides, grids, slices, or the edges of your document, enable the snapping for your selection:
    - Select View> Snap or choose View> Snap To and select a submenu command. Your marquee selection can snap to several Photoshop Extras and you can toggle that snapping on and off through the Snap To submenu.

HOW TO MAKE A SELECTION

To make a selection With the Rectangular Marquee tool or the Elliptical Marquee tool:

- Drag the Rectangular Marquee tool or the Elliptical Marquee tool over the area of your selection.
- To restrict the marquee to a square or circle while dragging, hold down the Shift key (release the mouse button before releasing Shift to maintain the constrained shape).
- To drag a marquee from its center, hold down the Alt key (Windows) or Option key (Mac OS) after you begin the drag.

A marquee selection is created a little differently when using either the Single Row or Single Column Marquee tool:

- Click near where you want to select and drag the marquee to the exact position. If you can't see the marquee, Zoom in on image view.

Note: To eliminate the selection from your image, pick Deselect from the menu.

MOVING A SELECTION USING SHORTCUT KEYS

To move selections around in your Photoshop document, use the following key shortcuts to do so:

- **Align Selection (in 1-pixel Steps):** Arrow Keys will move the selection one pixel at a time.
- **Align Selection (in 10-pixel Steps):** To do this, press the Shift Key + Arrow Keys to have your selection moved ten pixels at one time.
- **Marquee While Drawing Selection:** During selection, hit Spacebar which will toggle you into the Hand Tool from where you can reposition

the marquee for accurate placement. Release the spacebar to proceed with the selection.

USING LASSO TOOLS FOR SELECTION

There are a great number of selection tools in Photoshop. One of the best for creative, flexible selections is the Lasso tool. The Lasso tool offers the following:

- **Freehand Selection-Precision**: The default Lasso tool is your friend for freehand selections, giving you very precise control over selections. This freehand selection tool does not 'auto-snap' to object edges nor does it try to guess your selection. Your lasso shape stays wherever you draw it. However, Photoshop helps clean up your shape by filling in small gaps between your endpoint and starting point.

- **Selection Customization**: Similar to most selection tools within Photoshop, the Lasso tool contains additional functionality that allows one to work more efficiently. This includes adding to, subtracting from, and intersecting with previously made selections, adding greater precision and variability in edits.

- **Feather and Anti-Alias**: Use anti-aliasing to soften or feather the selection edges as per your requirement. High feathering gives you room for maneuvering with softer, fuzzier shapes, whereas anti-aliasing can make the edges of your selection smooth and accurate.

- **Maintain Precision**: Elevate the accuracy of your freehand selections by employing either the Magnetic Lasso tool or the Polygonal Lasso tool. The Magnetic Lasso tool harnesses AI capabilities to attempt snapping to object edges, while the Polygonal Lasso tool converts freehand lines into straight lines, crafting polygonal shapes with precision.

When to Use the Lasso

Wondering when to include the Lasso tool in your designs? Here's a rundown of some creative ideas that will spur you into action:

- **QEIRY Selections**: When shape selection isn't a perfect rectangle or oval, this is where the Lasso tools kick in. They're great for making creative, unique selections and are just ideal for composites.
- **Painterly Selections**: Combine the Lasso tools with Photoshop's Select and Mask features to operate within a separate selection environment. Herein, you can paint and refine selections artistically for greater control in your creative process.

MAKING LASSO TOOL SELECTIONS

To make selections with the Lasso tool you need to understand the simple three-step process:

- **Select Tool**: Click the toolbar and select the Lasso tool. Click and pull on the Lasso tool icon, and a fly-out menu will appear showing Magnetic or Polygonal Lasso tools.
- **Make Selection**: Drag, indicating the shape of your selection directly on your canvas.
- **Refine or Extend Selection**: If you need to make some adjustments to your selection, the Undo option can be availed by pressing Command + D for Mac users and Ctrl + D for Windows users to deselect the image and start over. You also have the "Select and Mask" option appearing on the top of your screen to refine your selection. Holding the Shift key will add new selections to an already selected one.

INTELLIGENTLY SWITCHING BETWEEN LASSO AND POLYGONAL LASSO TOOLS

By holding the Alt key down while making a selection, you can smoothly switch between the Lasso tool and the Polygonal Lasso tool. This provides an easy, fluid workflow for making selections. Selections come in all shapes and sizes, and often you'll use multiple techniques on one, and voilà, you achieve what you wanted. Although extremely powerful at selecting, the Magnetic Lasso Tool sometimes it's useful to have access to one of the other lasso tools within Photoshop. Here's how to switch intelligently between these tools:

- **Switch to Standard Lasso Tool**: While any of the lasso tools is active, hold down the Alt key (Win)/Option key (Mac), and click on the edge of

an object with the Magnetic Lasso Tool. Still holding down the mouse button after clicking, start dragging but let go of the Alt/Option key to switch to the Standard Lasso Tool. When done, let go of the mouse button. The toolset will now pop back to the Magnetic Lasso Tool.
- **Polygonal Lasso Tool**: Activating the Magnetic Lasso Tool, hold down the Alt / Option and click on the edge of an object. While holding the key, click, release the mouse button, then drag off away from the point clicked in. To add straight-line segments, click point to point while holding Alt / Option. To return to the Magnetic Lasso Tool, release the Alt / Option key, click on the object's edge to add a point, and release the mouse button.

SELECTING WITH THE MAGNETIC LASSO TOOLS

Make precise selections, by dragging your cursor, that automatically snap to the edges of an image.

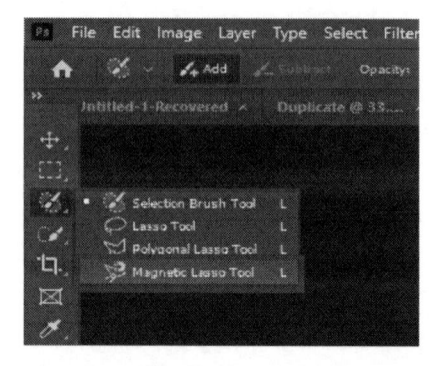

- Select the Magnetic Lasso tool (L) from the toolbar. If you don't see the Magnetic Lasso tool then click and hold the Lasso tool to show related tools and select the tool.

- Click your preferred choice option from among the list of possibilities that appear on the tool options bar: New Selection, Add to Selection, Subtract from Selection, or Intersect with Selection.
- More tool option parameters will be adjusted in the anti-aliasing, feathering, and settings for Frequency, Width, Contrast, and Stylus Pressure.
- Set your cursor anywhere in your image to set the first anchor point. As you move your cursor along the selected edge, the active segment of the selection will automatically snap to the strongest edge of the image.
- Click once to create an anchor point manually. Continue along the edge of the image, creating anchor points as needed to trace it accurately.

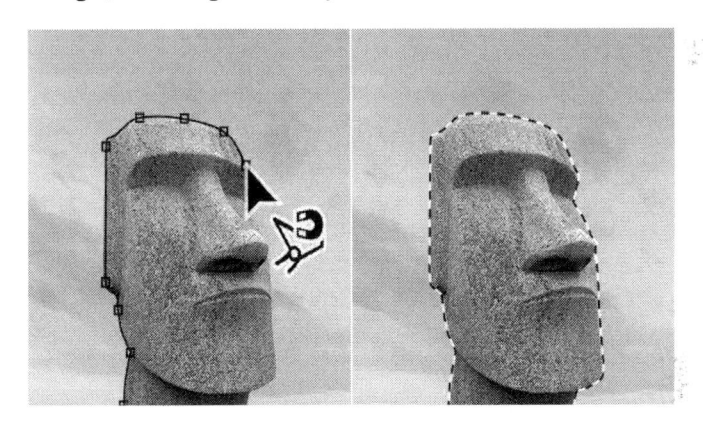

HOW TO ROTATE AND SCALE A SELECTION

Rotating Selection

A way of rotating selection is by using the Move Tool with the Transform Tool: The above method described is easier and quicker but has a disadvantage in that it clears the selection from the layer, which may leave a hole in your image that needs to be filled.

Luckily for you, this trick supports multiple select tools such as Lasso Tool L, Object Selection Tool W, Quick Selection Tool W, and all Marquee Tools M. Here's how:

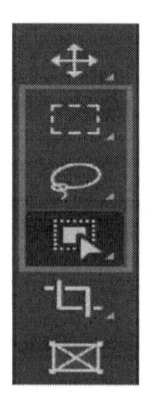

- Choose which tool you would like to utilize and make your selection in your picture or project. In this example, we will choose the Object Selection Tool, or (W).

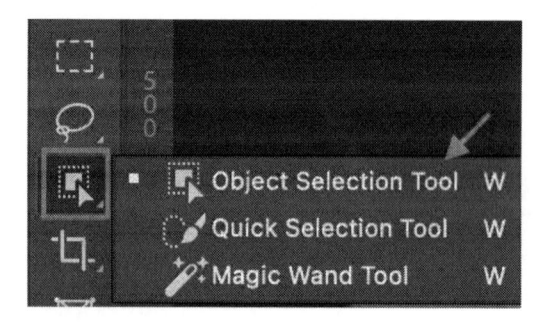

- With the Object Select Tool, define your selection either by clicking on objects that Photoshop has detected or by drawing a boundary in the image around an object you want to select. The identified objects will have pink after hovering over them; the marching ants start showing the active selection.

- To activate the Move Tool, click its icon or press the V key.

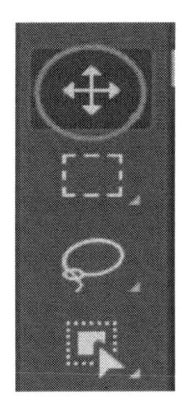

- To engage the Transform feature, hit Control + T for Win or Command + T for Mac. You'll see that your selection is now surrounded by a transform box.

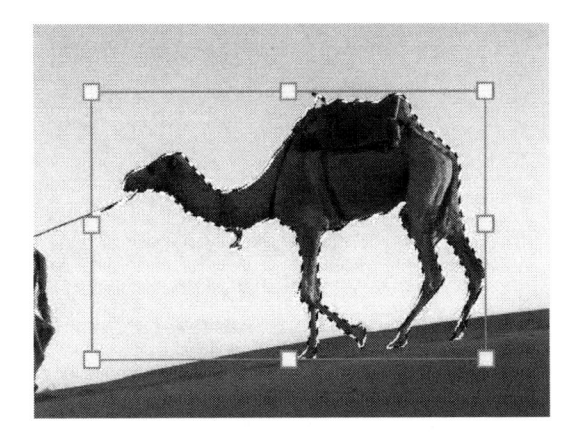

- To make the pointer change to a rotation icon, drag it over to, and just beyond, the corner of the transform box.

- Now, slide your pointer in the desired direction to rotate the selection.

- To remove the selection after rotating and moving it, press Control + D on Windows or Command + D on Mac.

Note: When rotating or moving the selection, it may seem to be cut out of its original area, leaving a gap. Employ techniques such as content-aware fill, layer duplication, and other fill-in methods to fix the problem.

Scaling Selection

Clicking on Transform Selection turns the transform box and handles on - as you know from Free Transform, but this time, while dragging a handle, the image is fixed and you resize the selection outline.

MAKING SELECTIONS WITH MAGIC WAND TOOL

Using cutting-edge machine learning, the Photoshop Magic Wand tool is an incredibly potent selection tool that can recognize and pick particular objects or regions inside your image on its own. For example, clicking on the sky chooses the entire sky rapidly, and clicking on someone's face selects the complete face properly in a matter of seconds. The following factors make the Magic Wand tool a great option.

- **Perfect for Novices**: For novices who want to begin picking out portions of their photos to modify further with tools like layer masks, the Magic Wand tool is a great option. It offers a simple gateway to the universe of options.

- **Professionals**: It is also professionally empowering, in that even though the Magic Wand is for beginners, a pro can control the selection process with fine-tuning by changing parameters such as tolerance, sample size, and anti-aliasing. It can change to suit the requirements of people with and without experience.

- **Choices Customizable**: If for some reason you are not happy with the choices that the Magic Wand is making, you can adjust its behavior. You can adjust how aggressively it selects which layers it focuses on, and a lot more.

- **Creative Problem Solving**: Choosing is not always a simple activity. You can attain the ideal solution to suit your needs by modifying, removing, or intersecting with options already selected using the Magic Wand tool.

- **Versatile Applications:** The Magic Wand tool offers fast and precise selections for your artistic work and may be used for a wide range of activities, including subject selection, color correction in photos, and much more.

Magic Wand Tool - How to Use It

Using the Magic Wand tool is extremely easy, as shown below:

- Select the Magic Wand tool from the toolbar and make sure the correct layer is active.
- The tool automatically selects whatever you click on by clicking in the area you want to pick.
- Inverse the selection by choosing the "Subtract from the Selection" icon in the Options bar to eliminate parts of your image you don't want in your selection. You can even use the Eraser tool among other tools, and edit when in Quick Mask mode, which can be accessed via the sidebar.
- You can also deselect by hitting Command+D (Mac) or Ctrl+D (PC) if your selection isn't ideal.
- To return your selection to its original position, select "Select › Inverse." This helps when you need to work in areas outside of your selection.

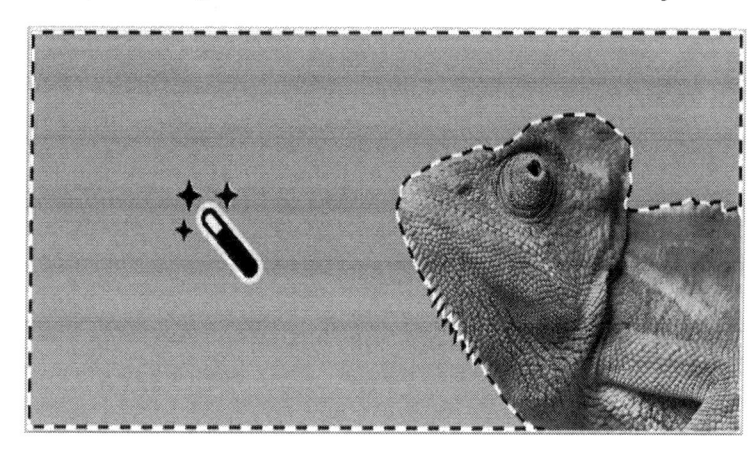

CHAPTER 5

EDITING IMAGES

EXPLORING VARIOUS IMAGE EDITING OPERATION

Learn how to quickly remove acne and other blemishes from your portraits and reveal glowing skin with the use of Photoshop's Spot Healing Brush. This is one such tool that can help in skin smoothening much quicker, thus refining your photo. Follow these steps:

- **Add New Blank Layer:**

Open your photo in Photoshop, then Create a new layer above the image so that you keep your retouching separate. Name this layer "Spot Healing."

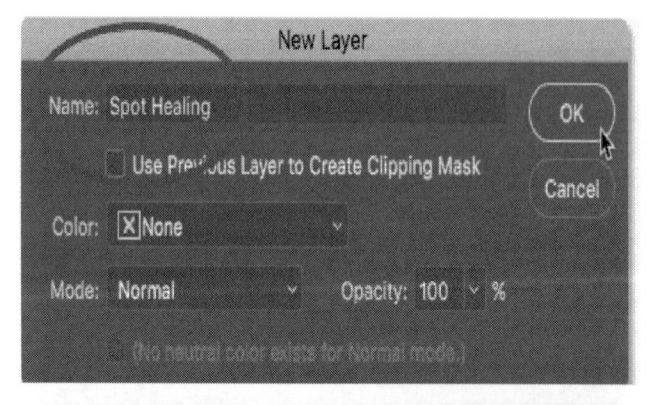

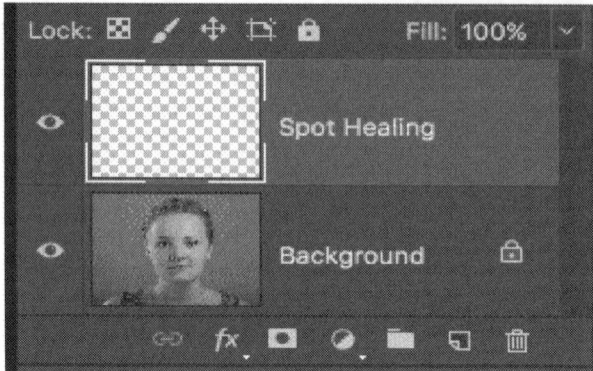

- **Next, the Spot Healing Brush Should be Selected**

Then select the Spot Healing Brush from the Toolbar. To make the retouching easier for you, it will automatically choose the texture.

- **Check "Sample All Layers"**

Click the "Sample All Layers" icon in the Options Bar so that it becomes highlighted. This tells the Spot Healing Brush to sample the texture on both the "Spot Healing" layer and the original underlying image.

- **Keep "Content-Aware" Selected**

In the Options Bar, keep "Content-Aware" selected as the Type setting. Photoshop can make better choices while attempting to change texture thanks to this handy function.

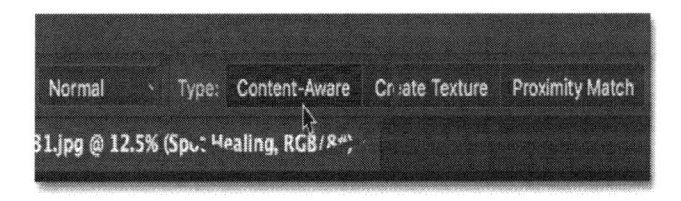

- **Heal Skin Blemishes**

Click on pimples and blemishes with the Spot Healing Brush, and make them all but disappear right before your eyes. To get the best effect, set your brush size just a little bit larger than the blemish.

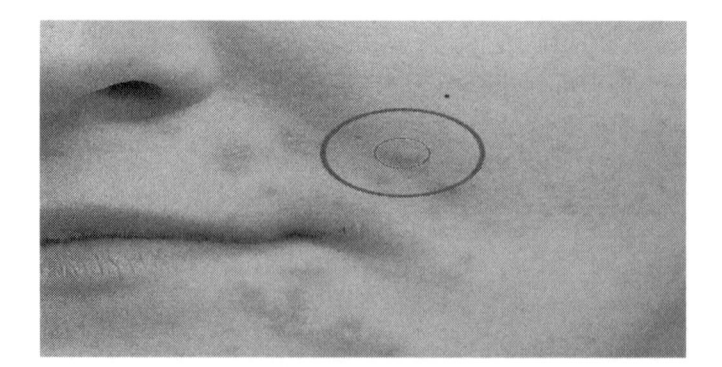

Tips:

- **Planning Mistakes**: If need be, hit Ctrl+Z (Win) / Command+Z (Mac) to undo and try again. Every time it clicks, something different pops out.

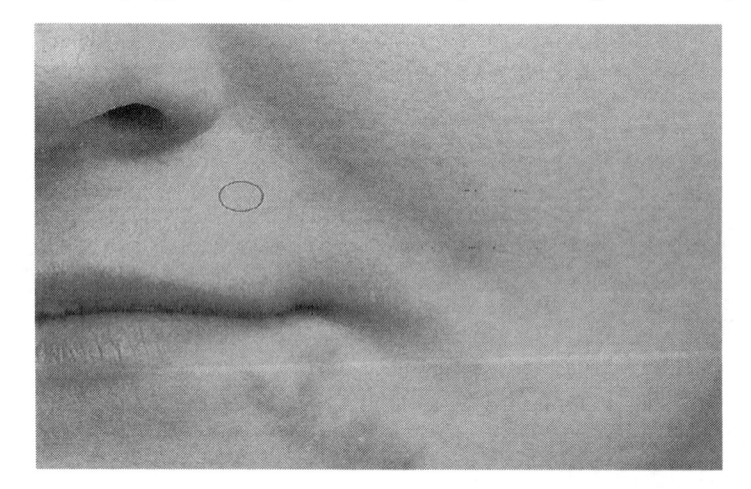

- **Larger Area Retouching:** First, go for the smaller problems and then the larger areas section by section. Click or drag the brush in short strokes, making gradual skin improvements.

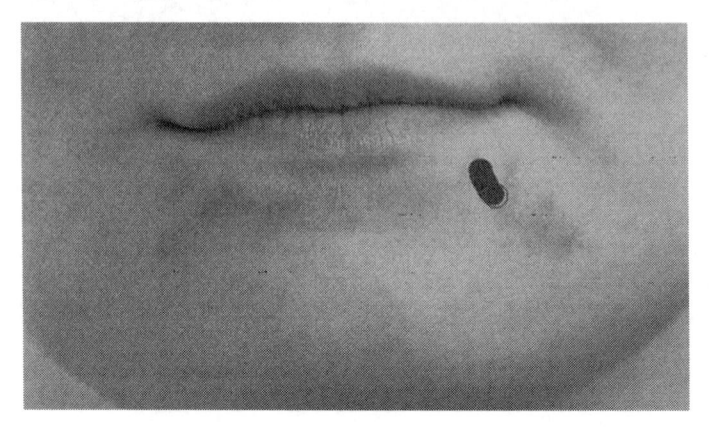

- **Retocar Touch:** Click or drag to remove remaining blemishes, feathering smoothly into the surrounding texture.

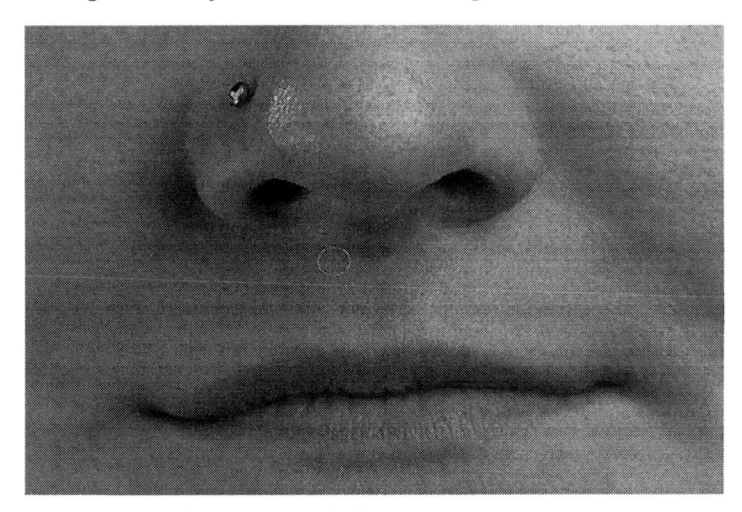

That is the way in a few simple clicks and strokes, your portraits will reveal perfect, naturally retouched skin. Master the Spot Healing Brush for professional results in Photoshop!

SHARPENING IMAGES IN PHOTOSHOP WITH A HIGH-PASS FILTER

High Pass works by laying a flat, mid-gray over the entire image and then identifies edges in those image areas where there is a significant jump in brightness between neighboring pixels and gives emphasis to them. This is done by lightening the light side of the edge and darkening the dark side, while areas with no edge continue as gray.

That's important because the setting of Radius controls how wide the edge sharpening will be by including how many pixels away from the edge, outward, will be included and sharpened as part of the edge. In other words, the smaller the Radius setting, the closer the High Pass filter is sharpening only one pixel on either side of an edge. In contrast, setting the Radius to 10 expands the highlighting effect to a width of 10 pixels on either side of the edge.

Sharpening just increases the contrast along edges, and the High Pass filter in Photoshop does an outstanding job of finding those edges. Now, let's see exactly how sharpening an image works with the High Pass filter. Open any image you think might benefit from some sharpening, and follow these steps.

Exploring Image Processing Filter With High Pass

First, you need to turn the image layer into a Smart Object by enabling it to support the High Pass filter as a non-destructive smart filter. Open an image on the Background layer of the Layers panel in the Layers panel.

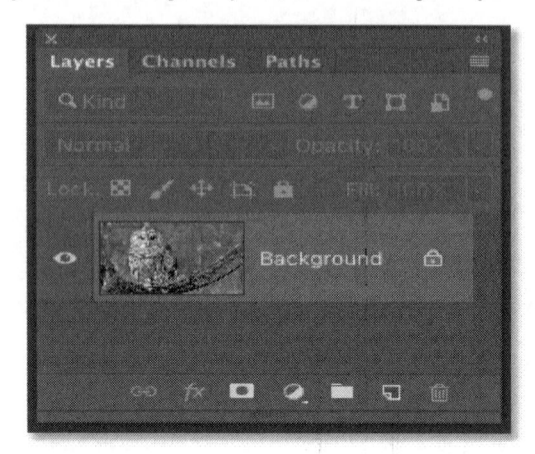

- Use the menu icon in the Layers panel's upper right corner to turn a layer into a smart object.

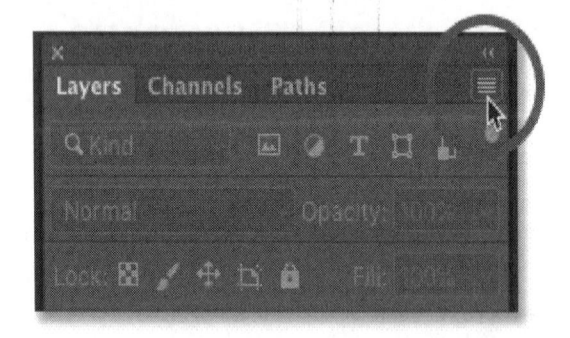

- Select "Convert to Smart Object" from the menu.

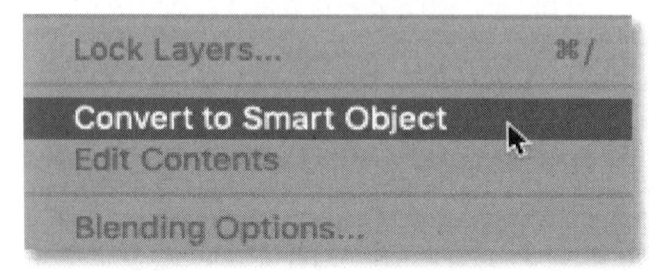

- To indicate that the image is securely hidden inside the smart object, a little icon is displayed to the lower right of the preview thumbnail. From this point on, any sharpening. Applying the High Pass filter to the smart object itself maintains the original image.

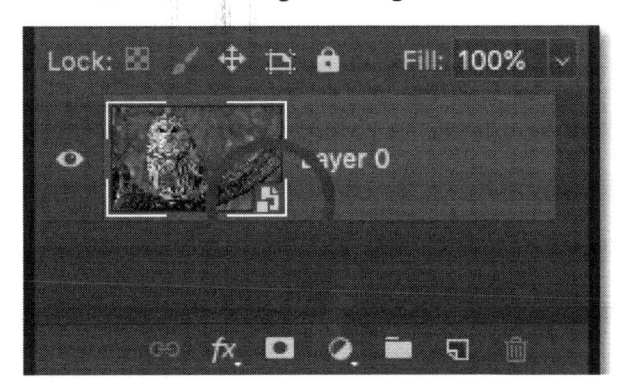

- Choose Filter > Other > High Pass from the Menu Bar to apply the High Pass filter. Select High Pass under Filter > Other.

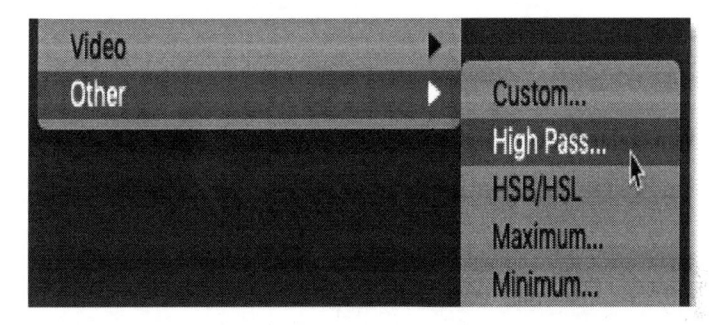

- Your image will turn grayscale if you select High Pass.

- Set the edges by moving the Radius value. High Pass filter dialog is very simple. In it, you can see a Radius slider below the preview window. Now let's take an in-depth look at how the High Pass filter works.

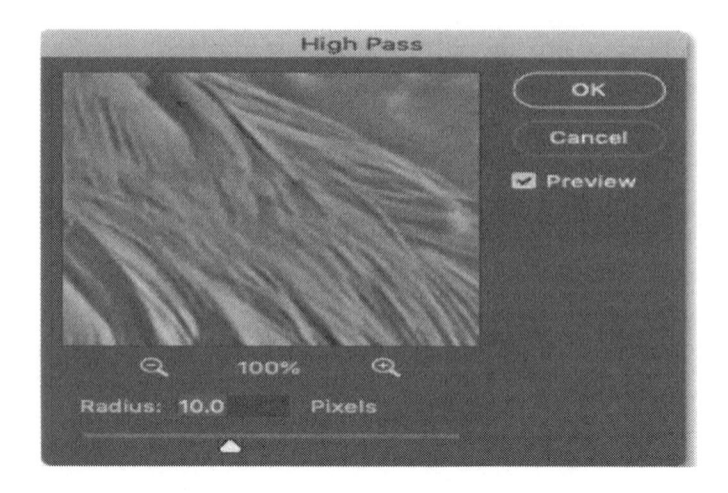

HOW TO USE GENERATIVE FILL INSTANTLY REMOVE PEOPLE OR ITEMS FROM PHOTOS

The Generative Fill tool in Photoshop allows for the removal of extra items or people in your pictures. While the video focuses on removing people, the process of content removal of any kind is the same.

Follow the steps below:

- Begin by selecting the Lasso Tool from the toolbar. Often this will be one extra step after having used either the Object Selection Tool or Select Subject for best outcome.

- For removing a person or an object, highlight it using the Lasso Tool and include a part of the space around in your selection so that Generative Fill understands how to meld AI-generated content.

- Locate the Contextual Task Bar below. If it is not there, then be sure the Contextual Task Bar is on by checking the Window/Contextual Task Bar. Click the button marked "Generative Fill."

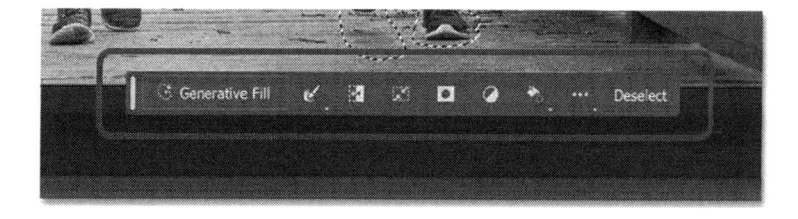

- A prompt box would appear; to remove a person or an object, it would be left empty. Tap the Generate button. Thereafter, Photoshop sends the image to Adobe's servers and shows a progress bar until Generative Fill renders the AI replacement content.

- Once the progress bar disappears, that would mean the 'thing/person' is successfully taken out and replaced with new AI-created content. The new content will perfectly merge with the surroundings, matching in detail the depth of field.

- A new layer, Generative, will appear above the original image in the Layers panel. In this layer, the AI-generated content is stored separately so that you can toggle back and forth between the original and edited version.

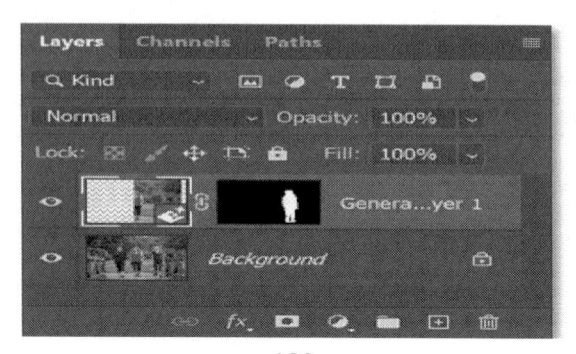

- You can see that Generative Fill has created three variations of replacement content in the Properties panel. Click each thumbnail to compare and select your preferred one.

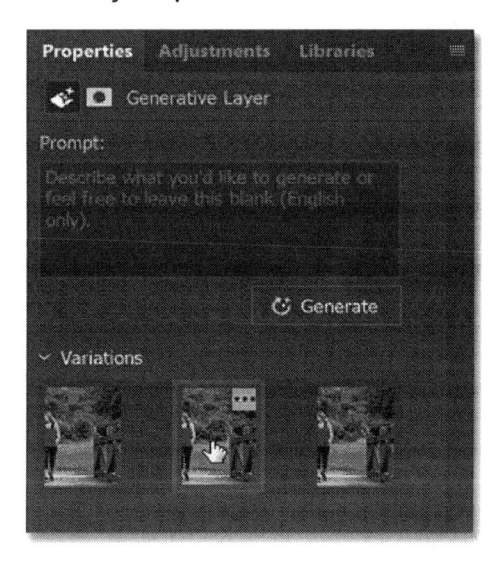

- To create three new options if you don't like the first set, tap the Generate button from the Properties panel. New iterations will replace the older ones. Repeat as necessary, until you're satisfied.

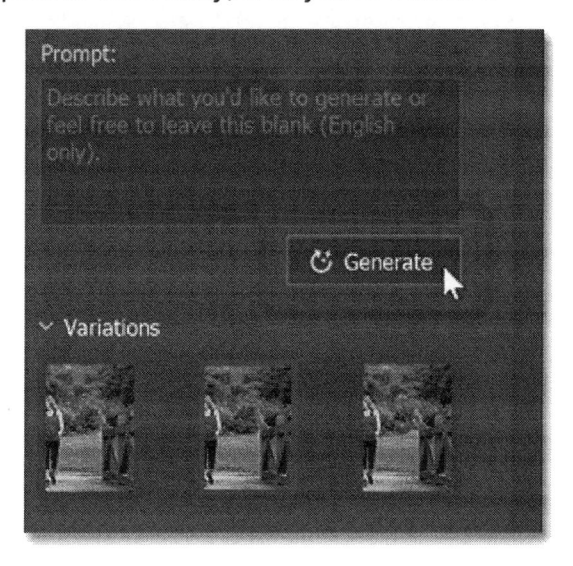

With all the variations that enable freedom and artistic expression, Generative Fill is a powerful option for smoothly erasing persons or objects out of photographs.

Tips:

The Lasso Tool is recommended for selections while using Generative Fill to remove people or items from photos. It has a lot of advantages by easily being able to include the areas around a selection. This can make a huge difference in yielding successful results. Conversely, if you want to use some of Photoshop's automated selection tools like Select Subject or the Object Selection Tool, you'll need an additional step to apply Generative Fill safely and avoid getting unexpected and undesirable results. Let me show you what I mean.

We then have an image that contains two people, whereby we're going to remove the woman wearing a red top.

EXPANDING THE SELECTION

Once you have your first selection with either the Select Subject or the Object Selection Tool, locate the Modify Selection button beside it and click it, then proceed with the Generative Fill.

- Select "Expand Selection" from the menu that appears.

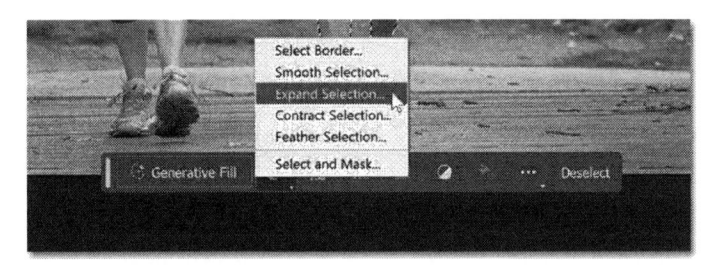

- To complete, click OK after enlarging the selection by 20 pixels.

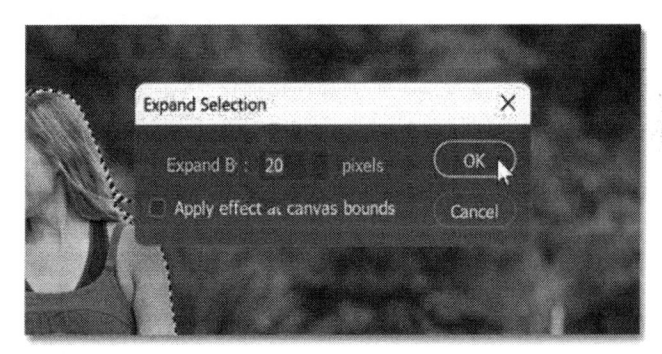

- By putting this expansion into practice, we include more neighboring places in the choice.
- Now, results are incredibly great when Generative Fill is used along with the Generate command, as opposed to the incredible results that are gotten when the Lasso Tool was employed as an initial selection.

CROP TOOL FOR IMAGE OPERATION

- **Choose Crop Tool**: Use 'C' or select the Crop Tool from the toolbar. By default, Photoshop will place a cropping border around an image opening in the last used proportions to crop a picture.

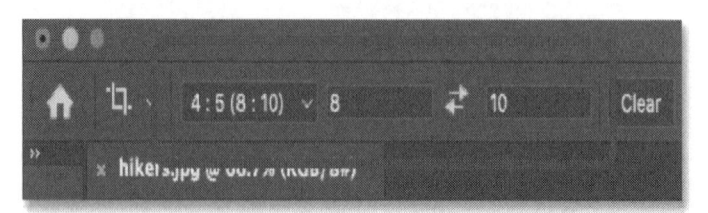

- **Reset the Crop Tool**: To return the Crop Tool to its default setting, click the tool icon in the Options Bar, right-click Windows/Control-click Mac, and choose "Reset Tool." This deselects the boxes for Width and Height and defaults the aspect ratio setting to Ratio.

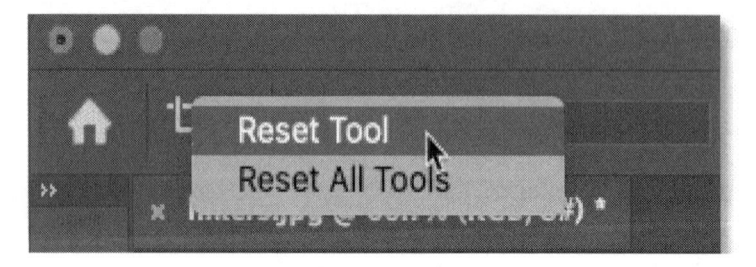

- **Resize Crop Border**: To resize the crop border, click on its handles and drag. For the aspect ratio to remain, you must hold down the Shift key. The image can be dragged and dropped inside the crop border to position it.

- **Canceling the Crop:** Click the Cancel button in the Options Bar to end the cropping process without applying it.

- **Drawing Your Crop Border**: Click anywhere within the image and drag it to draw your border. Now, edit its size and position as usual. Way better option than actually using the default auto-generated crop border.

- **Locking the Aspect Ratio**: By default, Photoshop has it set to allow unconstrained Crop border resizing. To lock the aspect ratio, hold the Shift key while you drag any of the corner handles.

- **Lock Aspect Ratio**: Photoshop by default allows unconstrained resizing of crop borders. To maintain the aspect ratio, while dragging any corner handle, press and hold the Shift key.

- **Aspect Ratio Lock and Center Resizing**: While dragging any corner handle with the Shift and Alt (Windows) / Option (Mac) keys held down, you can lock the aspect ratio and resize from the center.

- **Select an Aspect Ratio**: From the Aspect Ratio menu, which is available from the Options bar, choose a preset to choose common ratios like 8 x 10. If necessary, toggle width and height to switch the ratio, or enter values manually to choose an aspect ratio.

- **Saving a Custom Crop Preset:** If you frequently use a specific aspect ratio, use the Aspect Ratio option to save a custom preset.

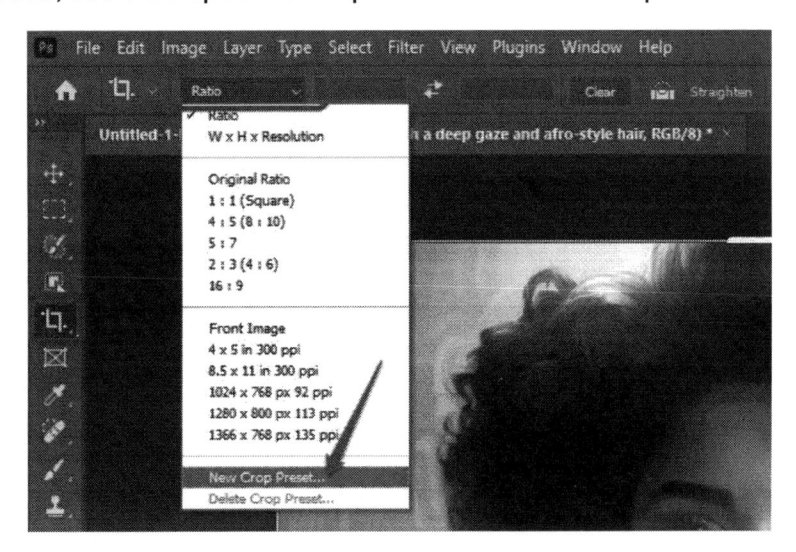

- **Cropping to a certain Image Size and Resolution**: To crop an image to a specific size and resolution, select "W x H x Resolution" from the Aspect Ratio menu. Adjust the crop border as needed after inputting the resolution, width, and height values.

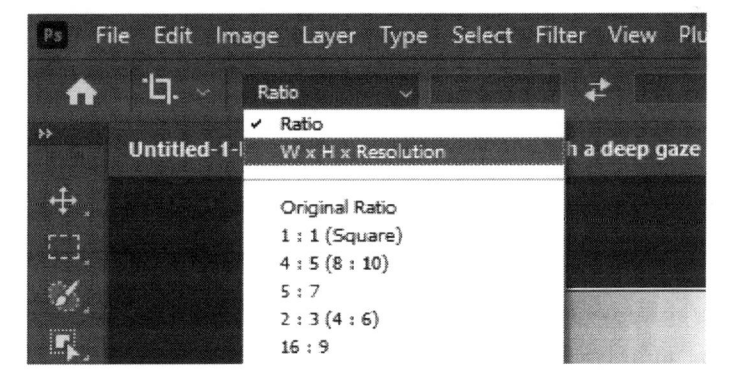

- **Picture Alignment**: In aligning any picture, use the Straighten Tool of the Crop Tool and draw a line between any two spots. Automatically, Photoshop will rotate and align the picture based on the drawn line.
- **Non-Destructive Cropping**: Avoid loss to your computer by ensuring the option "Delete Cropped Pixels" is unchecked. This ensures that the cropped pixels are merely hidden and not deleted; thus, re-cropping and editing are always allowed without deleting any part of the source image data.

- **Moving the Image Inside the Crop**: As non-destructive cropping conceals the cropped area, tap on the Move Tool to shift the image inside the crop.
- **Restoring the Whole Image After Cropping**: To restore the whole image if it was cropped non-destructively, go to the Image menu and select "Reveal All".

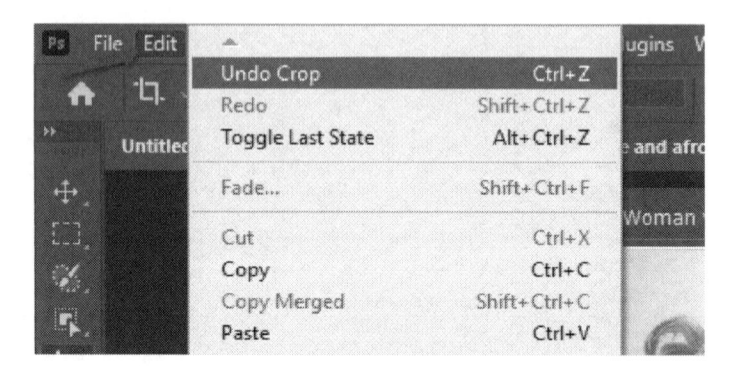

SMOOTHING WRINKLES FROM AN IMAGE WHILE MAINTAINING A NATURAL APPEARANCE

Wrinkles can be gotten rid of by following the steps below:

- **Introduce a New Blank Layer**

In applying a solution to wrinkles using Photoshop, clarity on the separation between the retouch and the original image must be sustained. Go ahead and create a new empty layer above the Background layer of the image from which you want to remove wrinkles. For clarity, let's call this layer "Reduce Wrinkles."

- **Choose the Healing Brush**

Select the Tools menu option and select the Healing Brush Tool. OR Press and hold on to the Spot Healing Brush (Win) or Control-click (Mac) and select the Healing Brush from the pop-up menu.

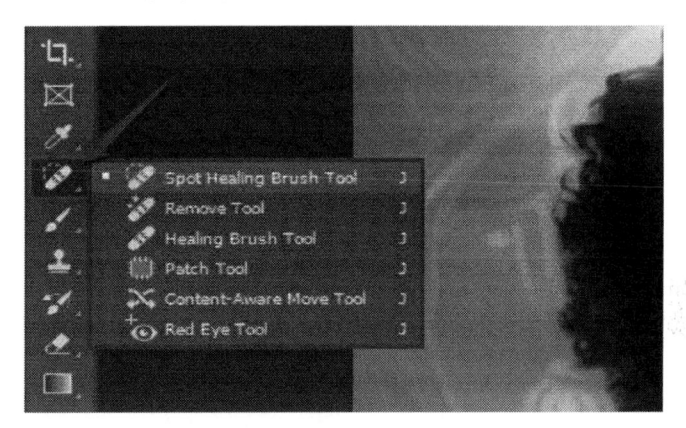

- **Change the Sample Option**

Set the Sample option in the Options Bar to "All Layers." This makes sure that the Healing Brush takes texture samples from the layer below (the Background layer containing the original image) as well as the layer that is now chosen.

- **Leave "Aligned" Unchecked**

Verify that the Aligned option in the Options Bar is not selected. This allows you to choose the source texture and the sampling point precisely.

- **Click on an Area of Good Texture to Sample It**

While holding down the Alt key (Windows) or Option key (Mac) the brush cursor will temporarily change to a target symbol; click in the vicinity of the wrinkle for a nice texture.

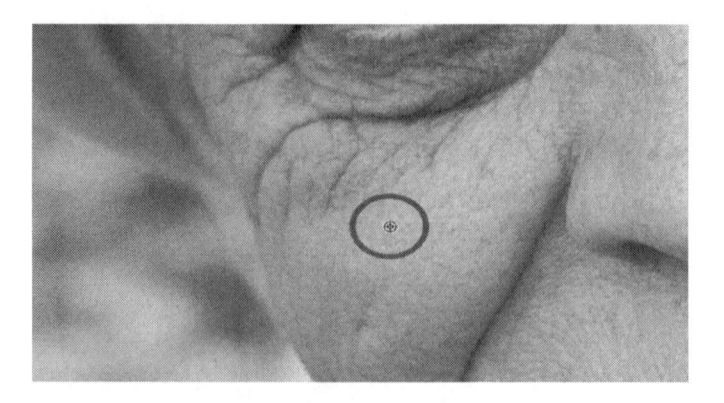

- **Paint Over the Wrinkle to Heal It**

From the thin, narrow end, paint over the wrinkle, releasing the Alt Win / Option Mac key. Using the bracket keys, adjust the size to a brush that is marginally broader than the wrinkle. As you paint, notice the + sign indicating what material is being sampled.

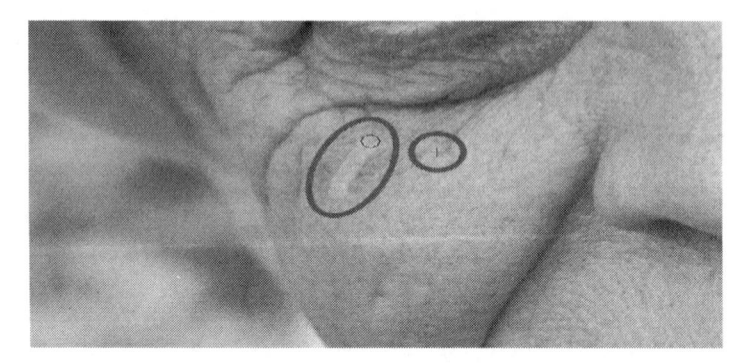

Tips:

- **Sampling Strategy**: To maintain consistency in texture, sample from sites close to but not on the wrinkle. Work toward the origin of the wrinkle slowly starting at the thin end.
- **Managing Errors**: If you've made an error, immediately press Ctrl+Z and try again using a smaller-sized brush.
- **Anti-Aging Big Wrinkles**: Work on bigger wrinkles into segments, starting at the youngest end of the wrinkle with short strokes and 'sampling' texture from around adjacent places.

- **Change the Layer Blend Mode to Lighten**

To give it a more organic feel, switch the blending mode from Normal to Lighten for the layer "Reduce Wrinkles"; that way, it keeps the naturally darker wrinkles yet allows any highlight to stay visible by letting lighter pixels through from the original image.

- **Lower the Layer Opacity**

Now, lower the opacity of the "Reduce Wrinkles" layer to allow wrinkles to come through subtler. Balance the effect out by setting the opacity to a figure between 40% and 60%, which will highlight wrinkles while allowing them to be seen.

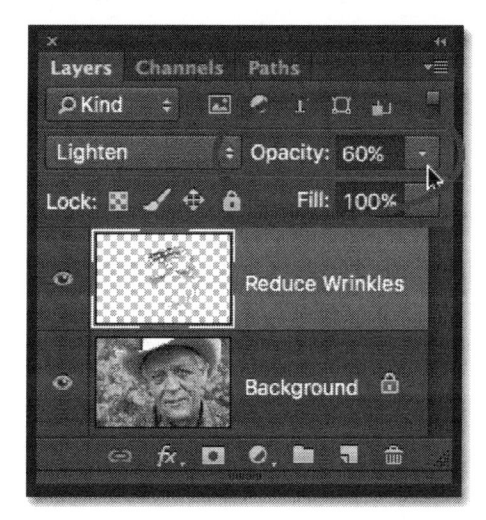

- **Final Result**

It would balance the mode and opacity in blending so the result will always look natural and not overly done.

SMOOTHING SKIN IN PHOTOSHOP

Here, you will learn how to remove blemishes using the Spot Healing Brush in Photoshop to achieve a smooth skin effect and do more to improve overall skin texture. Follow the steps below.

- **Make a Copy of the Image**

Pressing Alt (Win) / Option (Mac), click and drag the layer onto the New Layer icon. This allows you to save the original image. To be able to get it back later, create a new layer by clicking and dragging the background layer onto the New Layer icon, holding down Alt (Win) / Option (Mac). Name this new layer "Spot Healing."

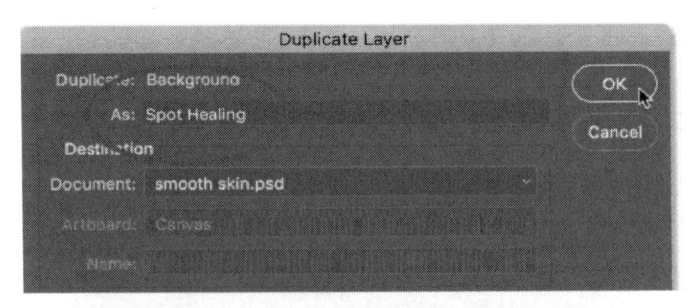

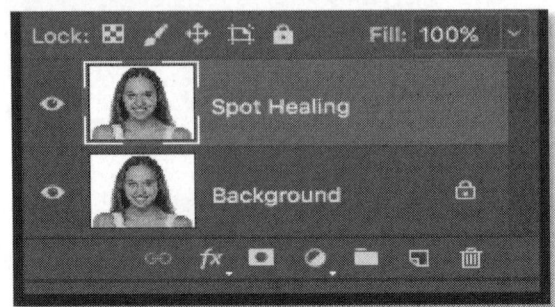

- **Choose the Spot Healing Brush from the Tools Bar**

Clicking the Spot Healing Brush on the toolbar; pull it over to the "Content-Aware" position in the Options Bar. Click over the blemishes to remove them, adjusting brush size for optimal results.

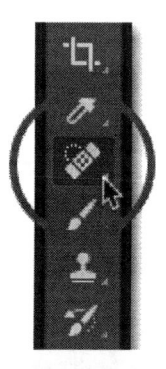

- **Initial Skin Cleanup**

Insisting on the importance of preserving the natural characteristics when carrying out the retouch, using the Spot Healing Brush to remove the defects and faults.

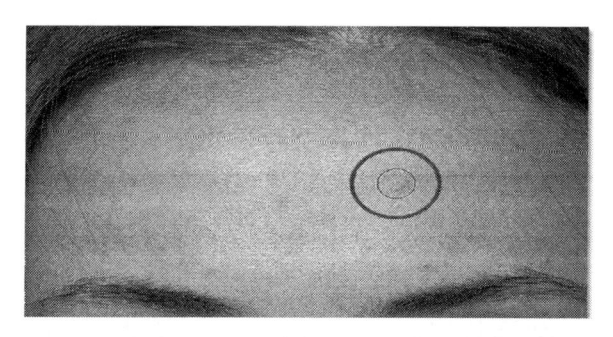

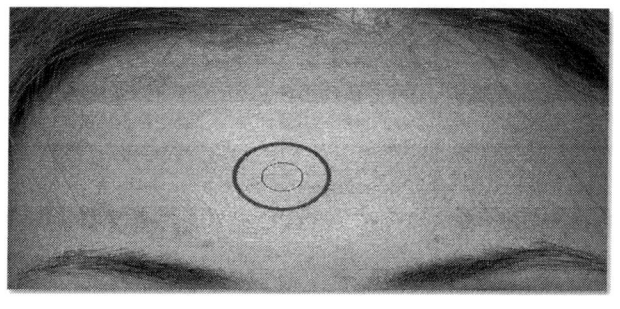

- **Duplicate the "Spot Healing" Layer**

The "Spot Healing" layer should be duplicated and titled "Smooth Skin" so that it can be processed further.

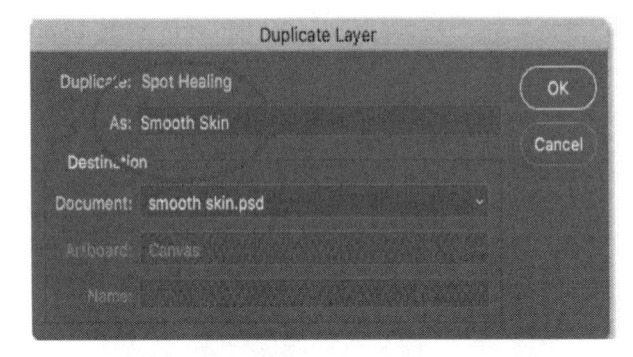

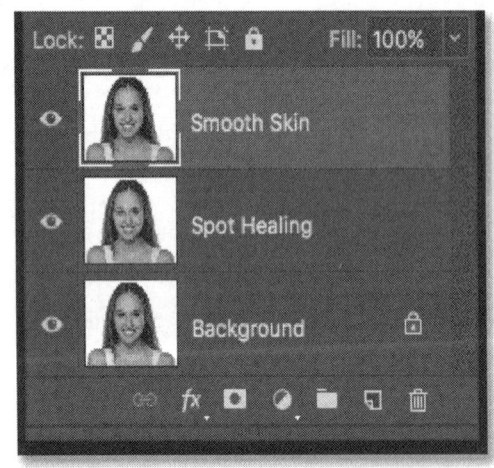

- **Apply High Pass Filter to the Image**

Apply the High Pass filter to identify edges.

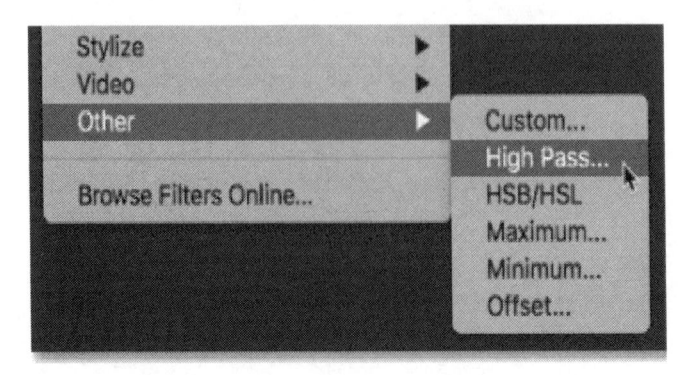

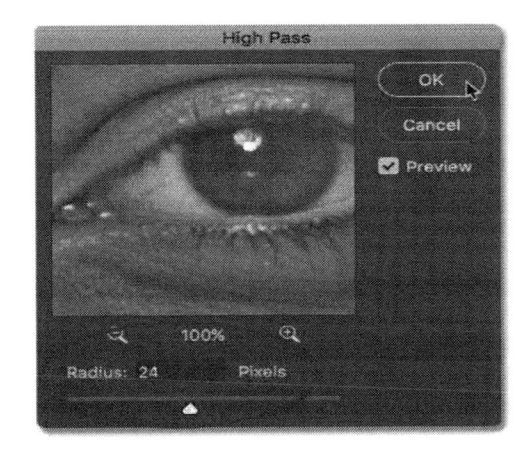

- **Apply the Gaussian Blur Filter**

Use the Gaussian Blur filter to reduce the High Pass impact and enhance skin texture.

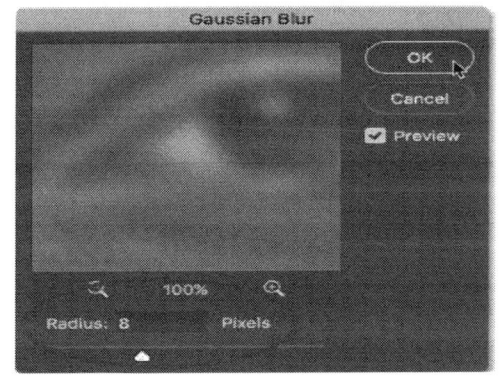

- **Select Linear Light as the Blend Mode**

Select Linear Light as the blend mode for the "Smooth Skin" layer to create a high contrast effect.

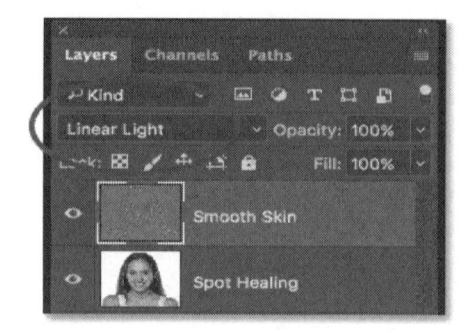

- **Invert the Layer**

To make more adjustments, flip the "Smooth Skin" layer over. Select Adjustments from the Image menu, then Invert.

- **Open Blending Options**

The Blending Options box allows you to change the layer's appearance.

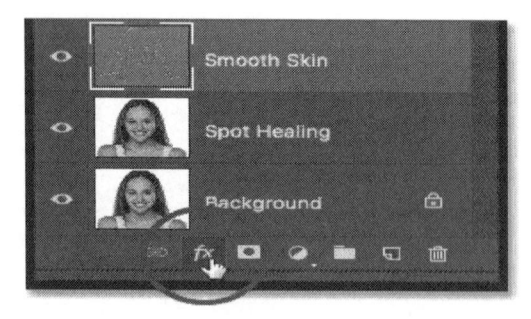

- **Drag the "Blend If" Sliders:**

Adjust the Blend Use the sliders to reduce unwanted halos for a smoother look.

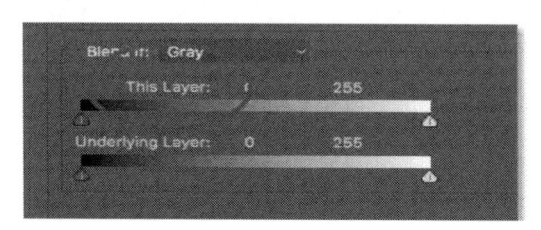

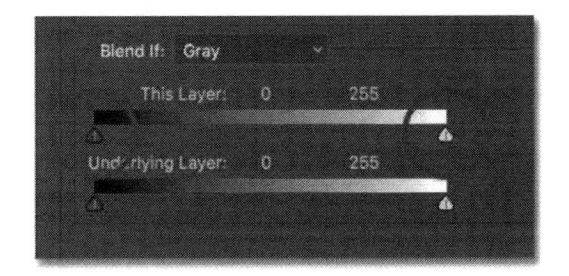

- **Add a Layer Mask**

Use a layer mask to give it a realistic look and limit the effect to specific areas.

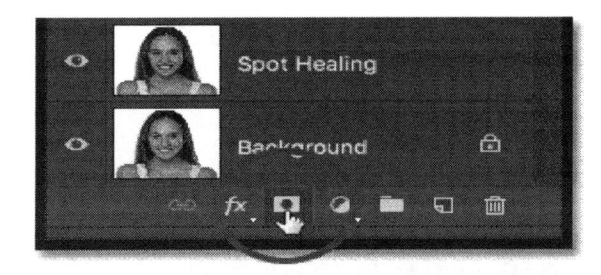

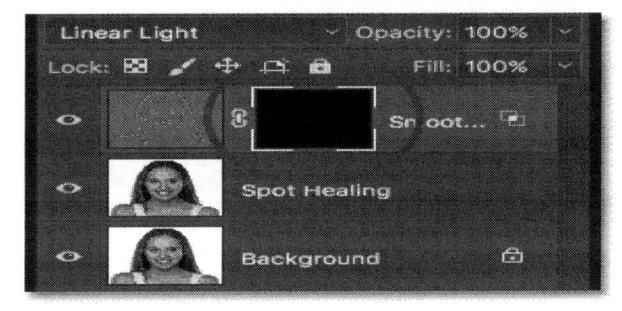

- **Select the Brush Tool**

Use the Brush Tool to adjust the skin-smoothing effect.

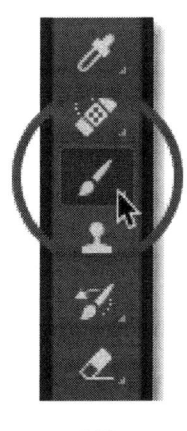

- **Set Brush Color to White**

To see the layer mask's smoothing effect, make sure the brush color is set to white.

- **Paint Over the Skin**

By using the brush to paint over areas of the skin, the desired level of smoothness is gradually revealed. Meanwhile, before painting, set the parameters of your brush to the following.

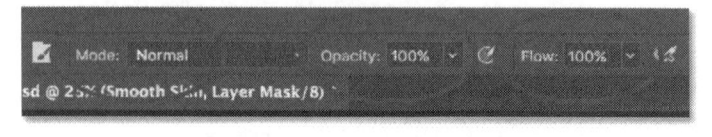

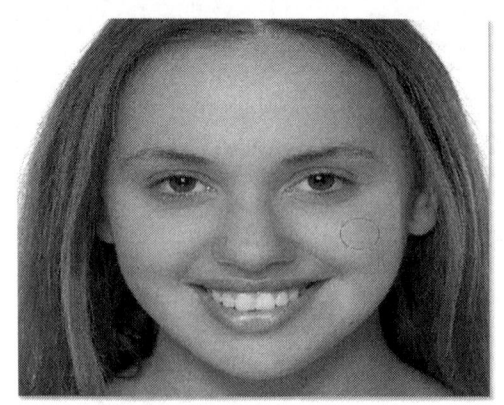

- **Lower the Layer Opacity**

Modify the layer opacity to fine-tune the overall strength of the skin-smoothing effect.

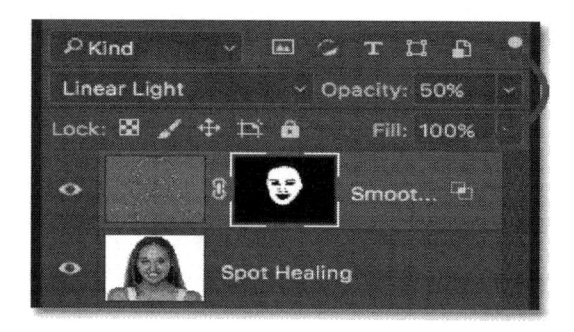

- The improved and natural appearance of your image should be as follows.

HOW TO CHANGE EYE COLOR WITH PHOTOSHOP

A new eye color in Photoshop is easily had via a Hue/Saturation adjustment layer. Whether you have in mind a certain color or are disposed to try a few different options, this is a quick and easy fun way to change eye color. Of particular note with this technique is that an adjustment layer is employed, so the changes you make are non-destructive, leaving your original, unchanged image and its original eye color intact.

Steps to Change Eye Color in Photoshop:

- Now zoom in closer to the eyes for a better view of how the editing is done. Choose the Zoom Tool from the Toolbar, then click between the eyes to zoom in on your subject. Having zoomed in, select the Hand Tool shortcut - press H - to center the eyes for fine-tuning.

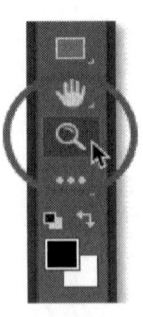

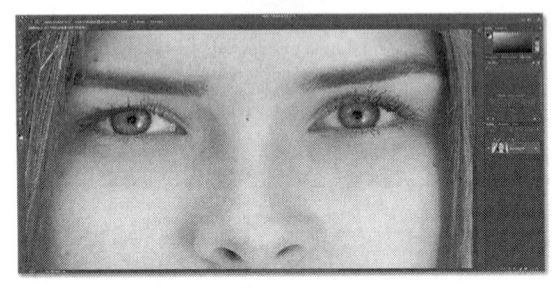

To change the color of one eye without affecting the rest of the image, use the Lasso Tool. Select it from the Toolbar.

- Make a selection in the center of the iris for each eye. Holding the Shift key while making the selection with the other eye will ensure that both eyes are chosen.

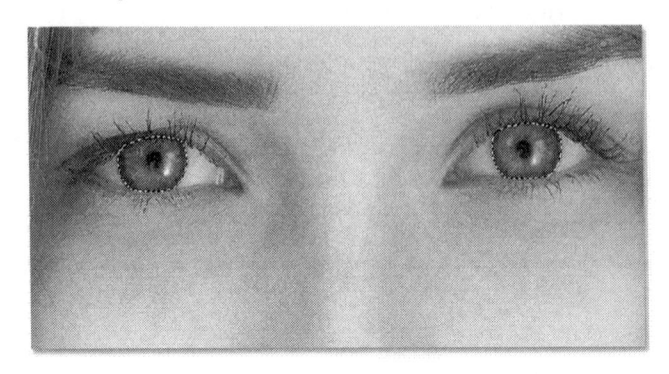

- Click the New Fill or Adjustment Layer icon from the bottom of the Layers menu and choose Hue/ Saturation. This creates the eye color adjustment layer.

- Choose the Colorize option after launching the Properties panel. At first, the eyes may turn red, but we'll change the hue in the next procedure.

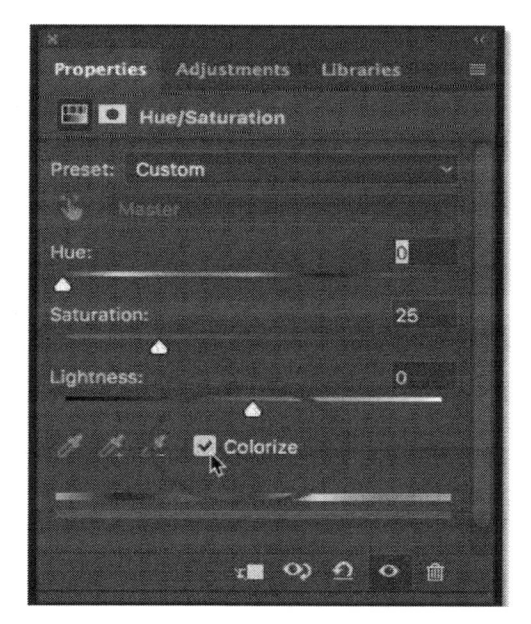

- To select the optimal color of the eyes, use the Hue slider. Observe how the image is changing in real-time. The sliders are moved until the color that suits them best has been achieved.

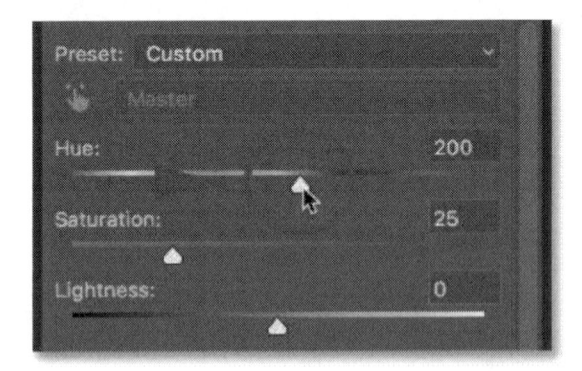

- Use the Saturation slider to reduce the saturation for a more realistic look. A score between 10 and 15 is what you want.

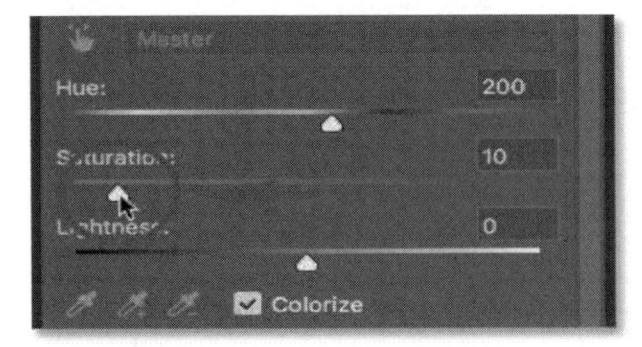

- Select Color as the blend mode for the Hue/Saturation adjustment layer in the Layers window. This ensures that just the color, not the brightness, is affected.

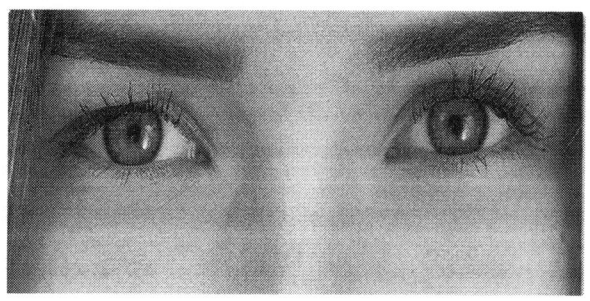

- Verify that the layer mask is chosen. Where the adjustment layer is applied is decided by the layer mask.

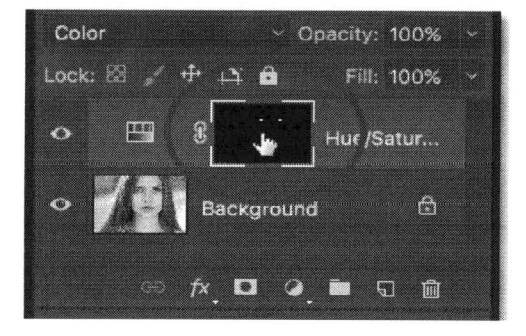

- Choose the Brush Tool to apply color more precisely. Any paint leaks into unexpected areas can be cleaned up with the help of this step.

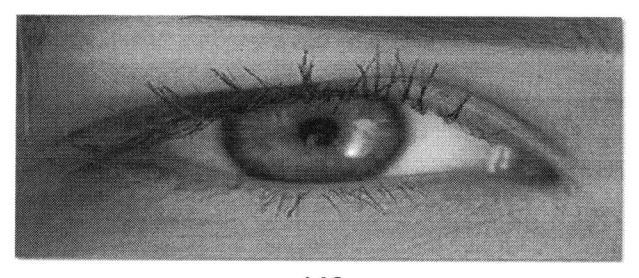

- Set the Foreground color to black and paint over the areas where you want to remove the new eye color.

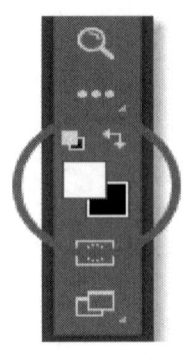

- Paint the region surrounding each eye's iris using the Brush Tool, making sure to remove any paint that may have bled into unwanted places. As necessary, change the brush's hardness and size.

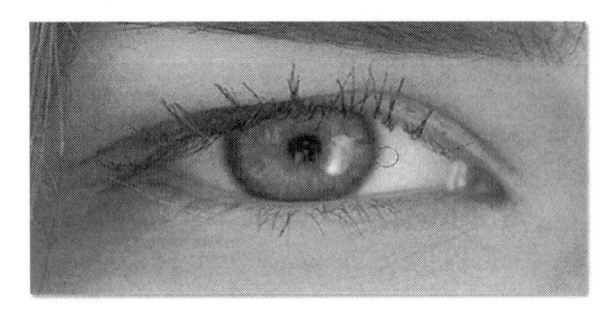

Tips:

If you oversharpen an area, just press X to switch to white and then paint over the gray area to fill it in with color again. Then just switch back to black and keep sharpening. To see before-and-after views of the new eye color and the old one, toggle the visibility of the Hue/Saturation adjustment layer in the Layers panel by clicking the visibility icon.

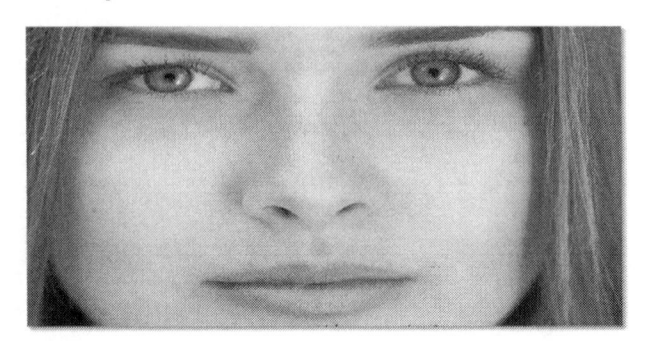

HOW TO CHANGE HAIR COLOR IN PHOTOSHOP

This tutorial will take you through the easy process of tinting hair in a photo and changing the color of your hair using Photoshop. The reason for this is that, with this method, we can control the process quite accurately and adjust the output in various ways. Also, the technique will make it easy to go back and alter the hair color at any time without having to redo the whole thing from scratch. This technique will allow you to try different shades of hair either in somebody else's images or your own.

How to change hair color in Photoshop:

- Open the image in Photoshop, and click the New Adjustment Layer icon available at the bottom of the Layers palette. In the list of adjustment layers, select "Hue/ Saturation".

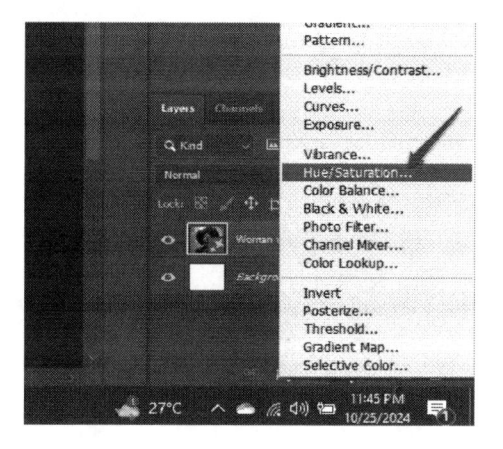

- Click within the checkbox next to the Colorize option in the lower right corner of the Hue/Saturation dialog box. This applies a preset red tone to the entire image instantaneously.

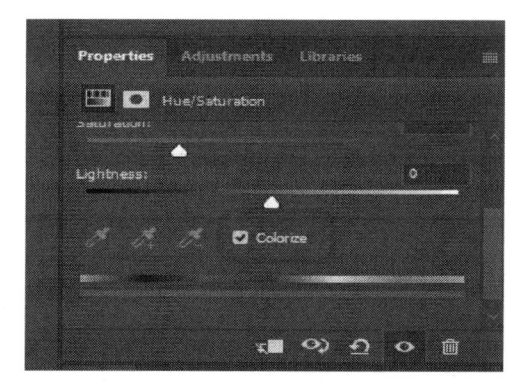

- To select the preferred hair color, drag the Hue slider to the left or right. Use the Saturation slider to change the saturation. Perfectionism is unimportant since corrections are simple to make afterward. To close the dialog box, click OK.

- The final product ought to resemble the picture below.

- Fill the layer mask with black to fix this problem, since the entire image was colorized. Once you have selected the layer mask, the keyboard shortcut Ctrl+Backspace for Windows, and Command+Delete for Mac will be used.

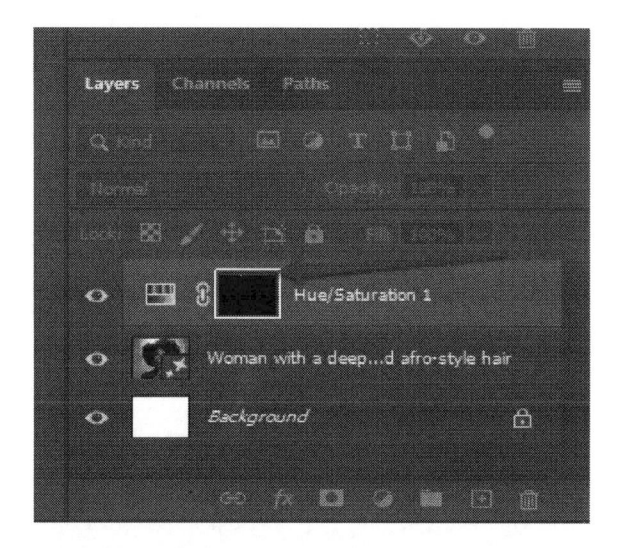

- Click the Brush Tool icon to select it. The colorizing effect will only appear where the Foreground color-white will be indicated.

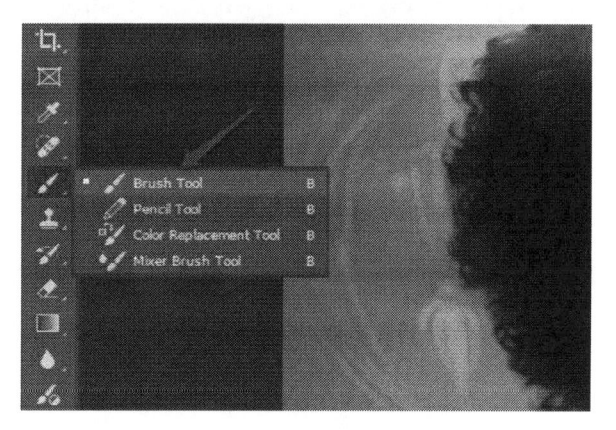

- Paint over the hair on the layer mask to reveal the colorizing effect. For more control, particularly around loose strands of hair, change your brush size and opacity.

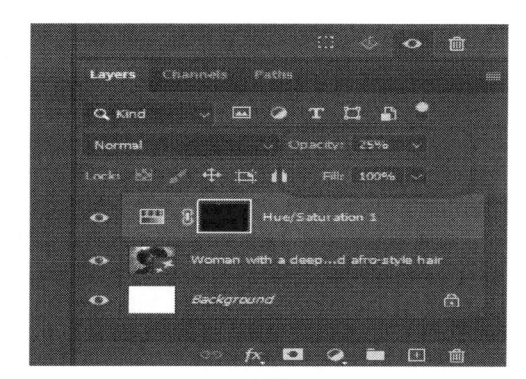

- Adjusting the adjustment layer's blend mode will yield the following effects: "Soft Light" yields a more dramatic effect while "Color" gives a colorizing effect.

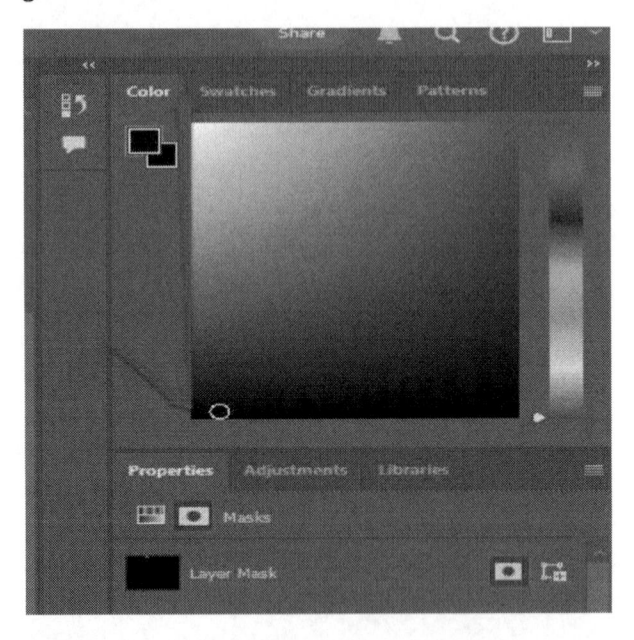

- See the effect of the result below.

- Adjust the vibrancy of the colorizing effect using the adjustment layer's opacity. Lowering the opacity produces a more subtle effect.

- Double-click the thumbnail for the Hue/Saturation adjustment layer in the Layers palette to re-open the Color Balance options and further refine the colors by activating both the Hue and Saturation sliders.
- Playing with having fun with your various colors, go back into your Hue/Saturation settings and adjust your blend modes and opacities to your taste View the result of the last adjustment made below.

HOW TO WHITEN TEETH IN PHOTOSHOP

To whiten your teeth in Photoshop, do the following steps:

- Select the area around the teeth using the Lasso Tool.

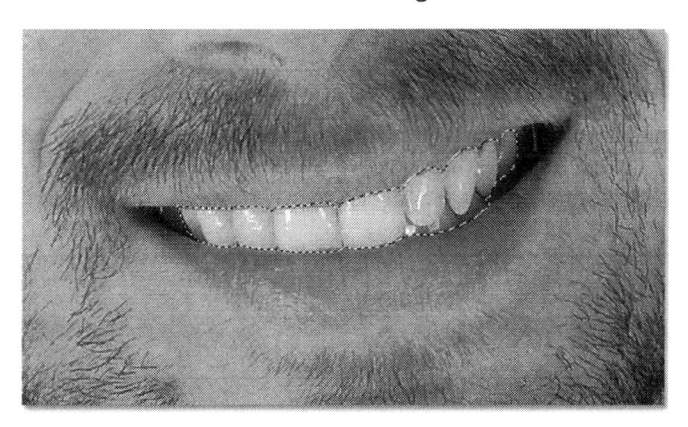

- After selecting the Layers panel, click the icon for the New Fill or Adjustment Layer. Choose a layer to modify the saturation and hue.

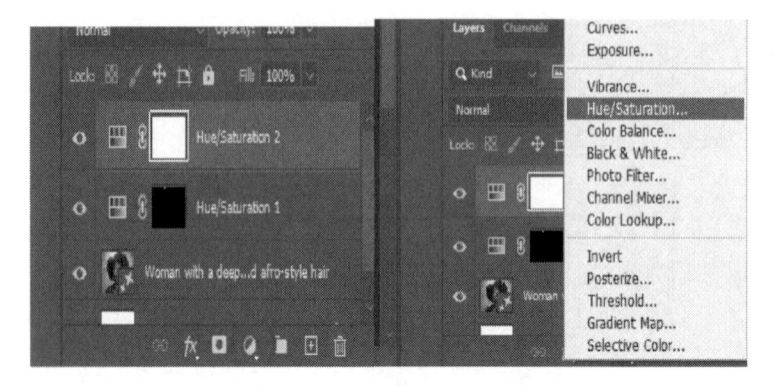

- Change the Edit option from Master to Yellows in the Properties panel.

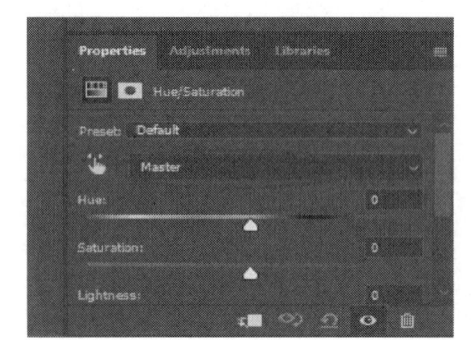

- To lessen the yellow tones in the teeth, move the Saturation slider to the left.

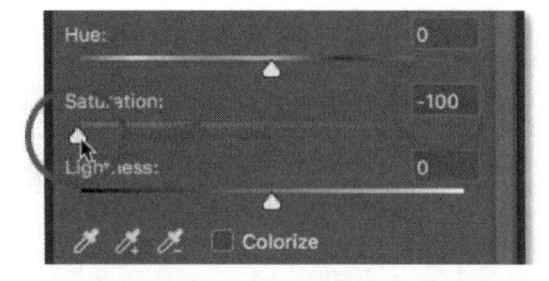

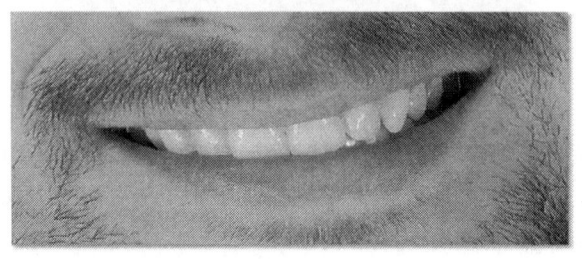

- Go back to the Properties box and select Master again under Edit instead of Yellows.

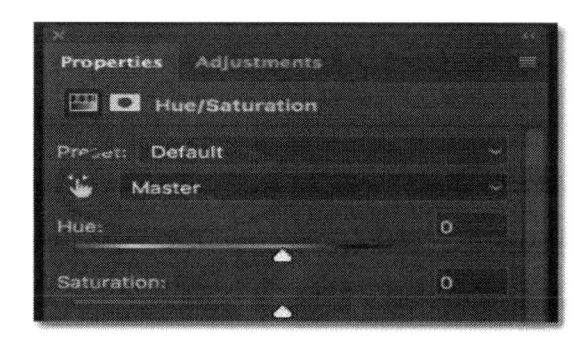

- To hide the effects of the adjustment layer on the lips and gums, select the Brush Tool, set your Foreground color to black, and paint around the teeth on the layer mask.

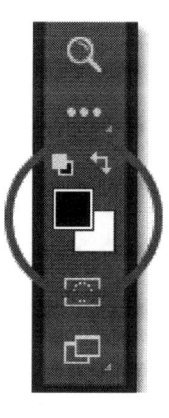

- Use distinct hue/saturation adjustment layers for each person in a photo to achieve the greatest effects.

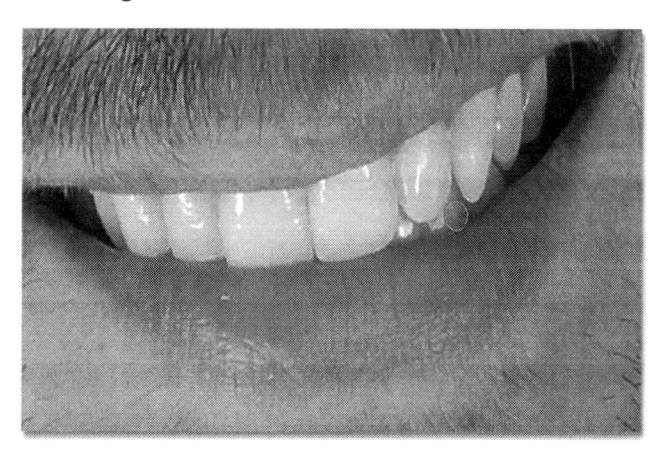

HOW TO USE THE COLOR REPLACEMENT TOOL IN PHOTOSHOP

By default, the Brush Tool in Photoshop is hidden behind the Color Replacement Tool in the Tools panel. Right-click (Windows) or Control-click (Mac) on the Brush Tool to reveal it, and select the Color Replacement Tool from the fly-out menu.

Like the other Photoshop Brush-related tools, you can change the size of the cursor using keyboard shortcuts. To make the size smaller, use the left bracket key ([); to make it larger, use the right bracket key (]). To adjust brush hardness, hold down the Shift key: Shift+left bracket ([) softens the edges, while Shift+right bracket (]) hardens the edges.

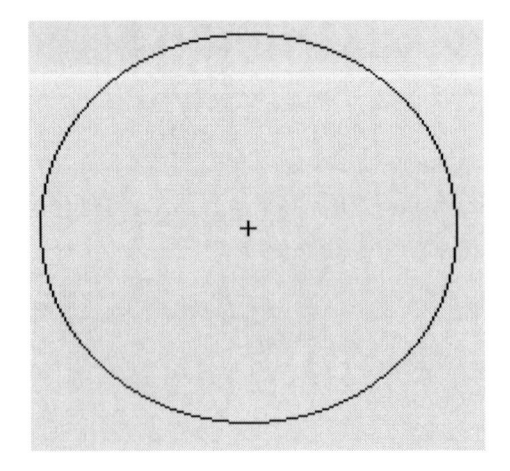

The Color Replacement Tool in Photoshop dynamically picks up the underlying color, at the center of the crosshair cursor as it moves over an image. This picked color is replaced and matched with your Foreground color. Pixels, inside the circle with a larger diameter than that of the crosshair, which also possess this replace color, are color transformed.

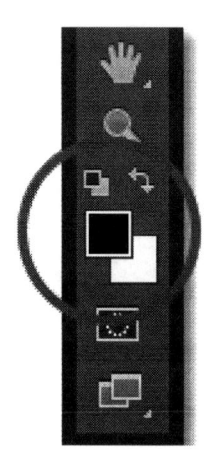

To determine what your active Foreground color is, first look at the Foreground color swatch in the Tools panel. This always appears to be set to black by default. To choose the Foreground color, click the swatch, select a new color via the Color Picker, then click OK to complete.

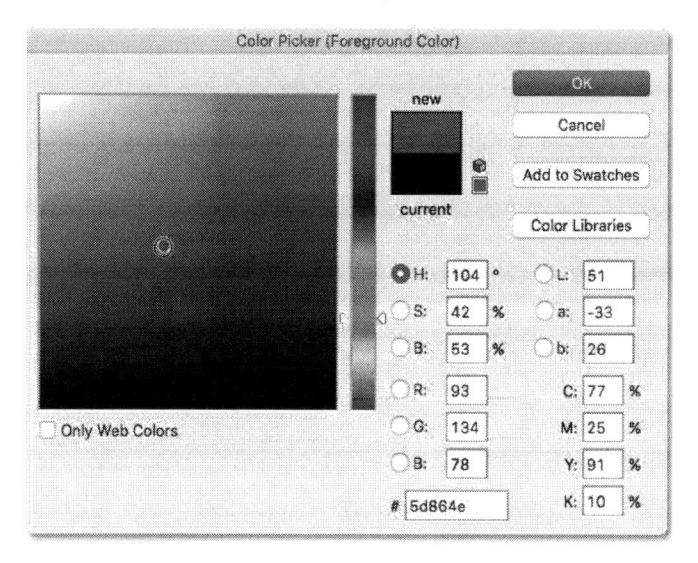

Alternatively, sample the color directly from the image With the Color Replacement Tool still selected but temporarily switched to, hold down the Alt key (Windows) or Option key (Mac) to toggle to the Eyedropper Tool. Click anywhere on the image on the color you want to sample. Let go of the Alt (Windows) or Option (Mac) key to return to the Color Replacement Tool. The new Foreground color is immediately updated to the color you just sampled.

The Color Replacement Tool uses different blend modes to allow the new color to blend with the object. In the Options Bar, there are four modes: Hue, Saturation, Color, and Luminosity. Color-the default adjusts levels of hue and saturation but maintains the brightness of the original underlying color. Select the blend mode to suit your specific editing requirement.

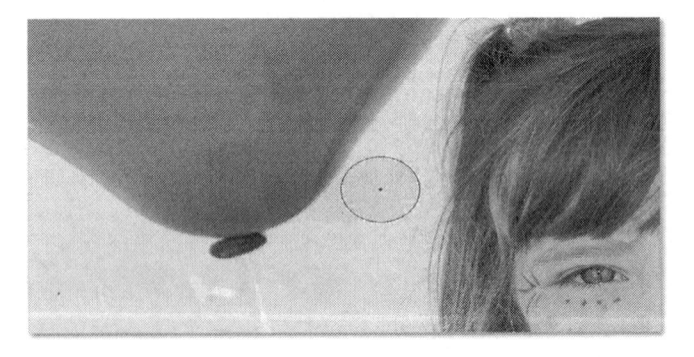

The Tolerance option within the Options bar defines the maximum color difference that is to be replaced. Although the default setting of 30% usually serves as an excellent starting point, pulling this value often yields a better outcome. The lower the tolerance, the more its range restricts the affected colors. Higher values increase the range.

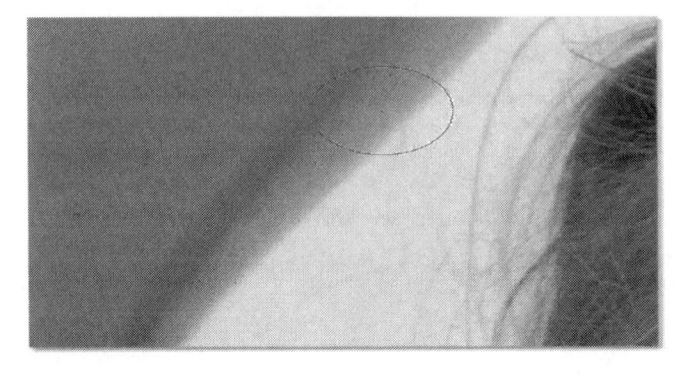

Sampling Options:

To the right of the blend mode are the sampling options: three icons, Continuous (default), Once, and Background Swatch. Continuous samples as you travel, Once samples the color of the original click, and Background Swatch replaces the background color with the foreground color.

- **Limits**

The Limits option of the Color Replacement Tool controls the area of search for colors and has options like Contiguous, Discontiguous, and Find Edges. Contiguous affects only connected pixels, while changes are made on unconnected pixels in Discontiguous, and Find Edges detects the edges and gives a clean adjustment.

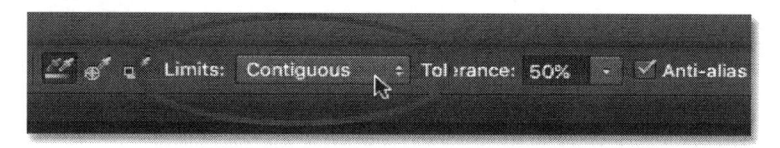

- **Anti-Alias**

Ensure that Anti-alias are checked to maintain smooth transitions around the affected areas, and to improve the general performance of the Color Replacement Tool.

HOW TO REMOVE BACKGROUNDS FROM IMAGES WITH BACKGROUND ERASER TOOL

Removing backgrounds in images can be a time-consuming activity, but it can be brought down to quite decent levels when the right tools and techniques are used. In this tutorial, we will dive deep into the processes of removing an image background using the Background Eraser Tool in Photoshop.

- Go to the Photoshop toolbar and click on the Background Eraser tool. You can select this tool by clicking the Eraser tool that would appear in the toolbar; hold the click and wait until the Background Eraser tool appears.

- Duplicate the Background Layer and hide the Bottom Layer. From the Options Bar, choose the desired size of a hard, round brush.

Set the settings as follows:

    a. **Sampling**: Contiguous
    b. **Limits**: Find Edges
    c. **Tolerance**: 50%

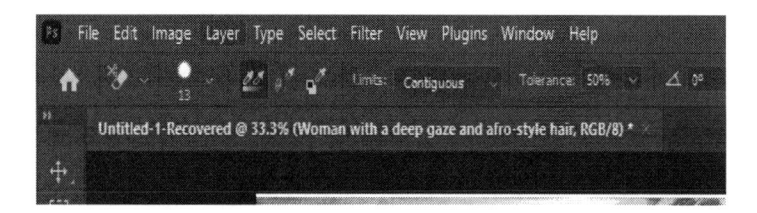

- With the Background Eraser tool, the back of an image can be automatically detected and removed. Try using a moderate brush size wherever possible to conquer difficult corners.

- After you're done, adjust the outcome to fix any flaws. If the background and subject colors are comparable, use the Protect Foreground Color option to sharpen the image.

HOW TO REMOVE GREY BACKGROUND WITHOUT AFFECTING HAIR

The image opens as the top layer in the layers panel. Here, it's our objective to keep the integrity of the hair but not the gray background. For this to work, Photoshop's Background Eraser Tool will always display a color sample just beneath the center crosshair of the circle.

- To get rid of the grey background, slide the cursor over the black hair. Over the column, move the crosshair until the black hair exactly aligns with the middle of the crosshair.

- When you right-click, the crosshair removes any matching grey pixels in the wider circle's range and picks the grey hues beneath it.

- To pick up even more grey, without right-clicking drag the crosshair to other locations over the grey background. Again, it is interesting to see that when the larger circle overlaps the black hair it does not get changed.

- That is, it will be selecting only the grey color, which makes removing the grey from corners and edges a lot easier. Of course, if you can manage to keep the crosshair inside the boundary area of the grey, then it will keep picking up the grey color.

It will erase black pixels if the crosshair extends into the black area, so be careful not to let that happen. If you make a mistake, you can always hit Ctrl + Z for Windows or Command + Z for Mac to go back. Hit Command + Option + Z for Mac or Ctrl + Alt + Z for Windows repeatedly to step back through many steps in case of multiple mistakes.

HOW TO REMOVE THE BACKGROUND OF A PHOTO USING THE QUICK SELECTION TOOL

The Quick Selection Tool enables fast backdrop selections and works especially fine with photos containing fine details. To remove a backdrop from an image in Photoshop using the Quick Selection Tool, follow the steps below:

- Select the Quick Selection Tool from the toolbar located on the left.

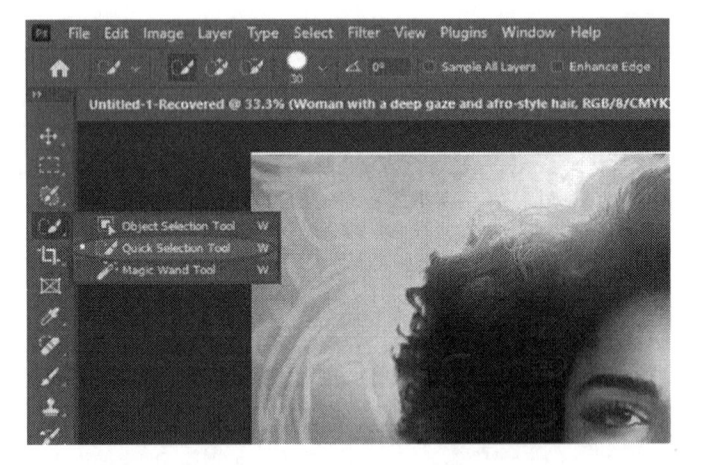

- Duplicate the layer after unlocking it.

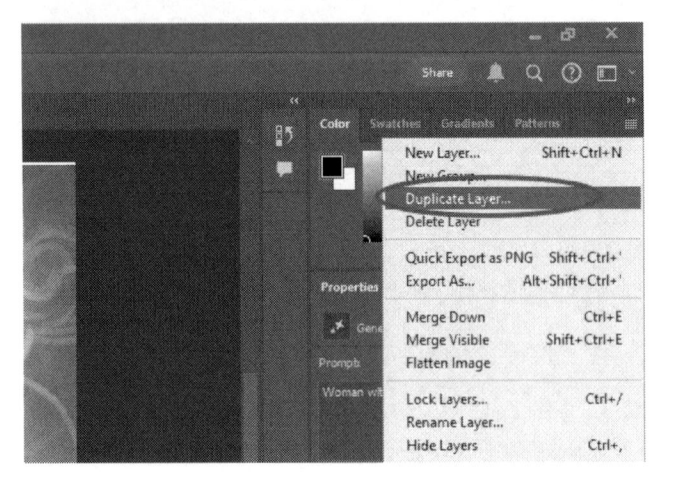

- Open the left-cornered menu and click on "Enhance Edge."
- Click and drag the tool over the subject to activate it.

- Refine the selection, using "Add to Selection" and "Subtract from Selection" in the top left menu.
- Go to the Layers menu, located on the right-hand toolbar.
- Then click the icon to "Add Layer Mask" - this looks like a little rectangle with a circle in the middle.
- After that, click on the "create new fill or adjustment layer, then solid color to give your picture a fresh background.

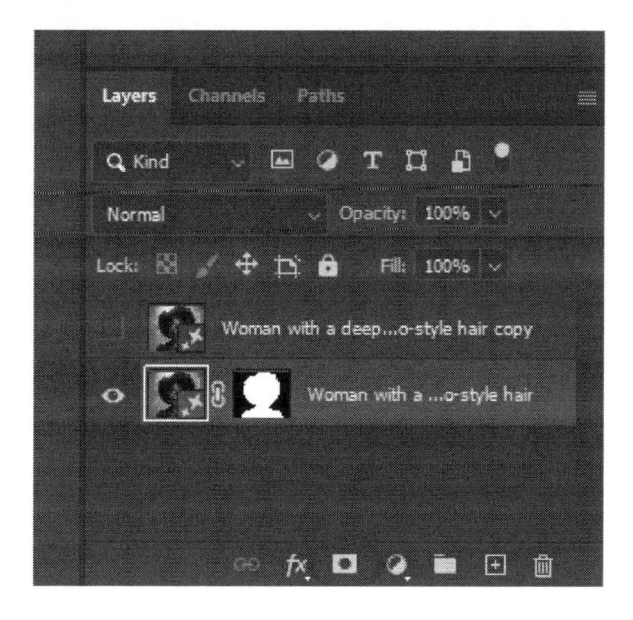

- Your result should appear as the one below.

HOW TO REMOVE PHOTO BACKGROUNDS IN ADOBE PHOTOSHOP USING THE PEN TOOL

The Pen tool is a sure and painstaking way to remove backgrounds in photos when making use of Photoshop, a way in which control over the result could be considered unparalleled. Timely and with lots of precision, when compared to fast-moving tools such as Quick Selection or Background Eraser, the Pen tool proves to be irreplaceable at times when either the subjects or backgrounds of a picture have lower contrast, or other ways around simply do not work out. Follow the steps for detailed guidance:

- Open your image in Photoshop. Right-click on the Background layer and select "Duplicate Layer." In the dialog box that appears, enter the name for your layer and click OK. Click the eye icon to the left of the original layer to disable it.

- Choose the Pen tool from the left-hand toolbox, which is located above the Text tool in the toolbox. Zoom into part of your image and click to set the first anchor on your subject's edge, or wherever will be a good starting point for you. Continue around your subject adding new anchors until you have outlined its contour.

- When dealing with curved lines, utilize the click-hold-drag technique. Adjust the curve by moving the mouse accordingly.
- Refine anchor points or straight lines using the Direct Selection tool, located in the toolbox under the Path Selection tool.
- Eliminate an anchor by employing the keyboard shortcut (Command + Z for macOS, Control + Z for Windows) or navigating to File > Undo.
- Ensure you return to the starting point to complete the path. Save the path once satisfied by selecting Window > Paths, opting for New Path from the three-bar menu, and assigning a name.
- Right-click the new path in the Paths panel, choose Make Selection, and click OK in the dialog box (keeping default settings). This reveals the location of your path.
- To encompass everything except the subject, choose Inverse under Select. The marching ants will now surround the entire image, effectively highlighting the background.
- Press Delete to erase the background, unveiling a white and gray striped background in place of the original.

While the Pen tool might not be good enough by itself, combining it with other techniques will make some features better. Perhaps some other approach would be more effective in refining an eyelash area of a specific image.

USING THE RED-EYE CORRECTION TOOL

The photos clicked under low light conditions, especially when the subject is standing near the flash, will tend to show the bright red color of the pupils instead of black due to light reflection from it. This may look pretty irritating for your subjects. Luckily, Photoshop has a tool solely for this purpose, and that is the Red-eye tool.

Procedure for using this tool:

- Open a picture that has a red-eye effect in Photoshop.
- Select the Red Eye Tool from the Toolbar.

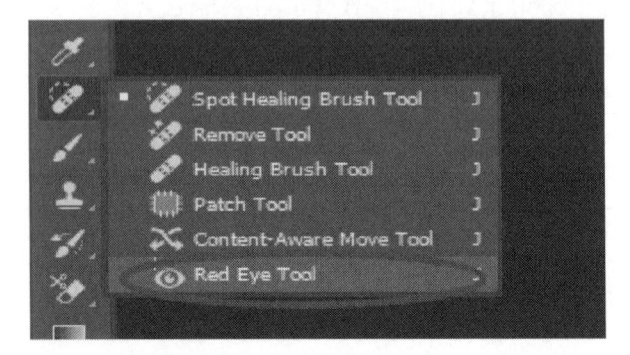

- Use the Red Eye Tool to click on the red pupil.

- Photoshop will rapidly remove the unwanted red-eye appearance.

- You may also use the Options Bar to adjust the Darken Amount and Pupil Size to further fine-tune the correction.

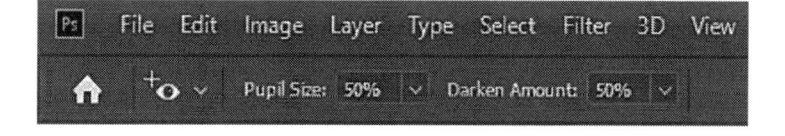

USING DODGE AND BURN TOOLS FOR IMAGE OPERATIONS

Dodging and burning are techniques that enhance the appeal and life of an image. These techniques can easily be effective in bringing about striking changes. The Dodge and Burn tools in Photoshop offer an easy yet effective way to make some power punches. The reason designers just love them is that they allow targeting just the desired area of the image for brightening or darkening. And because there is a natural tendency to move the viewer's attention away from darker areas, this is an intentional leading of viewer attention.

Dodge Tool:

- This tool will lighten areas selected by you without desaturating the colors or affecting the hue.
- Opening your image, the Dodge tool is available under the Toolbar option.
- Drag it across those places you feel need brightening to give an excellent look to your image. 
- The result of the operation is displayed below.

Note: Use the provided configurations to create a new layer and tweak things like brush size in the Options Bar without changing the source image.

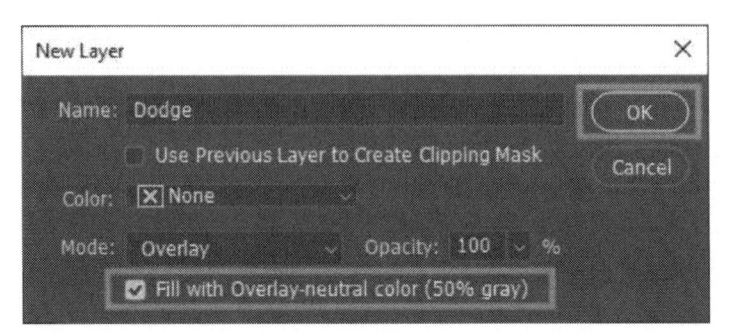

UNDERSTANDING THE BURN TOOL

The Burn tool darkens parts of an image, while the Dodge tool lightens other areas. The Burn tool works just like the Dodge tool but can also be found under Toolbox End.

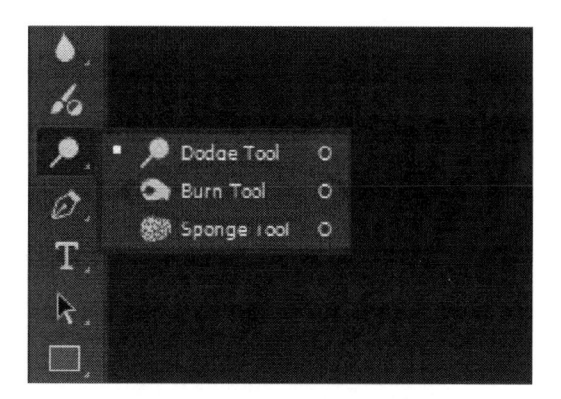

UNDERSTANDING THE SPONGE TOOL

Like the Dodge and Burn tools, the Sponge Tool affects slight hue and saturation color changes. You simply choose it from the Toolbar and enter the other settings, along with the Mode - Saturate or Desaturate via the Options Bar.

UNDERSTANDING THE SPOT-HEALING BRUSH TOOL

Small imperfections are creatively removed with the Photoshop Healing Brush Tool by effectively blending them into the pixels of the backdrop image. The tool is similar to the Clone Stamp Tool; however, this tool also aligns the texture, shading, and lighting of source pixels.

How the Spot Healing Tool Works

- Zoom in to your desired magnification and then select the Spot Healing Tool from the Toolbar.
- Open your picture, create a new layer, and then switch this latter off to keep the original intact.

- Modify the brush's size and properties, such as Blend Mode, Sample All Layers, and Brush Type, in the Options Bar.

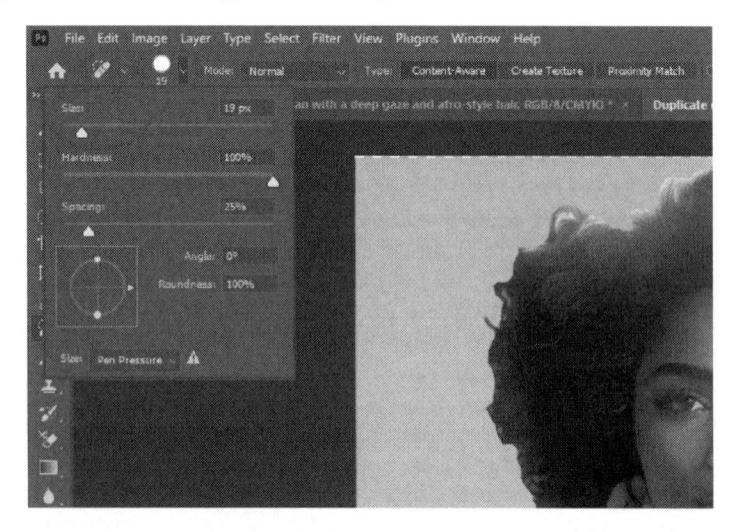

- Click the areas that require healing in the document area. You could wish to alter the selected Brush Type if nothing changes.

UNDERSTANDING THE PATCH TOOL

The Patch Tool is one of the most important healing brushes for improving and repairing your images. It is particularly effective in correcting more serious errors or eliminating flaws and distractions.

- After opening your picture, choose the Patch Tool from the Toolbar.

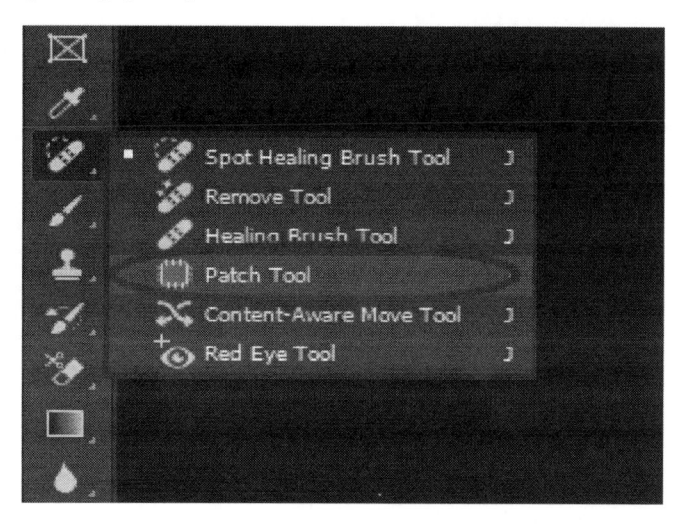

- Make sure the "Content Aware" Patch option in the Options Bar is chosen.

- Identify the area of the image that requires correction.

- Click in the middle of the selection and drag the pointer to the surrounding area for a smooth matching of the selected area to another portion of the image.
- To remove the selection line, click the Delete or Ctrl + D.

HOW TO ADD OR DUPLICATE OBJECTS BY CLONING WITH THE PATCH TOOL

- Select the area that needs to be copied by drawing a selection around the region.
- Select a location using the Options Bar.

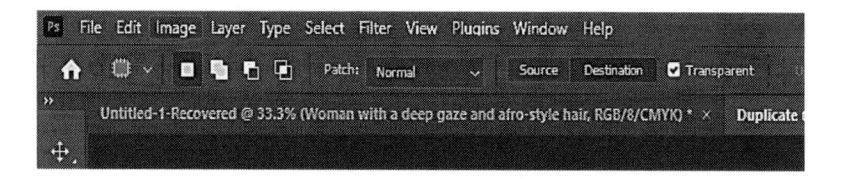

- Use the Patch Tool to relocate the selection to the desired location by placing your mouse over it.

WHAT CAN YOU DO WITH THE CLONE STAMP TOOL?

The world of perfecting advertising or fashion photos is marred by imperfections and distractions that take away their flawless appeal. But there is one powerful ally-the Clone Stamp Tool-that offers a remedy that can easily and effectively be performed. It does quick work of unwanted details such as distracting wires, ugly dust stains, hair strays, or even unwanted people by skillfully duplicating the pixels from another part of the image.

To make use of the Clone Stamp Tool in Blender, follow the steps below.

- Open an image that you want to enhance and, if you haven't already, duplicate it to preserve the original integrity.

- From the Toolbar, choose the Clone Stamp Tool, then modify the brush parameters in the Options Bar.

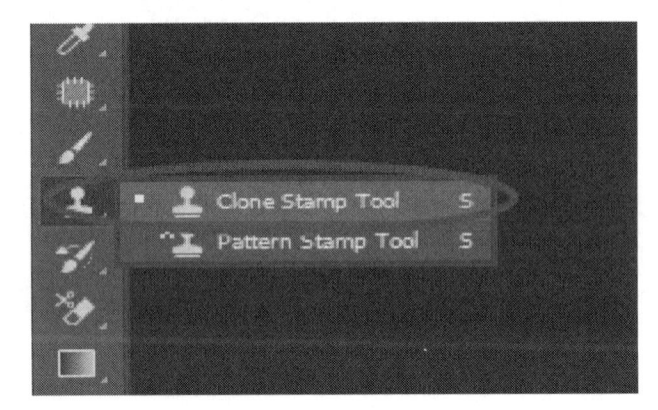

- While cloning, move your cursor over the area of the image from which you want to choose, click while holding the Alt key down, and select pixels from that selection.

- Click over the image where a region is desired that needs cloning of a pixel then start painting over it.

- While painting, everything should look very natural. If needed, make use of the Undo option for restoration.

HOW FILTERS WORKS IN PHOTOSHOP

- Photoshop filters offer an easy way to alter the contents of layers; they can be used for more complex tasks like offsetting pixels or adding high-pass filters, or they can be used for simpler effects like image sharpening. Filters can affect the active layer in the active selection or the layer mask. The filter is applied to the entire layer mask or layer if no selection is made.

- How to Use Photoshop's Filters:

- Hovering over the selections will allow you to explore more options.
- Before applying a filter, use the Filter Gallery option to see how it will affect your image.

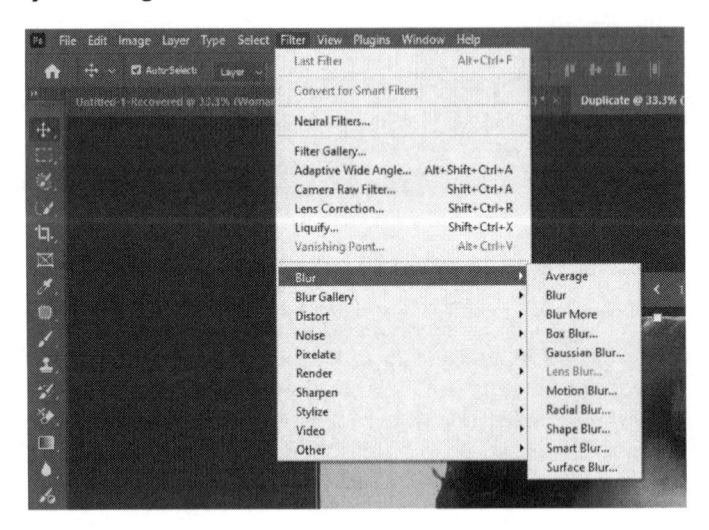

WORKING WITH THE OIL PAINT FILTER

The Oil Paint filter can be used to give a photograph the appearance of a genuine oil painting. To achieve desired effects, this tool offers sliders for changing brush scale, cleanliness, stylization, and more.

The Oil Paint Filter can be used as follows:

- Open the image and select the Filter tab.

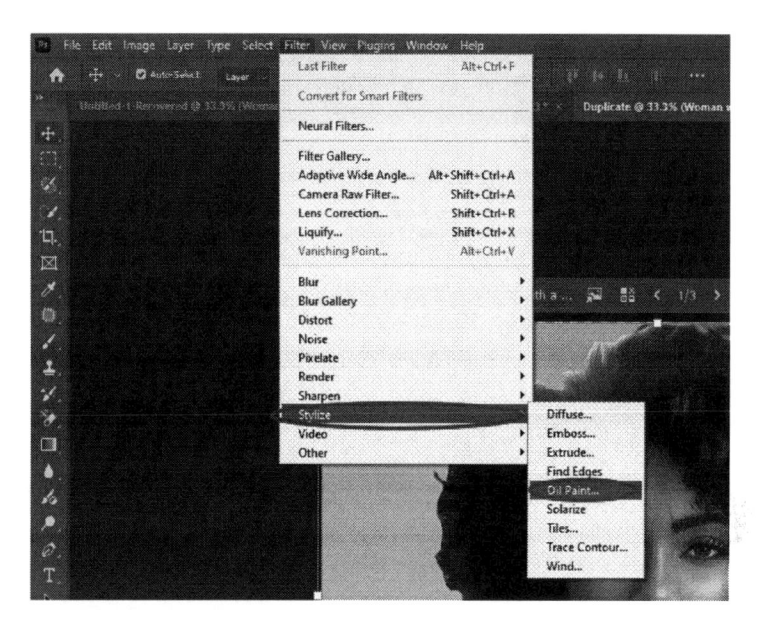

- Go to Stylize and select Oil Paint.
- Move the sliders in the Oil Paint Filter panel to achieve your desired painterly effect.

UNLEASHING THE POTENTIAL OF THE LIQUIFY TOOL

The Liquify tool is thus about versatile, ranging in scope from subtle manipulations such as that of muscle tone or adjusting the dimensions of the eyes of the subject to more complex manipulations. If done in a very cautious manner with much attention to detail, the changes this tool can make might appear low-key yet entirely believable. Nonetheless, aside from simply manipulating bodies, the Liquify tool's potential also greatly extends into the realms of pixel manipulation in various imaginative ways.

Mastering the Liquify Tool and Advanced Features

Apply the following steps to make the most of the Liquify tool:

- Open your image, start transforming it, and convert it into a smart object; right-clicking on the layer and selecting "Convert to Smart Object" will enable you to work flexibly without losing any information or performing any destructive edits.

- Click the Filter tab, then choose Liquify.

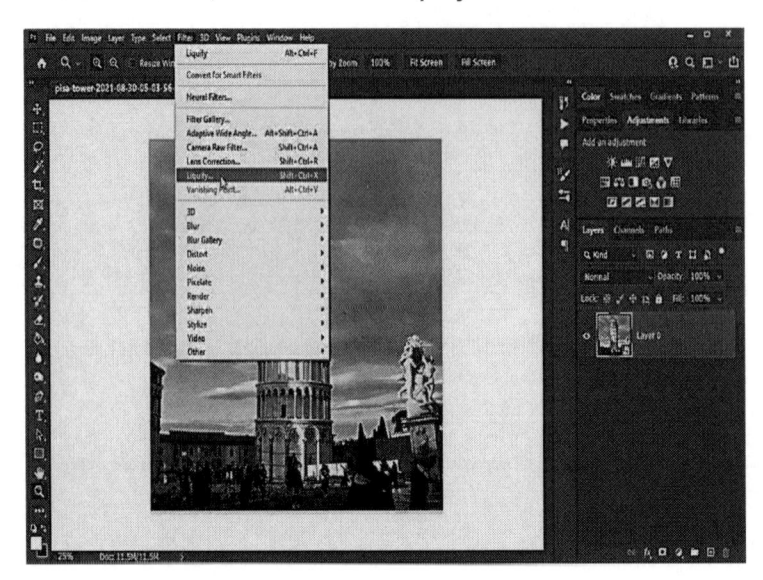

- Review tools in the Liquify window such as the Push Left, Reconstruct, Forward Warp, and Smooth Effect among others.
- From the left pane, adjust the parameters of the brush.

HOW BLURRING WORKS IN PHOTOSHOP

The Blur tool is available within Photoshop under the Filters tab. The Gaussian Blur tool allows for blurring over an entire photo by adjusting the radius value. If you want to do a selective blur, select the area with one of the selection tools and then use the Gaussian Blur tool.

CHAPTER 6

EXPLORING THE TYPE TOOL

WHAT CAN YOU DO WITH THE TYPE TOOL

The Type tool is a tool that can be used to easily add text to projects; in fact, an entire world of creative possibilities opens up when designing everything from posters and holiday cards to invitations. Here's how the Type Tool can be used:

- You can find the Type tool in the Tools panel or simply select it by using the T key on your keyboard to save time.

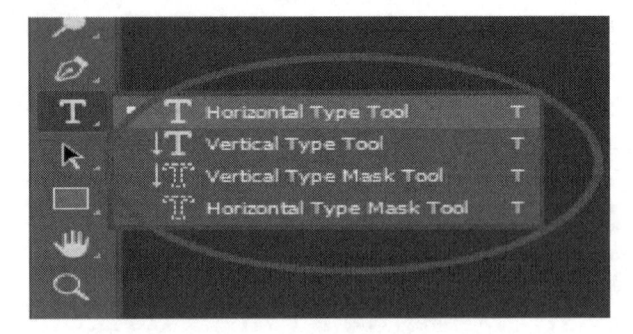

- Choose the preferred font and text size from the Control panel located at the top of the screen.
- Within the dialog box, click the Text Color Picker and select the color you want.
- To create a text box in the document window, click and drag.

- A new text layer has been added to your document, in which you can begin typing and adding text.

- If your document is heavy with text, you may want to work on multiple text layers. As you see here, we have added a second text layer for the term "mountains".

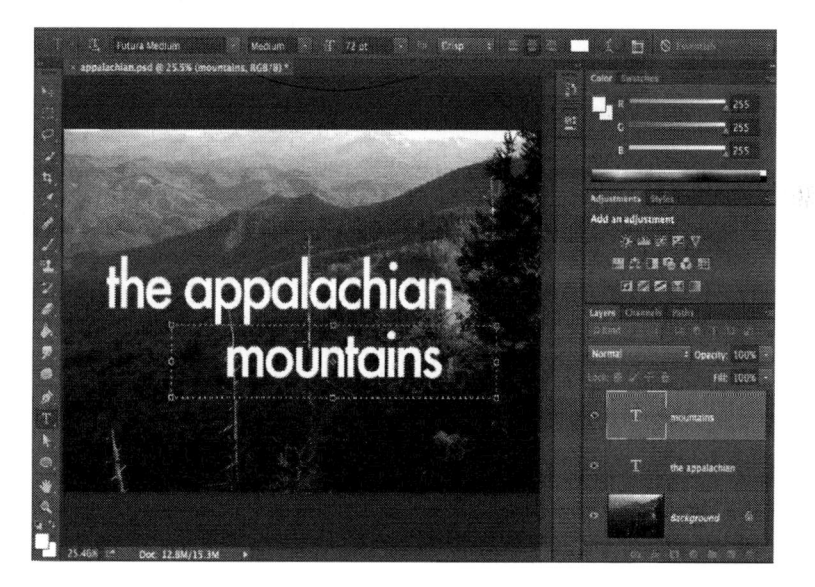

TEXT MANIPULATION IN PHOTOSHOP

To select Text in Photoshop, follow these steps:

- Open the document in Photoshop containing the text that will be edited. Make sure it is on a type layer, or proceed with step 2 and then step 3 to add text.

182

- To select all text or paragraphs on a type layer, with the Move tool choose and double-click on text. If it doesn't work that way, check your Photoshop version. Otherwise, choose the Type tool, click on the text, and then choose Select > All from the menu.
- To select certain characters, choose the Type tool, click, and drag across the characters.
- After selecting, you can perform editing functions such as changing color, size, copy and paste, etc.

Editing Text within Photoshop:

- Open the Photoshop document containing the text to edit on a type layer. If necessary add text by following steps 2 and 3.
- Select the Type tool in the toolbar
- Click and highlight the text to edit.
- Utilize the options bar for font, size, color, alignment, and style changes. Among them are text orientation, font style, size anti-aliasing, alignment color, warping text, and also view character and paragraph panels.
- More text editing can be done using the Character and Paragraph panels.
- Clubs Save your edits by clicking the checkmark icon in the options bar.

Copying and Pasting Text in Photoshop:

Copy and Paste from a Non-Photoshop File:

- Highlight and copy the text from the non-Photoshop file, whether it is a Word, PDF, or web page.
- The Photoshop document opens. Then select the Type tool and select the type layer.
- StepThrough Go to Edit > Paste or Command+V (macOS) or Control+V (Windows) to paste the text.

Copy and Paste from Another Photoshop Document PSD:

- Open the source PSD, select and copy the text.
- Open the target PSD select a type layer and select Edit > Paste. Or select Edit > Paste Special > Paste in Place for the same position.

Working with OpenType SVG Fonts:

- Photoshop allows you to work with OpenType SVG fonts such as Trajan Color Concept and EmojiOne. These fonts allow multiple colors and gradients in a single glyph.

To use OpenType SVG fonts:

Create a paragraph or point-text type layer. Typically OpenType SVG fonts appear differently.

- Choose an OpenType SVG font.
- Type any text through the keyboard or your own choice of glyphs by opening Glyphs Panel via Window> Glyphs or using Window> Workspace> Graphic and Web then click the tab Glyphs.

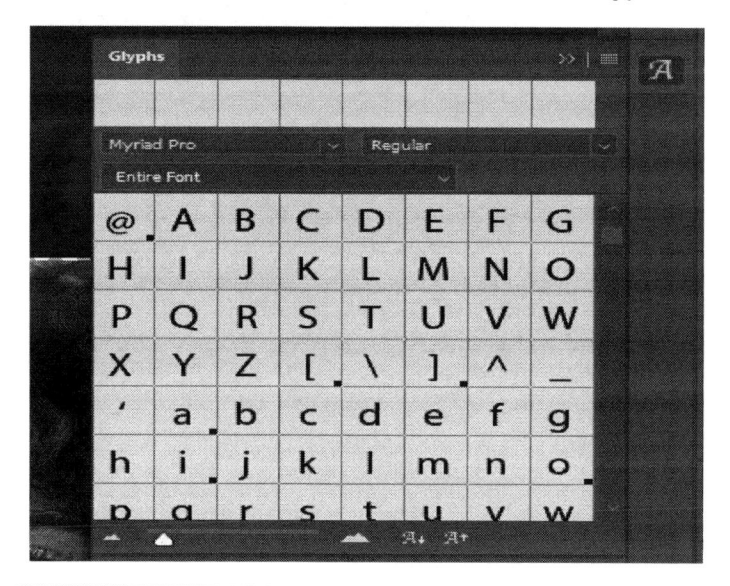

UNDERSTANDING CHARACTER PANEL IN PHOTOSHOP

The Character Panel is an advanced feature that allows users to pay closer attention to the appearance of text within their designs. It allows users to manipulate and have full control over the basic properties of typography, which include font style, size, spacing, and alignment. The following listed are the most important features that could be adjusted in the Character Panel.

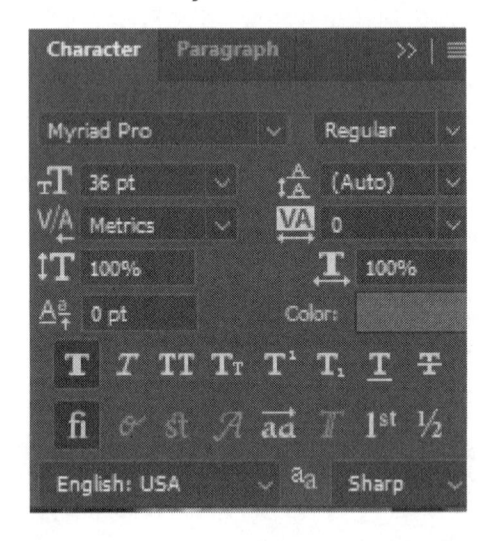

Key Features of Character Panel

- **Font Type**: Select one of the various types of fonts in Photoshop or import and modify fonts you like.
- **Font Style**: Bold, italic, or underlined, depending on the font face.
- **Font Size**: Enlarge or shrink your text according to your design requirements.
- **Leading (Line Spacing)**: Adjust the vertical spacing between lines of text.
- **Tracking (Letter Spacing)**: Adjust character spacing in a word or block of text.
- **Kerning**: This is used to adjust the distance between certain pairs of characters for even typography.
- **Baseline Shift**: Allows to move selected text upwards or downwards relative to baseline for alignment purposes.
- **Color**: Fills the text with pure colors, gradients, or patterns. Anti-aliasing Options: The edges are smoothed to make it look finer.

How to Access the Character Panel in Photoshop

Follow these few easy steps to open the Character Panel:

Via Menu Bar:

- Go to Window at the top menu.
- From there, select Character from the drop-down menu.

Via Type Tool:

- Click on the Type Tool via the toolbar or use the hotkey T.
- When the Type tool is selected, click anywhere on your canvas to start typing.
- The Character Panel will sometimes pop up automatically. If it does not, go through the menu method above.

Via Shortcut Windows/ Mac:

You can activate text transformation options by pressing Ctrl + T (for Windows) or Cmd + T (for Mac) while working with the Type Tool. It's also easy to access the Character Panel via the Properties tab.

You can open it and dock, drag and drop the panel in a comfortable position, allowing you to change text on the fly.

ORGANIZATION OF PHOTOSHOP TEXT ELEMENTS

Font:

It is the entire character set of letters, and numbers, along with all the symbols, which a typeface possesses. It has similar characteristics in weight, width, and style. Example - 10-pt Adobe Garamond Bold.

Typeface:

Typefaces, also called font families, are sets of fonts that are designed to be consistent in appearance. A typeface is Adobe Garamond. In addition to regular characters, typefaces can include ligatures, fractions, swashes, ornaments, ordinals, titling and stylistic alternates, superior and inferior characters, old-style figures, and lining figures.

Glyph:

A glyph is a specific form of the character. Various fonts might offer variations in style for the capital letter A to be used for swash or small cap.

Type Style:

A type style is a derivative of one font in a font family. The Roman or Plain font is common as the base font from which other styles are available; these can be but are not limited to regular, bold, semibold, italic, and bold italic. If a font style has not been professionally produced, some faux styles can be activated which mimic bold, italic, superscript, subscript, all caps, and small caps.

SELECTING CHARACTERS

To designate a type layer, do one of the following:

- Choose the Move tool and then double-click the type layer on the canvas.
- Choose the Horizontal or Vertical Type tool. Either select the type layer in the Layers panel or click inside the text flow to automatically activate a type layer.
- Place the cursor in the text and:
    a. Drag to select one or more characters.
    b. Click in the text, then Shift-click to highlight a range of characters.
    c. Highlight all characters in the layer by choosing "Select All" from the menu.
    d. Select all characters in the bounding box, double-click a word, triple-click a line, quadruple-click a paragraph, or quintuple-click anywhere in the text flow.
    e. Hold down Shift and press the arrow keys to select characters, or hold down Shift+Ctrl (Windows) or Shift+Command (Mac OS) and press an arrow key to select words.

To select all characters in a layer without setting the insertion point, double-click the layer's type icon in the Layers panel. Note that selecting and formatting characters activates the edit mode of the Type tool.

APPLYING UNDERLINE OR STRIKETHROUGH TO TEXT

- Choose text to be underlined or struck through.
- To strike through, select the Underline button in the Character panel.
- To enter a horizontal and/or vertical line: click the Strikethrough button or select it from the menu.

APPLYING ALL CAPS OR SMALL CAPS TO TEXT

- Highlight the text that you want to change.
- Click the All Caps or Small Caps button on the Character panel or choose either option from the menu.

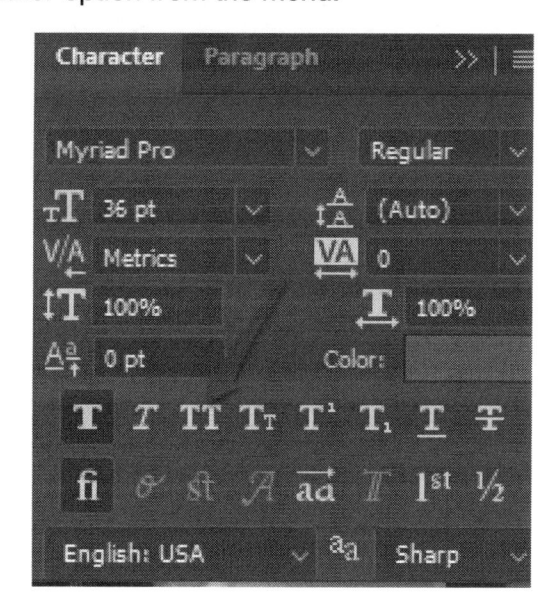

CREATING A POINT TYPE

There are two types of text layers available to the designer when designing in Photoshop: point text and paragraph text. Each of these can be set in either a vertical or horizontal orientation within the Design Editor. One important consideration is that the orientation set within the PSD is absolute and cannot be adjusted by the end user. Text layers, as they are placed on the canvas, become editable.

Sometimes, scaled text appears blurry within the Design Editor, while the very same text scaled identically with the same font settings in Adobe Photoshop may not show any blurring. So, to avoid such situations, it is better not to use any scale transformations for text layers while creating PSD templates and try changing the font size instead.

In the Design Editor, to smoothly appear any point text field must have one font style. If multiple styles are used for this type of layer, only the first one is used for the whole text, and the rest are ignored.

To start a point text layer in Photoshop:

- Choose the Type Tool on the Tools panel
- Do one of the following to switch to a Horizontal Type Tool or Vertical Type Tool.

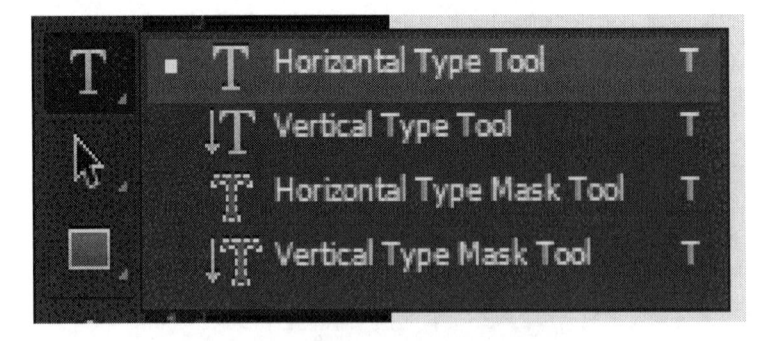

- Click on the canvas and type the necessary text there to choose it. To start a new line, press the Enter key.

Some point text
Each line has its own length

- When you're done, click "Done".

- Here are three types of text: point, paragraph, and path. Point text can be converted to paragraph text. To change a selected point text layer that has been selected via right-clicking use "Convert to Paragraph Text." To change the orientation between horizontal and vertical click the Options Bar.

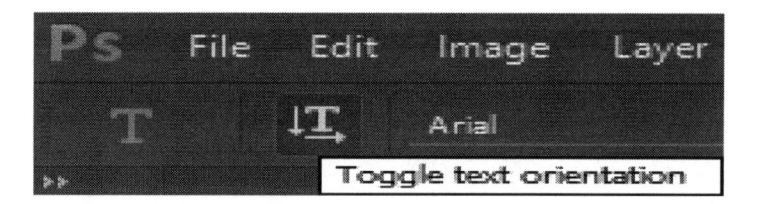

- The snapshot below shows the text that was previously created and imported into the editor.

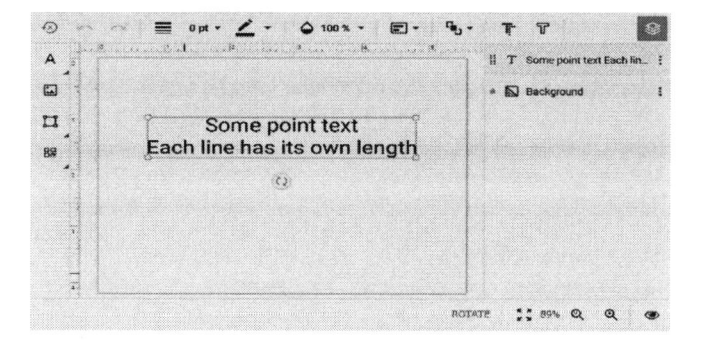

ALIGNING TEXT WITHIN A PARAGRAPH

In Photoshop you can easily specify alignment in a paragraph with the left, center, or right type for horizontal text and the top, center, or bottom type for vertical text. Adjustments to alignment apply only to paragraph type.

To set alignment:

Choose a type layer to specify all paragraphs on that layer or select one or more paragraphs. In the Paragraph panel or options bar, select one of the following options from the alignment icon menu: Horizontal type options:

- **Left Align Text**: This will align text to the left and the right will therefore be ragged.
- **Center Text**: This will align text to the center; both the left and the right will therefore be ragged.
- **Right Align Text**: This will align text to the right and the left will therefore be ragged.

Vertical type options:

- **Top Align Text**: This will align text to the top and the bottom will therefore be ragged.
- **Center Text**: Centers the text, leaving rough edges on both the top and bottom.
- **Bottom Align Text**: Bottom aligns text with a ragged edge at the top.

APPLYING JUSTIFICATION FOR PARAGRAPH TYPE

Specify justification for paragraph type by aligning text with both edges. Options include justifying all lines or excluding the last line, affecting horizontal spacing and overall aesthetic appeal.

To set justification:

- Choose a type layer to affect all paragraphs within it or select specific paragraphs.
- In the Paragraph panel, select a justification option:

Horizontal type options:

- Justify Last Left
- Justify Last Centered
- Justify Last Right
- Justify All

Vertical type options:

- Justify Last Top
- Justify Last Centered
- Justify Last Bottom
- Justify All

Note the following:

- Adjusting the spacing of the words and letters in the justified text controls the spacing between characters. To do so, you can set Word Spacing, Letter Spacing, and Glyph Scaling to specify a range for justified paragraphs. This applies only to Roman characters.
- Paragraph indentation: Specify the amount of space between the type and the bounding box or line containing the type. Set indention options for the left margin, right margin, and the first line of the paragraph.
- Adjust paragraph spacing: Choose values to add space before and after paragraphs.
- Turn on Roman fonts to have hanging punctuation, which allows punctuation marks to align outside the margin. Choose Roman Hanging Punctuation from the Paragraph panel menu to set the option for all paragraphs in a type layer or for selected paragraphs. Some Asian fonts, such as those for Japanese, require options available in the Type preferences for double-byte punctuation marks.

CREATING A CLIPPING MASK AND APPLYING A SHADOW

Mastering Photoshop essentially entails editing an image, whereby a basic technique is to make use of the clipping mask to hide areas of a layer that are essentially not necessary to be seen in a final design or document. It constitutes one of those vastly utilized techniques while availing of any Photoshop masking service. To create a clipping mask:

- Open the picture you want in Photoshop.

- Find the horizontal tool icon or hit 'T' Once any of the tool icons is at the top of the screen, there are choices to select one out of many typefaces. The color of the text does not matter, pay close attention to making anti-aliasing strong.

- To start inputting the text, click the image. A new Text layer will appear in the Layer Panel.

- Centre the text inside the image or a chosen area of interest by using the Move Tool (shortcut 'V').
- In the Layer Panel, drag the freshly made text layer underneath the image layer. Make sure the image is clipped underneath the first image so it fits the text's shape.

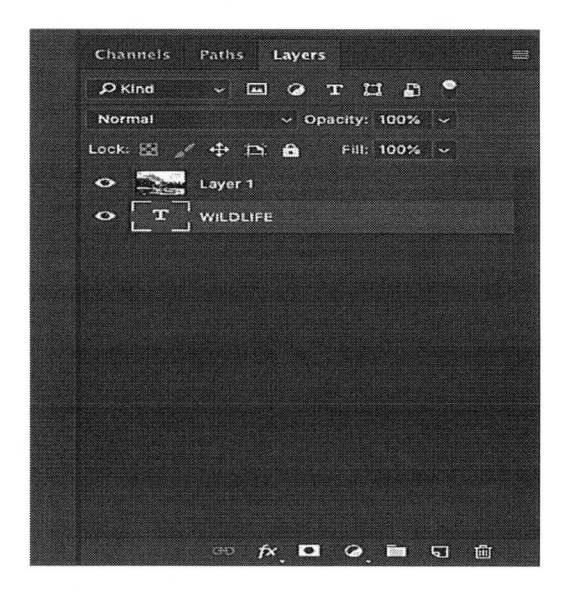

- After selecting the Image Layer, click the hamburger menu button in the Layers Panel's top right corner, and choose "Create Clipping Mask." An alternative shortcut is Alt+Ctrl+G (Windows) or Option+Cmd+G (Mac).

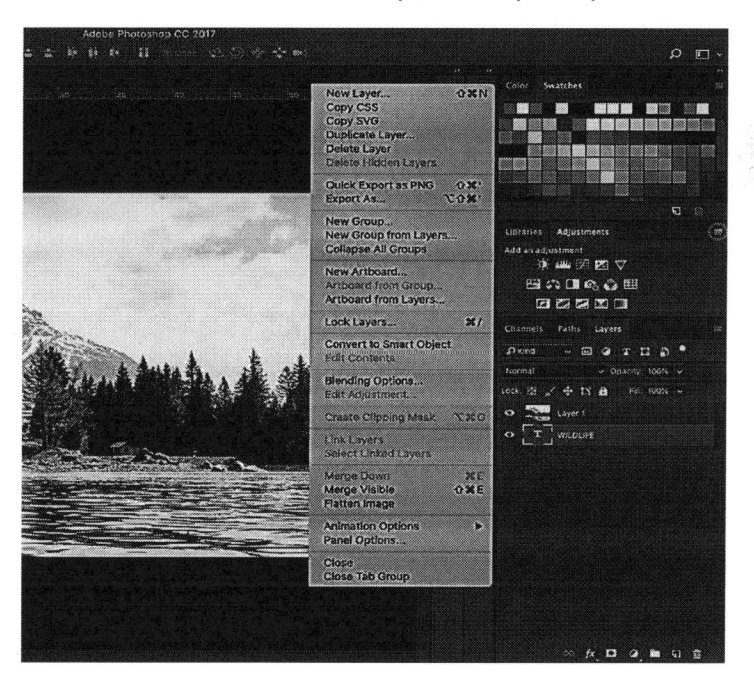

- Upon clipping, besides the image layer, there will be a small arrow in the Layers Panel. Now select the Move Tool (V) and align the needed parts of the image with the text. The clipping mask shows the text where it's filled up with bits of the image, its rest hidden.

Include Drop Shadow

- To add special effects to the image, add a drop shadow to the Text layer.
- Click the Text layer and in the Layers Panel click on the small triangle icon beside "Add a Layer Style," then select "Drop Shadow."

- Adjust the Drop Shadow parameters in the Layer Style dialog box to your preference.

Including Additional Text

- To enlarge your design, include more text:
- Use the Type tool (T) in the options bar to find and choose the font, size, and color.

- Choose the image and type the necessary text. The Move Tool (V) can be used to position the new text.

HOW TO PUT TEXT ALONG A PATH IN PHOTOSHOP

The process of setting text along a path is the same, regardless of the tool that you have used to construct it. To simplify things for this tutorial we will use the Ellipse Tool. To access the Ellipse Tool, right-click (Windows) or control-click (Macintosh) on the Rectangle Tool in the Tools panel.

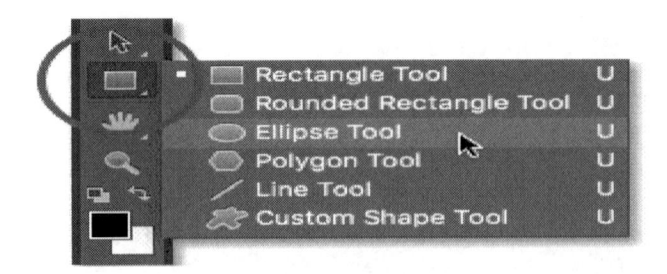

- While the Ellipse Tool is selected, set the Tool Mode in the Options Bar to "Path" to guarantee that we draw a path rather than a form.

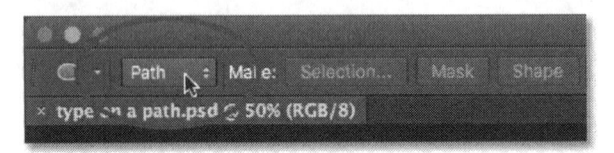

- Click and hold the mouse pointer in the center of the golf ball, then press Shift+Alt (for Windows) or Shift+Option (for Mac) and drag outward to create a perfect circular route. Let go of the keys and mouse button once the path encircles the ball.

- After drawing the path, choose the Type Tool from the Tools menu.

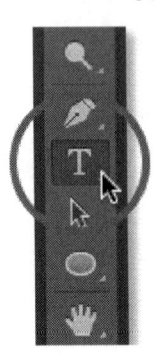

- In the Options Bar, adjust the font specifications. For example, choose the font, size, color, and text alignment.

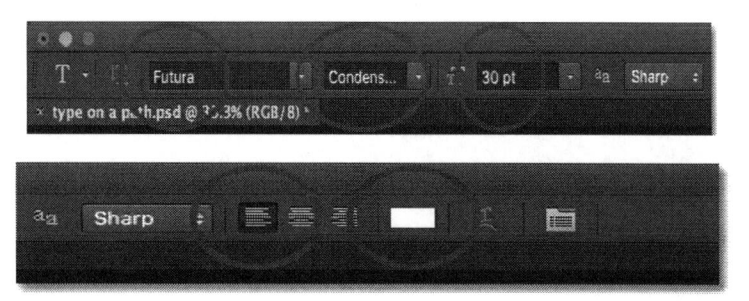

- Place the Type Tool over the path to add text directly to it. An I-beam with a dotted, wavy line will appear where the cursor was.

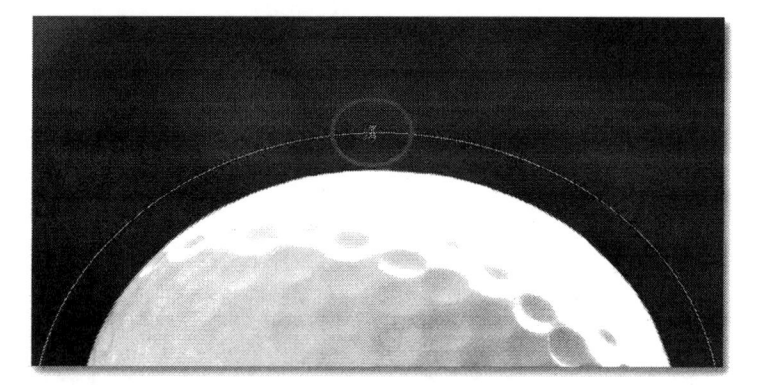

- To start typing, click anywhere on the path. The text flows in the direction of the path. When you have finished typing your text, click the checkbox in the Options bar.

- You can move text along the route by using the route Selection Tool located in the Tools panel.

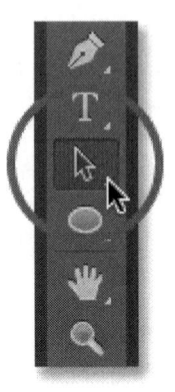

- To animate the text along the path, hover the Path Selection Tool over the text and click and drag. Be careful not to drag across the route because it can flip words.

- To avoid accidentally 'flipping' the text so that it is backward, drag it across the route without dragging it down or high. If it does flip, drag it back across the route and it will return to normal orientation.

- Once you are happy with the position of the text, choose any layer but the Type layer within the Layers panel to hide the path.
- Follow these steps, and you will be able to add text to a path in Photoshop and have a professional result at the end.

APPLYING WARPING AND DISTORTION TO TEXT

Now let's learn how to bend and distort text in Photoshop. It is a very straightforward technique that allows you to choose one of many warp effects to make your design more interesting.

- Open Photoshop and create a new backdrop layer with the size you want initially. Type on the canvas the text you want to warp. You can change the color of the background layer if necessary for your design.

- Click the "Type" tool, and you will notice a series of selections pop up in a dropdown menu. Select and click on "Warp Text" from the populated list. In just a few seconds, you will notice a small window pop open featuring a host of different warp effects. Take a look at your options and decide which one you feel works best for the intended design.

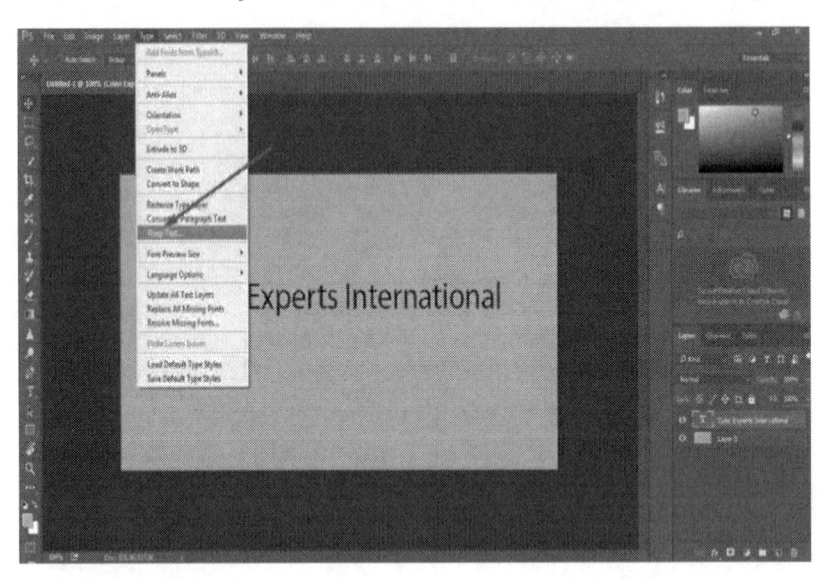

- There is bend, vertical distortion, and horizontal distortion in the window. You can directly use the sliders for adjustments and changes in distortion imposed on your text in real-time.

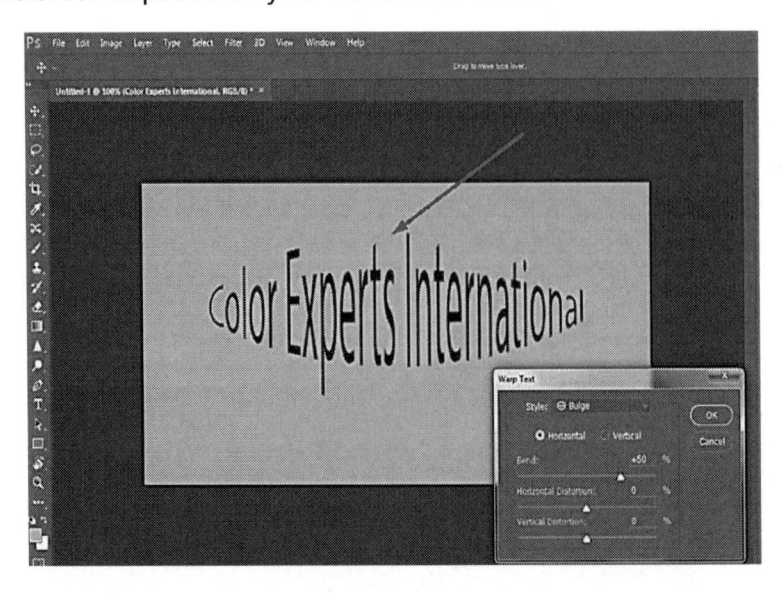

- Analyze several types of warp effects: wave, flag, fisheye, arc, and arch. You can try each kind of warp effect and its features with the help of visual tools. Pick up the most appropriate one regarding your idea about your design.

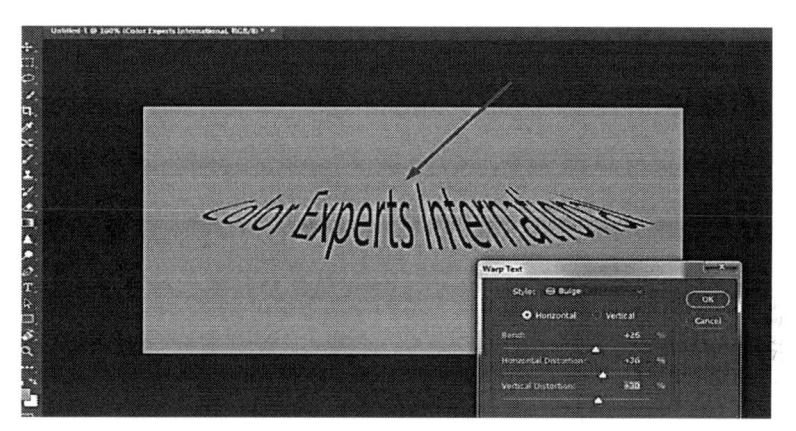

CHAPTER 7

UNDERSTANDING PHOTOSHOP DRAWING

EXPLORING BITMAP IMAGES

A bitmap or raster picture represents the picture information as a two-dimensional array of colored pixels. Each pixel has a position and color value, which together create the detailed pattern of the image. To illustrate this, in a bitmap rendering, the tire of a bicycle would be represented merely by a carefully selected collection of pixels, precisely placed at the appropriate location. In bitmap editing, the single pixels are the primary units of manipulation, instead of objects or shapes.

Such types of images are vastly used in the digital realm, especially concerning continuous-tone visuals like photographs or digital paintings. The power of bitmap images is actually to show subtle gradients of shades and colors. However, it should be mentioned that a bitmap image is resolution-dependent; it contains a fixed number of pixels. Because of this, bitmap images tend to lose a bit of their detail and get 'pixelated' if they are blown up on-screen or perhaps when they are printed at a lower resolution than they were initially set up. A practical application of bitmap images is in the preparation of images for laser engraving. In such a process, an image needs to be converted to a bitmap format to proceed with it. Since learning this conversion through Photoshop can be of great assistance in this regard, step-by-step instructions follow:

- Begin with an image already in existence or one you have taken.
- Open the selected image in Photoshop.

- To convert the image to grayscale, select Image > Mode > Grayscale.

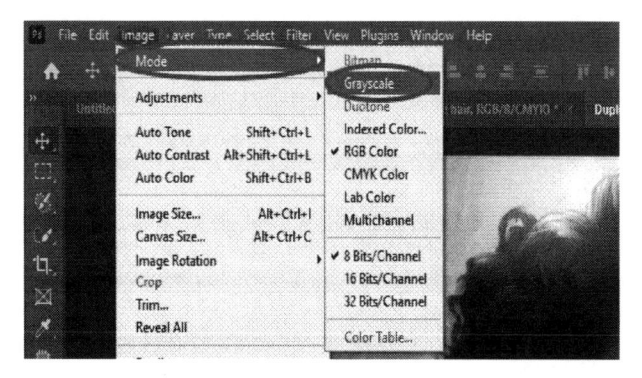

- Choose Image > Adjustment > Levels to alter the image's contrast.

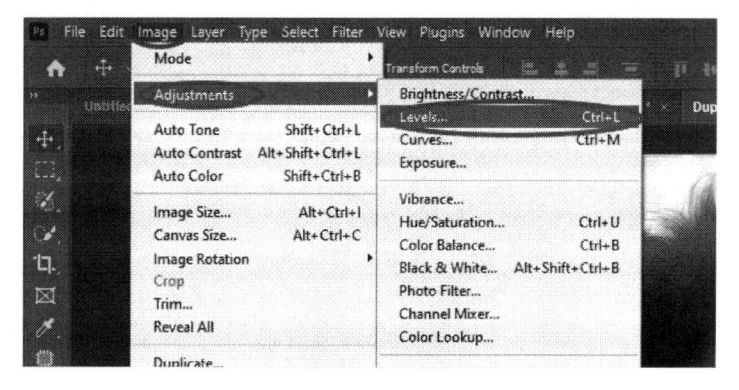

- After the grayscale image is ready, choose Image > Mode > Bitmap to turn it into a bitmap.

- Browse through the list of available bitmap styles and choose your favorite. You may try different styles to see what works best with your taste.
- Now you have successfully made your image into a bitmap. Save as a JPEG to easily use, or as a Photoshop file that you will use in Illustrator later..

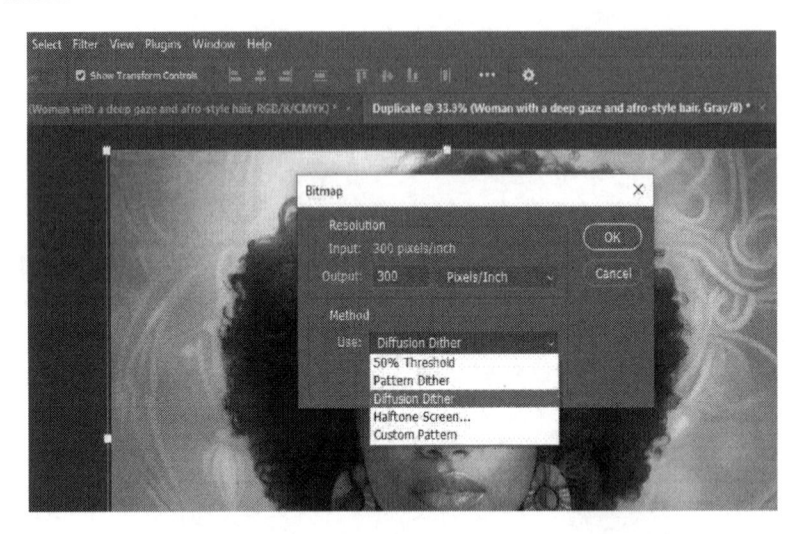

EXPLORING VECTOR GRAPHICS

The uniqueness of vector graphics is that they retain their sharpness regardless of the size. This is in contrast to raster images, better known as bitmap images. Unlike raster images, whose size is fixed with pixels, therefore becoming grainy when zoomed into, vector images are designed with geometric polygons and color, and maintain sharpness at any scale since they are based on mathematics. Graphic designers and digital artists generally use vector graphics when creating logos, fonts, and icons.

How to vectorize an image in Photoshop step by step:

- Import the image in Photoshop which is to be used.
- According to your requirement, select the region with any selection tool, like the Rectangular Marquee tool Magic Wand tool, or even the Select Subject option.
- Click on the New Threshold layer in the Layers panel to make the selection a one-color image. The slider sets the threshold: all lighter pixels turn white and the others turn black.

- The Color Range command selects the pixels of similar color in a very easy way. Then select either a white or black area using the Eyedropper tool by choice.
- After the selection, right-click and select "Make Work Path." This will form a path with a predetermined value of tolerance. The value of tolerance designates exactly how well the path fits into the contours of selection.
- On the Layers panel, click to add a new Fill layer or Adjustment layer. From the menu, choose "Solid Color." This will be the vector shape over the top of the Threshold layer and can be any color you choose.
- Right-click on the layer and choose "Export As." Choose the SVG file format for your image to be saved as a vector file.

WHAT IS YOUR UNDERSTANDING OF PATHS?

Primarily a raster-based application, Photoshop makes a comfortable use of vector-based functionality, and Paths is one of the most obvious. Paths consist of vector lines comprised of segments that are joined together by what are called anchor points. Segments take two forms: straight lines and curves, or mixtures of both. One of the qualifications an entity has to meet to be considered a path is that an entity has to form one closed loop. That is, every anchor point is connected to another anchor point.

The most important advantage of Paths is that they are vector-based, and as such, possess the major advantage of always remaining sharp and clear no matter if any size or resolution changes are done. This ensures consistency in detail and quality which is so valuable in design workflows. A second point to touch on is the capability of paths to enable users to create their custom shapes.

Even though Photoshop does have a set of pre-defined shapes, users can create and save custom shapes as paths.

In practice, paths have various applications, which enhance the professional aspect of the artwork. Some typical uses of paths among graphic designers include creating curved or circular text, selecting objects from backgrounds with extreme accuracy, and stylizing type with Bezier Points to achieve artistic typography. Paths prove especially useful for creating logos and graphics scalable in different sizes for future projects. Digital Artists also embrace the use of paths to transform a freehand drawing into an accurate, manipulable, vector-based image added with an extra layer of precision and flexibility during their creative process.

CREATING PATHS IN PHOTOSHOP

There is more than one way to create paths in Photoshop; paths can be created in different ways. Below are just a few ways to create paths:

- **Pen tool**: Lines drawn with anchor points are created while using the Pen Tool to make a path.
- **Shapes tool**: Any shape can be made as a path by selecting the Paths option with the Shapes tool.
- **Create as a path**: A path can be created intentionally with the Pen Tool or Shapes tool.
- **Convert to Path**: This enables the user to take an already existing image, graphic, or text and convert it into a path to continue editing it.

Like many of the design elements within the program, the user can set a fill color for the path, and determine the color and weight of a path's stroke. While little known and underused, Paths is an extremely useful and diverse tool within Photoshop, enabling new creative possibilities in design and artwork.

CREATING A SHAPE USING THE PEN TOOL

The Pen Tool in Photoshop is the best tool to produce smooth paths, which are defined by different anchor points as well as handles. To use the Pen Tool effectively, follow these steps:

- Select the Pen Tool [P] from the toolbar.

- In the Options bar, select settings for the tool: Drawing Mode and switch states of Auto Add/ Delete anchor points, thereby creating what you want.
- Choose the Pen Tool and create a path by placing anchor points and handles wherever needed to form your path.
- Complete the path by selecting either to close or to leave open, depending on what you're trying to achieve with your design.

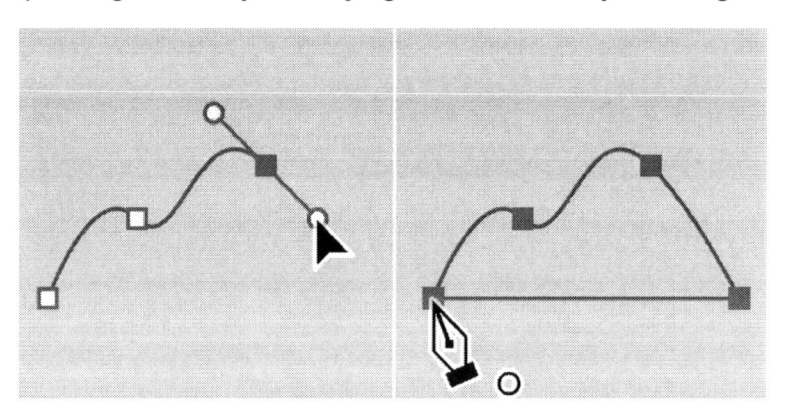

These techniques will enable you to use Photoshop's Pen tool efficiently and create intricate pathways with accuracy.

HOW TO DRAW A CURVE

Drawing smooth curves using the Pen tool in Photoshop requires that you strategically create anchor points and adjust the associated direction lines. To do this,

- Click the Pen tool in the toolbar to activate it.
- Click to place the first anchor point.
- Click and drag to establish the direction and slope of the curve.
- Allow the direction line to extend about one-third the length to the next anchor point.
- Use as few anchor points as possible to make the path highly editable and fast. Place the anchor points carefully so that unnecessary bumps are avoided.
- Refine the shape of the curve by adjusting the length and direction of the direction lines.

- To switch the Pen tool to constrain it at multiples of 45°, use the Shift key while dragging.

Following them means you will be able to draw curves with accuracy for maximum editability, and also it will contribute to a smoother display or printing experience. Placing the anchor points and carefully adjusting direction lines are just the keys to achieving your required curve shape.

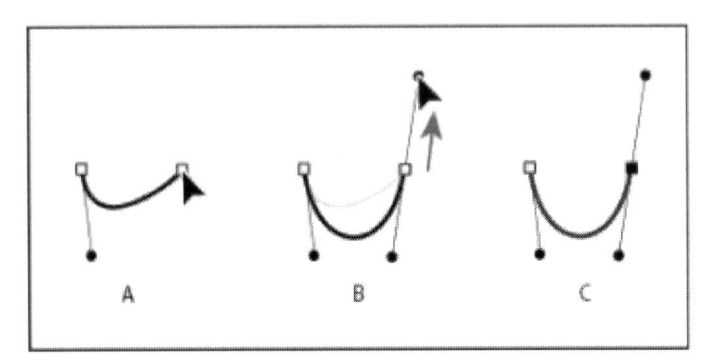

To complete a curve segment of your path:

- Drag the Pen tool to the end of where you want the curve segment of your path to be.
- Still holding down the mouse button drag in the opposite direction of the previous line of path, creating a C for the first half of the curve, or drag in the same direction, creating an S for the second half of the curve,
- Release the mouse button.
- Drag the Pen tool from various points to create smooth curves. The start and end of each smooth segment are anchored by an anchor point. To create a sharp curve, release the mouse button, Alt-drag (Windows) or Option-drag (Mac OS) the direction point in the desired direction, reposition the pointer, and drag in the opposite direction.

To complete the path:

- Move the Pen tool over the initial anchor point and either click or drag.
- To exit, Ctrl-click (Windows) or Command-click (Mac OS) outside of objects or select another tool.

Combining straight lines and curves:

- Click on corner points to create a straight segment.

- Place the Pen tool over the endpoint, click, and drag the direction line in the desired position for the curved segment.

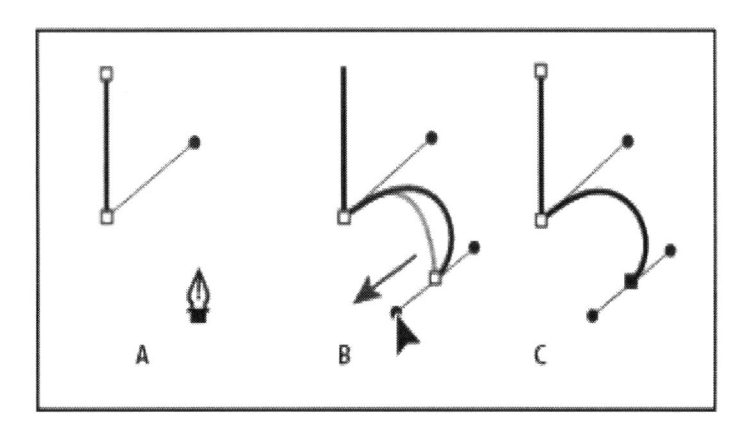

For curves followed by straight lines:

- Drag to produce the first smooth point.
- Move and drag to complete the curve.
- Select the endpoint with the Convert Point tool to convert it to a corner point.
- Click where the straight segment should end with the Pen tool.

For two curved segments that meet at a corner:

- Drag to produce the first smooth point.
- To convert to the slope and reposition, drag to set the second smooth point, while holding down Alt (Windows) or Option (Mac OS).
- Release the mouse button and the key.
- Drag the Pen tool to a new location and then drag it to create another smooth point to complete the second curved segment.
- Drag to create the first smooth point.
- To convert the slope, drag to reposition and set the second smooth point, holding down Alt (Windows) or Option (Mac OS).
- Release the mouse button and the key.
- Drag the Pen tool to a new location and, holding down the mouse button, drag to create another smooth point to complete the second curved segment.

FAMILIARIZING YOURSELF WITH COLOR MODE

Various color modes in Photoshop direct different ends:

RGB Mode (Millions of Colors):

- Utilizes the RGB model; and assigns intensities to pixels in red, green, and blue channels.
- Intensity values range from 0 (black) to 255 (white) for each component in 8-bit-per-channel images.
- With three channels, it can reproduce as many as 16.7 million colors per pixel.
- This is best suited for on-screen display and is also the default in opening or creating new images in Photoshop.

CMYK Mode (Four-Printed Colors):

- Assign percentage values for process inks-cyan, magenta, yellow, black- to every pixel.
- Used in the creation of images for printing with process colors.
- To produce pure white, all four components must have a value of 0%.
- To get color separation for printing, one must convert from RGB to CMYK.

Index Mode 256 Colors:

- A color palette consisting of 256 indexed colors is used.
- It can be widely applied because optimization of basic color representation to file size is possible.

Grayscale Mode 256 Grays:

- Grey levels are represented-256 levels of grey can be supported in 8-bit images.
- Luminance levels vary between 0 (pure black) and 255 (pure white).

Bitmap Mode (2 Colours):

- Pixels are represented in pure black and white.
- An image in Bitmap mode is a 1-bit image with a bit depth of 1.

Lab Color Mode:

- Based on the CIE Lab Color model, which reflects how humans perceive color.
- Considers colors in respect of their lightness, L, on the green-red axis, a, and on the blue-yellow axis, b.
- Was once considered device-independent in color model terms about Color Management Systems.

Every color mode option in Photoshop greatly affects color detail and file size. CMYK would be the best color mode for print, while RGB is generally the best color mode for the web, considering a tradeoff between color integrity and file size. The Lab Color color mode represents colors in a device-independent way, matching human color perception. Grayscale and Bitmap mode have their purpose and are, therefore, appropriately represented depending on the nature of the image being grayscale or binary. A complete understanding of the modes will provide a basis for comprehensive editing and optimization of images.

WHICH COLOR MODE DO I NEED TO SELECT?

The choice of Photoshop color option depends on how and where the photos are going to be used and what the output is. Here are some basic tips that will guide you to determine the best color mode:

RGB Mode, or Red, Green, and Blue

Ideal For: Digital media, web graphics, and on-screen displays.

When to Decide: Most people will be viewing your photos on a computer, tablet, or smartphone.

CMYK Mode: Cyan, Magenta, Yellow, Black

- **Best Used For**: Print products, such as posters, flyers, and brochures.
- **What to Consider When You Come to a Decision**: Whether professional printing of your images will include the four-color process so widely used in commercial printing.

Lab Color Mode

- **Best For**: Color correction and modification work where color perception accuracy is critical.
- **When to Pick**: When to perform an advanced color correction and for a color-managed process.

Grayscale Mode

- **Optimal For**: Monochrome photographs and other black-and-white images.
- **When to Use**: When you want to show imagery with shades of gray, and color information isn't necessary.

Bitmap Mode

- **Ideal For**: Straightforward logos, line art, or pictures that simply use black and white.
- **When to Pick**: When printing text or line drawings, for example, you require a 1-bit image for a specific reason.

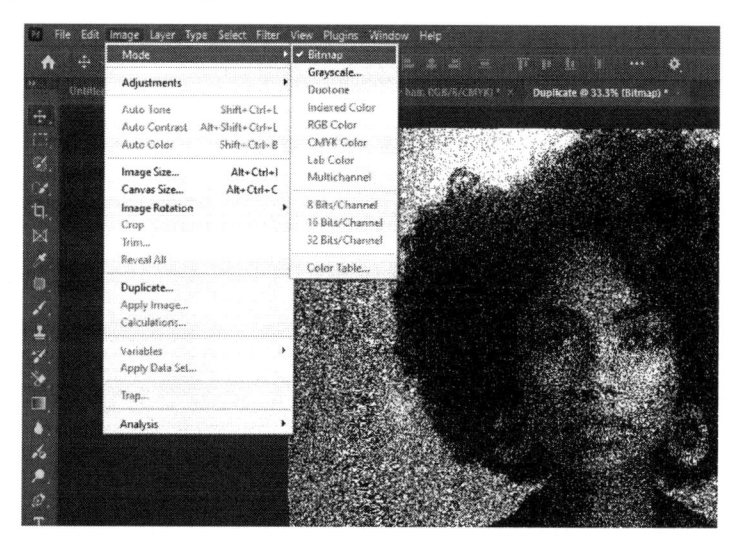

Think about the intended use and destination of your photos when making your decision. If you're not sure, start with CMYK for printing or RGB for digital media since those tend to be the most common uses. Second, color conversions will always matter because once you change the mode you're working in, colors can show up differently.

HOW TO CHANGE COLOR MODE IN PHOTOSHOP

Changing the color mode in Photoshop is pretty easy; all you have to do is:

- Select Image > Mode.
- Choose from the available options regarding your preferred Color Mode.

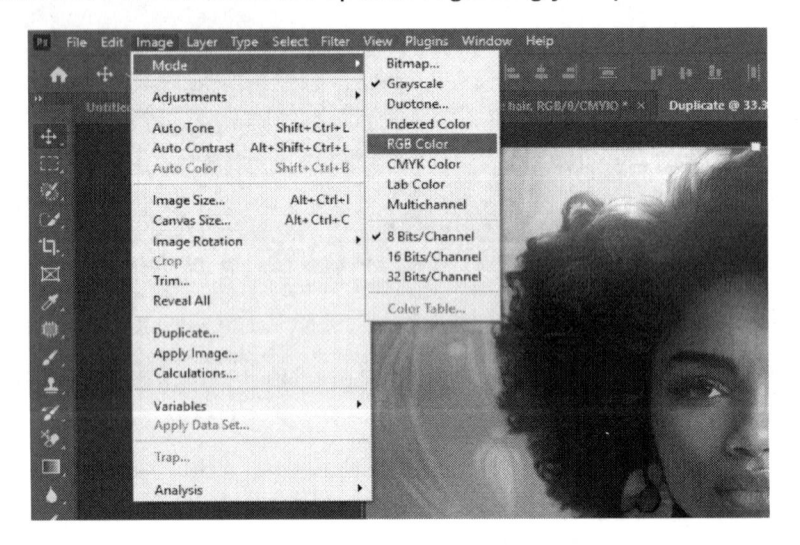

CALIBRATION AND PROFILING GRASPING

Understanding Calibration

One of the fundamentals in digital imaging involves calibration, a process that corrects variability that may be reflected on the monitors. This is because of manufacturing differences, and most monitors will have some differences regarding color accuracy and brightness. To overcome these problems, the monitors can be calibrated with the aid of colorimeters or spectrophotometers. These are devices that measure colors displayed on the monitor and create a profile that compensates for the inaccuracies. Without calibration, the colors that a user may see on the screen are not necessarily indicative of their true colors as represented in the digital images. This is why there exists an Adobe

Photoshop setting to calibrate the monitor, through which the user can define the color parameters for consistent viewings.

Understanding Profiling

While calibration focuses on the precision of the monitor, profiling extends the concept to other devices that can take part in the imaging process, like printers and cameras. Each of the devices in question has its distinctive way of displaying or reproducing colors, and profiling is a means of creating a very specific description of these characteristics. A profile, after calibration, is generated for monitors to get the colors as close to exact as possible. Similarly, printers need to be profiled on the specific ink and paper being used in combination with one another so the resulting printed piece is a true representation of the digital image. Of course, cameras can be profiled too, which is useful in controlled applications where color accuracy from capture is important.

CONVERTING RGB IMAGE TO CMYK MODE

- Open Photoshop and select the image.
- To change the mode of the image in Photoshop, go to Image > Mode
- From the menu, select "CMYK Color" to convert it into a CMYK image.

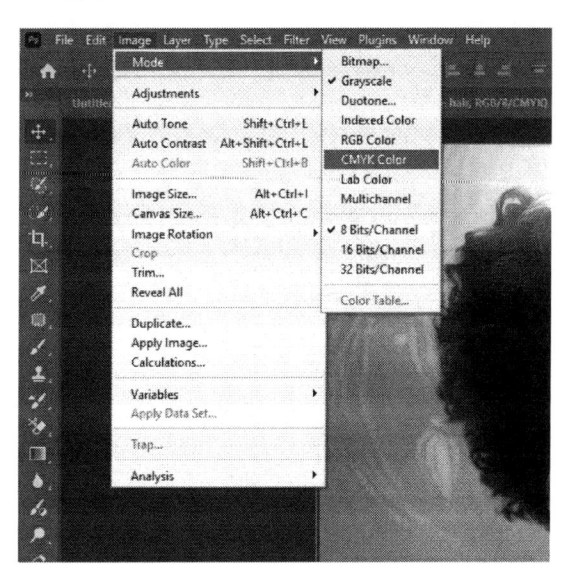

- There are colors that the conversion might not be able to maintain.
- Note that modern processes often avoid the necessity of making images CMYK before printing.

- Alternatively, select Edit > Convert to Profile in case of any advanced CMYK Color Profile settings.

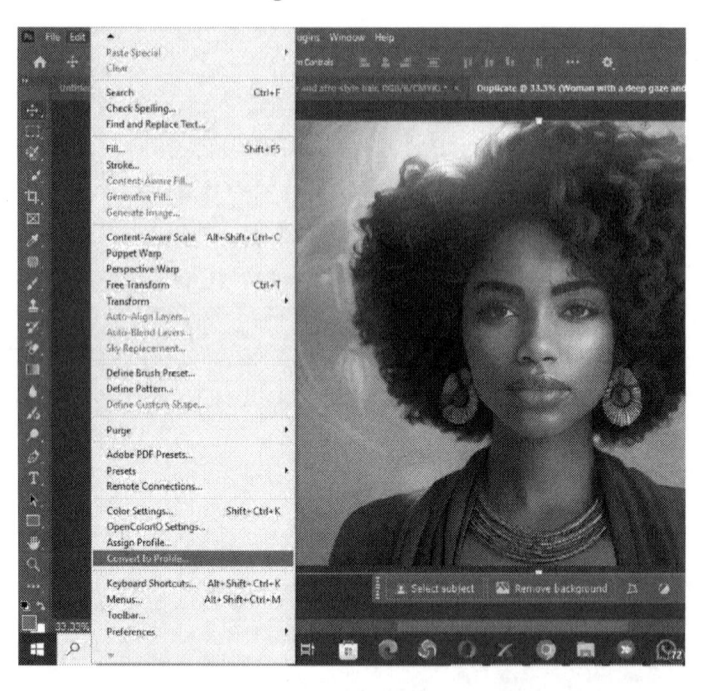

- In the newly opened window, choose your desired CMYK profile from the Destination Space drop-down menu.

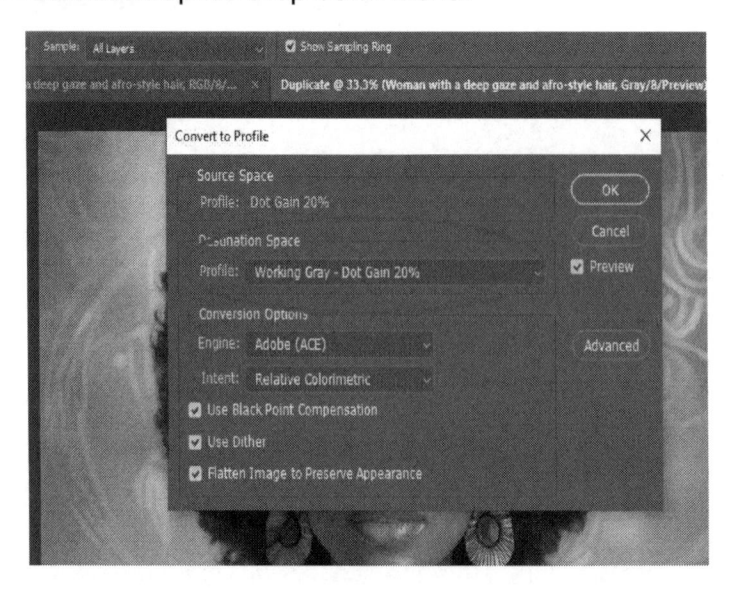

SAVING YOUR IMAGE AS PHOTOSHOP PDF

Note that the color profile will also change, possibly leading to a loss of color, from RGB to CMYK. Proof these photographs in advance to avoid anomalies you may not be prepared to handle.

The final step to convert the image into CMYK is to save it in the right CMYK format. To do so, head over to File > Save As and choose the kind of file you would prefer to work with.

HOW TO EXPORT YOUR WORK

Exporting your projects the right way is about making sure that it is of high quality but optimized for a particular platform. Here's how you can do this more efficiently.

- Go to File > Export > Export As.
- Choose the format needed: JPEG, PNG, GIF, or SVG.
- Change the size and quality where needed.
- Click on Export; choose the location where you will save the file.
- You can also Save your work in a format called a Photoshop Document which retains all layers and adjustments that you can reopen and edit sometime later by going through File > Save As and selecting the PSD format.

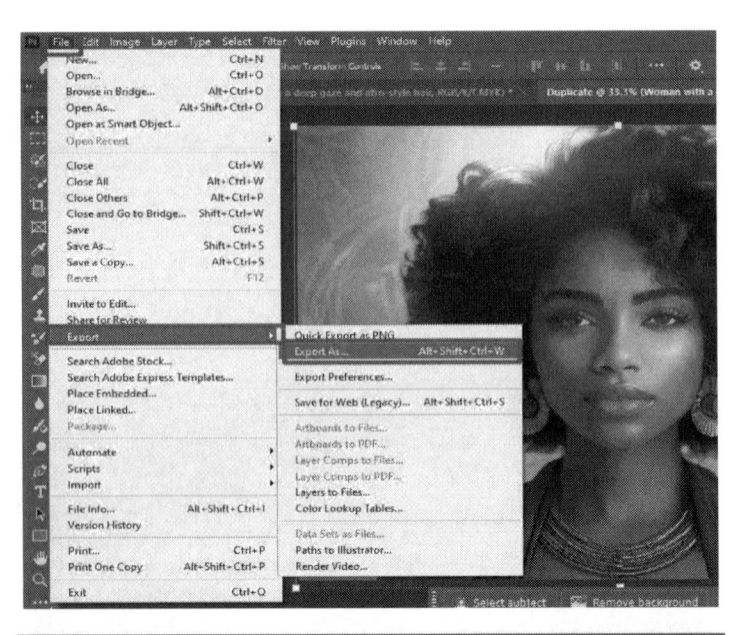

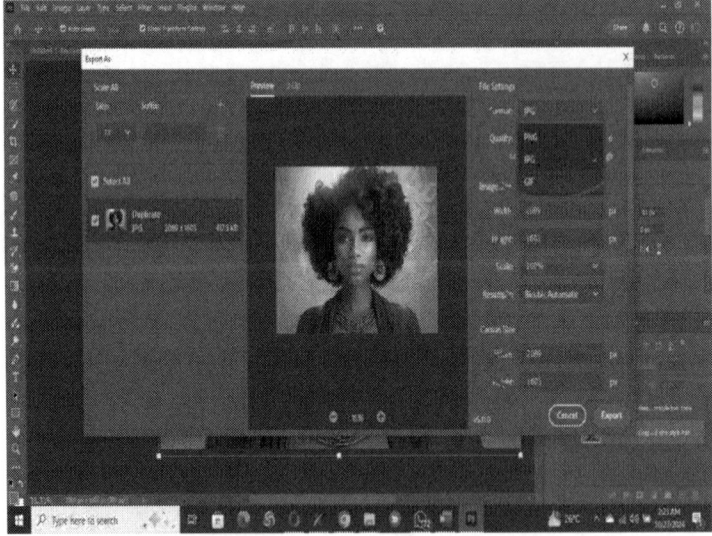

PRINTING YOUR WORK IN PHOTOSHOP

Printing directly from Photoshop ensures your design maintains the colors you want, the best resolution, and the way it has been laid out. Follow these steps to print your work effectively:

Prepare the Document for Printing:

- Go to File > New and set the resolution to 300 DPI dots per inch for high-quality prints.
- Use the CMYK color mode if printing with commercial printers or RGB for standard printers.
- Also, make sure your canvas size is equal to the print dimensions.

Check Image Resolution and Size:

- Image > Image Size. Make sure the resolution is at 300 pixels/inch.
- Adjust document dimensions if needed to ensure it's the same size as the paper or print output.

Configure the Print Setup:

- Click on File > Print.
- In the print dialog box, from the dropdown, select your printer.
- Choose the right paper size and orientation.
- In the Scaling options, set to fit the design on the paper correctly.

- Inside the print dialog box, click on Print Settings.
- Choose the right paper type, such as glossy or matte.
- For the best quality print output, choose High Quality.

- Under Color Handling, choose either, Photoshop Manages Colors for precise color control. Or Printer Manages Colors to print using the printer's default.
- If Photoshop Manages Colors, select the right printer profile.
- Once all settings are confirmed, click Print.

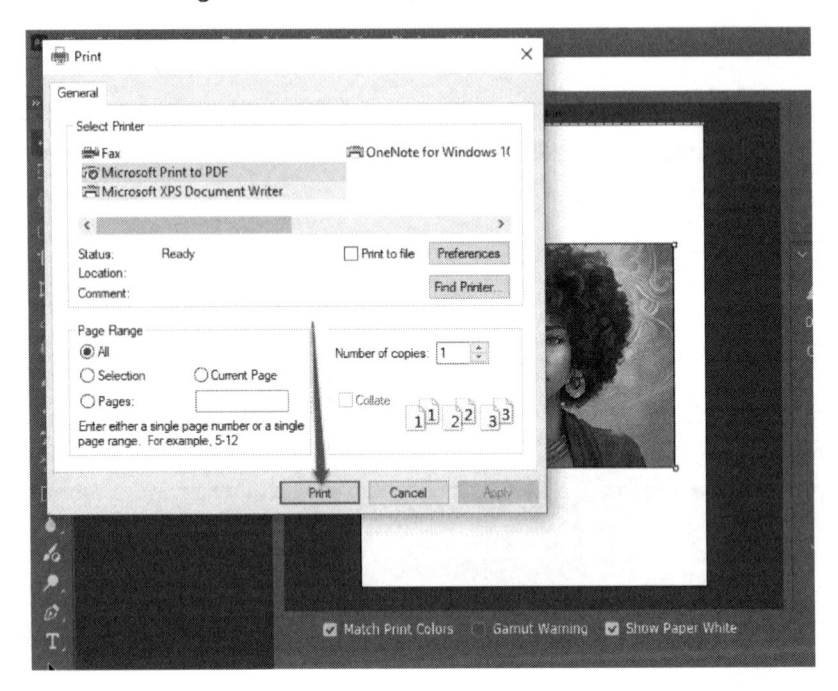

CONCLUSION

Adobe Photoshop 2025 is indeed a cornerstone for professional and amateur creative people; its powerful functionalities offer endless possibilities to edit photos, make digital designs, and express artistic ideas. Having passed through this step-by-step guide, you have learned about the key features, mastered the interface, and applied practical tricks to enhance your creative projects. You are now prepared for different kinds of tasks, starting from simple image adjustments and complex manipulations to high-end retouching.

One of the major strengths that work for Photoshop 2025 is that it keeps getting better. New AI-driven features, smoother workflows, and broader compatibility make high-quality results easier and faster to get. This program caters to both experienced users and beginners with intuitive tools for experimentation, exploration, and skill building. Working your way through with Photoshop, the secret of mastering lies in practice and curiosity.

More than just photo editing, Photoshop opens the floodgates to try your hand at digital painting, graphic design, web layout, and even animations and 3D. Every project you work on will be different from others, and it will give you a different experience, yet at the same time provide satisfaction in doing something that will be new and different. Equipped with such versatility and precision, Photoshop can be a lifetime tool that enables you to refine your craft and push the bounds of your creativity.

The demand for engaging visual content is on the rise, as the digital world is huge and getting bigger. Be it a personal project, an assignment at work, or creating a creative portfolio, the skills you have built up in this tutorial will empower you to give back to the world. Keep updating yourself with the new software updates and go through tutorials to connect with the larger Photoshop community.

Thank you for taking that initial step to mastering Adobe Photoshop 2025. This is only the beginning of your creative journey. Make use of every given opportunity, be fearless in experimenting, and let your imagination shape the future of your designs.

INDEX

A

adjustment, 82, 161
Adjustment, 6, 76, 80, 82, 84, 85, 86, 151, 155, 160, 211, 213
Adobe, 1, 4, 5, 7, 10, 13, 14, 15, 16, 17, 18, 19, 22, 23, 24, 25, 35, 48, 61, 67, 73, 93, 97, 129, 193, 196, 222, 229
application, 5, 18, 22, 25, 41, 46, 48, 95, 103, 210, 213
art, 4, 5, 27, 65, 221
artist, 8
attributes, 77

B

background, 8, 9, 10, 12, 29, 31, 39, 41, 79, 82, 90, 95, 98, 99, 104, 142, 165, 166, 168, 169, 172, 173, 207
Background, 4, 10, 12, 29, 39, 98, 126, 138, 139, 165, 166, 167, 168, 172
Bar, 8, 9, 10, 12, 19, 20, 22, 23, 24, 25, 40, 46, 92, 94, 123, 127, 129, 134, 135, 139, 143, 164, 166, 175, 176, 177, 178, 179, 180, 182, 193, 197, 204, 205
batch, 6
Bitmap, 69, 211, 218, 219, 221
Black, 83
blemishes, 6, 28, 122, 123, 125, 142, 143
blend, 6, 52, 76, 88, 89, 90, 91, 93, 95, 145, 152, 158, 159, 164, 165
Blend, 140, 146, 178
Blending, 75, 88, 89, 95, 146
Blur, 6, 145, 187
Bottom, 166, 198
brightness, 6, 31, 52, 76, 85, 89, 125, 152, 164, 222
Brush, 19, 20, 25, 27, 28, 46, 80, 108, 122, 123, 125, 139, 142, 143, 147, 148, 153, 154, 157, 161, 162, 177, 178
brushes, 25, 28, 31, 179
brushing, 8

C

Calibration, 222
canvas, 98
capabilities, 5, 10, 51, 68, 111
Clipboard, 47
Clone, 182
Cloud, 16
CMYK, 64, 65, 218, 219, 220, 222, 223, 224, 225, 227
color, 49, 81, 82, 83, 99, 120, 156, 161
Color, 19, 29, 31, 33, 39, 42, 43, 53, 64, 65, 81, 90, 91, 99, 148, 149, 152, 158, 159, 162, 163, 164, 165, 168, 188, 191, 192, 213, 218, 219, 220, 222, 223, 224, 227, 228
Compatibility, 7, 14
complex, 4, 5, 8, 21, 69, 93, 183, 185, 229
compression, 57, 63, 66, 68, 69
Content Aware, 179

Content-Aware, 123
Contextual, 8, 9, 10, 12, 129
Contiguous, 165, 167
Control, 40, 41, 45, 96, 102, 116, 117, 134, 139, 162, 173, 188, 190
correcting, 179
creative, 16
Creative, 16
creativity, 4, 7, 8, 28, 95, 229
Crop, 9, 71, 134, 135, 137, 138
Customize, 34

D

damaged, 6
designer, 4, 12, 196
digital, 4, 5, 7, 19, 27, 32, 52, 54, 60, 62, 63, 64, 65, 67, 68, 69, 95, 100, 210, 212, 222, 223, 229
dimensions, 8, 9, 25, 54, 57, 59, 60, 61, 63, 65, 70, 185, 227
Dimensions, 54, 55, 57, 58
distortion, 6, 208
distraction, 8
Distraction, 4, 7
distractions, 7, 48, 179, 181

E

Edges, 165, 167
Edit, 8, 19, 22, 23, 30, 34, 35, 45, 46, 72, 94, 108, 160, 161, 190, 224
editing, 4, 5, 6, 10, 13, 14, 19, 22, 23, 25, 30, 52, 56, 62, 67, 68, 73, 76, 80, 95, 137, 149, 164, 190, 199, 210, 214, 219, 229
Editing, 1, 5, 19, 52, 76, 106, 190

edits, 6, 10, 21, 31, 32, 79, 110, 186, 190
effects, 6, 10, 13, 21, 22, 25, 27, 29, 73, 75, 76, 87, 88, 89, 92, 93, 95, 100, 158, 161, 183, 184, 202, 207, 208, 209
elements, 4, 5, 6, 10, 22, 25, 27, 28, 29, 38, 69, 70, 71, 73, 95, 214
enhancements, 4, 7, 10, 15
Eraser, 19, 29, 46, 120, 166, 167, 168, 172
Expand, 4, 9, 10, 133
Export, 7, 47, 67, 81, 213, 225
Exporting, 225

F

features, 4, 6, 7, 10, 14, 15, 19, 24, 25, 38, 41, 73, 93, 112, 174, 192, 209, 229
files, 5, 6, 7, 13, 14, 22, 23, 24, 25, 48, 63, 64, 65, 66, 81
Fill, 4, 8, 10, 19, 46, 74, 82, 84, 85, 86, 95, 128, 129, 131, 132, 133, 151, 156, 160, 213
Filter, 144, 145, 184, 186
filters, 6, 14, 22, 183
Firefly, 4, 8, 9
Flatten, 79, 82, 98
Flyers, 65
formats, 7, 9, 63, 66, 67, 69, 79

G

gallery, 6
general, 5, 19, 48, 86, 165
General, 47
Generative, 1, 4, 8, 9, 10, 128, 129, 130, 131, 132, 133
GIF, 7, 63, 66, 68, 225

Gradient, 95
graphic, 4, 5, 28, 52, 214, 229
graphics, 5, 6, 19, 29, 68, 76, 212, 214, 219
Grayscale, 221
Group, 42, 67, 77
guide, 4, 70, 71, 72, 219, 229
guides, 23, 70, 71, 72, 109
Guides, 71, 72

H

heading, 54, 56
healing, 6, 28, 178, 179
Healing, 6, 28, 122, 123, 125, 139, 142, 143, 144, 177, 178
heights, 5
High Pass, 144
History, 20, 31, 32, 44, 45, 46

I

Illustrator, 5, 212
image, 41, 69, 82, 83, 139, 149, 155, 168, 173, 184, 211, 221
images, 4, 5, 8, 9, 14, 21, 22, 25, 26, 28, 29, 52, 53, 54, 59, 60, 63, 64, 65, 68, 69, 93, 95, 105, 106, 155, 166, 179, 210, 212, 218, 219, 220, 221, 222, 224
imperfections, 6, 177, 181
innovative, 5, 7
install, 16
installation, 16
integration, 4
Invert, 146

J

JPEG, 7, 57, 63, 67, 68, 79, 212, 225

K

keyboard, 24, 34, 39, 45, 78, 93, 156, 162, 173, 188, 191

L

Lab, 220
launched, 5
layer, 49, 82, 98, 99, 139, 161, 170, 198
Layer, 5, 19, 21, 22, 73, 74, 76, 77, 79, 80, 82, 84, 85, 86, 92, 95, 98, 122, 138, 140, 141, 142, 144, 146, 147, 148, 151, 155, 160, 166, 171, 172, 200, 201, 202
layers, 5, 6, 19, 20, 21, 22, 25, 27, 30, 31, 41, 44, 63, 67, 68, 73, 74, 76, 77, 78, 79, 80, 81, 82, 88, 94, 95, 98, 104, 107, 119, 155, 161, 168, 183, 189, 196, 225
Layers, 6, 20, 21, 31, 32, 33, 44, 49, 73, 74, 75, 76, 77, 78, 79, 80, 81, 82, 88, 92, 94, 95, 98, 99, 101, 104, 107, 123, 126, 130, 139, 151, 152, 154, 155, 159, 160, 171, 178, 194, 201, 202, 207, 212, 213
license, 16
Lighten, 140
Lightroom, 5
location, 5, 20, 32, 33, 67, 69, 173, 180, 181, 210, 217, 225
Lock, 72, 77, 136
logos, 6, 29, 68, 69, 212, 214, 221

M

macOS, 5, 13, 19, 39, 79, 173, 190
Magazines, 65, 66
Magic, 120
manipulate, 4, 25, 26, 30, 77, 101, 192
manipulating, 5, 20, 186
manipulation, 5, 186, 210
Mask, 28, 40, 76, 101, 103, 105, 106, 107, 112, 113, 120, 147, 171, 201
matches, 9, 58
Measure, 70
Medium, 49
membership, 16
Memory, 51
Menu, 19, 20, 22, 24, 25, 46, 92, 127, 193
Merging, 78
Mode, 40, 65, 70, 89, 103, 140, 145, 177, 178, 204, 211, 215, 218, 219, 220, 221, 222, 223
Model, 8, 9

N

naming, 74

O

Objects, 67, 77
Opacity, 74, 96, 141, 148
options, 11, 19, 20, 21, 22, 23, 24, 25, 28, 30, 31, 38, 39, 41, 44, 46, 49, 50, 57, 66, 81, 82, 96, 97, 104, 105, 106, 107, 108, 114, 118, 119, 131, 149, 159, 165, 184, 190, 193, 197, 198, 199, 203, 208, 222, 227

original, 5, 6, 9, 33, 36, 42, 56, 76, 77, 81, 91, 100, 117, 121, 123, 127, 130, 138, 139, 141, 142, 149, 164, 165, 173, 178, 181
Overlay, 75, 90

P

Paint, 140, 148, 184
palette, 34
panel, 12, 20, 29, 31, 32, 35, 41, 42, 43, 44, 45, 46, 49, 73, 74, 76, 77, 79, 80, 81, 82, 88, 92, 96, 99, 101, 126, 130, 131, 151, 154, 160, 162, 163, 168, 173, 185, 188, 193, 194, 195, 196, 197, 198, 199, 203, 206, 207, 212, 213
Panels, 42, 43
panoramic, 9
patch, 6, 28
Patch, 181
Path, 173
PDF, 225
performance, 13, 14, 15, 46, 47, 165
Performance, 50
permanently, 82
photo, 4, 5, 6, 8, 10, 19, 20, 23, 28, 54, 56, 59, 64, 66, 68, 90, 91, 122, 155, 161, 187, 229
photographer, 4
Photoshop, 1, 4, 5, 6, 7, 9, 10, 11, 13, 14, 15, 16, 17, 18, 19, 20, 21, 22, 23, 24, 25, 26, 27, 28, 29, 30, 31, 32, 35, 36, 39, 40, 41, 42, 44, 45, 46, 47, 48, 49, 50, 51, 52, 53, 54, 56, 58, 61, 63, 64, 65, 66, 67, 69, 70, 72, 73, 76, 87, 92, 93, 94, 95, 97, 98, 103, 107, 108, 109,

110, 112, 113, 115, 118, 122, 123, 125, 128, 129, 132, 134, 135, 136, 137, 138, 142, 149, 155, 159, 162, 166, 168, 170, 172, 174, 175, 177, 183, 184, 187, 189, 190, 191, 192, 193, 196, 197, 199, 203, 207, 210, 212, 213, 214, 215, 218, 219, 222, 223, 225, 226, 228, 229
picture, 6, 29, 45, 52, 54, 55, 57, 58, 62, 67, 73, 76, 85, 99, 100, 106, 107, 115, 134, 137, 156, 172, 174, 178, 179, 199, 210
pixel, 5, 27, 52, 53, 54, 56, 59, 60, 61, 62, 63, 78, 108, 109, 110, 125, 183, 186, 210, 218
pixels, 5, 6, 27, 28, 52, 53, 54, 55, 56, 57, 58, 59, 60, 61, 62, 63, 64, 65, 76, 81, 88, 89, 90, 91, 98, 101, 108, 110, 125, 133, 137, 141, 165, 168, 170, 177, 181, 182, 183, 210, 212, 213, 218, 227
Pixels, 52, 55, 64, 137, 162, 218
PNG, 7, 63, 66, 68, 79, 225
portraits, 4, 8, 105, 122, 125
PPI, 63, 64, 65, 66
preference, 49
Preferences, 19, 46, 47, 72, 108
preset, 96, 155
Preset, 137
Print, 65, 66, 220, 227, 228
printers, 64, 65, 68, 223, 227
Printing, 64, 65, 226
professional, 5, 7, 64, 125, 207, 214, 220, 229
professionals, 4
projects, 4, 5, 23, 24, 25, 67, 74, 77, 93, 188, 214, 225, 229
prompts, 4, 8, 11

properties, 6, 31, 40, 178, 192
property, 5

R

RAM, 13, 14, 51, 56
rectangle, 76, 102, 104, 108, 112, 171
Redo, 45
refine, 6, 105, 112, 113, 159, 229
refinement, 8, 9, 22, 105, 107
Removal, 4, 7
remove, 6, 8, 30, 61, 81, 117, 122, 125, 129, 132, 138, 142, 143, 154, 170, 172, 175, 180
Remove, 4, 7, 12, 72
rename, 21, 74
resolution, 14, 21, 52, 53, 54, 56, 57, 58, 59, 60, 61, 62, 63, 64, 65, 66, 68, 137, 210, 213, 226, 227
Resolution, 14, 53, 54, 56, 57, 59, 61, 62, 64, 66, 69, 137, 227
restored, 42, 46
Retouching, 6, 28, 124
RGB, 53, 64, 65, 218, 219, 222, 223, 225, 227
Rulers, 69, 71

S

Sampling, 140, 165, 167
Save, 173
Scaling, 117, 199, 227
Select, 106, 147
Selection, 6, 19, 27, 76, 102, 103, 104, 105, 106, 107, 108, 110, 112, 114, 115, 117, 120, 128, 132, 133, 170, 171, 172, 173, 206
selections, 120, 184

Selections, 6, 101, 102, 112, 113
Shadow, 202
shape, 6, 10, 21, 29, 76, 93, 100, 109, 110, 112, 200, 213, 214, 215, 216, 229
Shape, 6, 21, 29, 76
shapes, 5, 6, 27, 29, 33, 76, 108, 111, 113, 210, 214
sharpening, 6, 125, 127, 154, 183
Size, 56, 57
smooth, 6, 13, 15, 28, 64, 93, 111, 142, 165, 180, 214, 215, 216, 217
Spot, 143, 144
squares, 52, 54, 108
Stamp, 182
standard, 5, 64, 227
Subject, 106
subscriptions, 16
SVG, 69, 191, 213, 225

T

tab, 33, 42, 43, 44, 45, 50, 82, 98, 184, 186, 187, 191, 193
Text, 203
theme, 48
Thomas, 5
TIFF, 7, 63, 68, 79
Tool, 4, 7, 8, 9, 10, 12, 19, 25, 27, 28, 29, 39, 70, 71, 72, 93, 95, 107, 110, 112, 113, 115, 116, 120, 128, 129, 132, 133, 134, 137, 138, 139, 147, 149, 150, 153, 154, 157, 159, 161, 162, 163, 164, 165, 166, 168, 170, 174, 176, 177, 178, 179, 181, 182, 186, 188, 193, 196, 200, 201, 203, 204, 205, 206, 214, 215

toolbar, 7, 9, 10, 24, 26, 27, 29, 30, 34, 35, 36, 95, 103, 105, 107, 112, 114, 120, 128, 134, 143, 166, 170, 171, 190, 193, 214, 215
Toolbar, 34, 182
tools, 4, 5, 6, 7, 8, 10, 13, 14, 15, 16, 19, 20, 21, 22, 25, 26, 27, 28, 29, 30, 31, 35, 36, 38, 39, 50, 76, 93, 101, 106, 108, 110, 112, 113, 114, 115, 118, 120, 132, 162, 166, 172, 175, 177, 187, 209, 229
Tools, 1, 6, 19, 20, 27, 28, 29, 35, 36, 39, 115, 139, 143, 162, 163, 188, 196, 203, 204, 206
transform, 4, 116, 117, 214
transformations, 6, 196
transparency, 68, 75, 89

V

vector, 5, 6, 29, 68, 69, 76, 212, 213, 214
vectors, 6, 76
version, 4, 7, 13, 45, 46, 100, 130, 190
View, 19, 22, 66, 69, 71, 72, 109, 159, 227
visible, 34

W

White, 83, 148
wide, 5, 7, 12, 28, 55, 58, 95, 120, 125
Window, 173
Windows, 5, 13, 19, 37, 39, 40, 41, 45, 46, 71, 74, 77, 79, 102, 108, 109, 113, 117, 134, 136, 139,

156, 162, 163, 170, 173, 190, 193, 194, 201, 203, 204, 216, 217
workflow, 5, 7, 15, 19, 20, 25, 30, 31, 46, 113
works, 5, 10, 28, 30, 125, 127, 170, 177, 208, 212

Z

Zoom, 5, 19, 29, 38, 66, 109, 149, 173, 178

Printed in Great Britain
by Amazon

55a4cb7e-e6af-48c4-a1b7-be3a65bd82b3R01